MONTLAKE LIBRARY

JUN 1 0 2017

NO LONGER PROPERTY OF
SEATTLE PUBLIC LIBRARY

D0536699

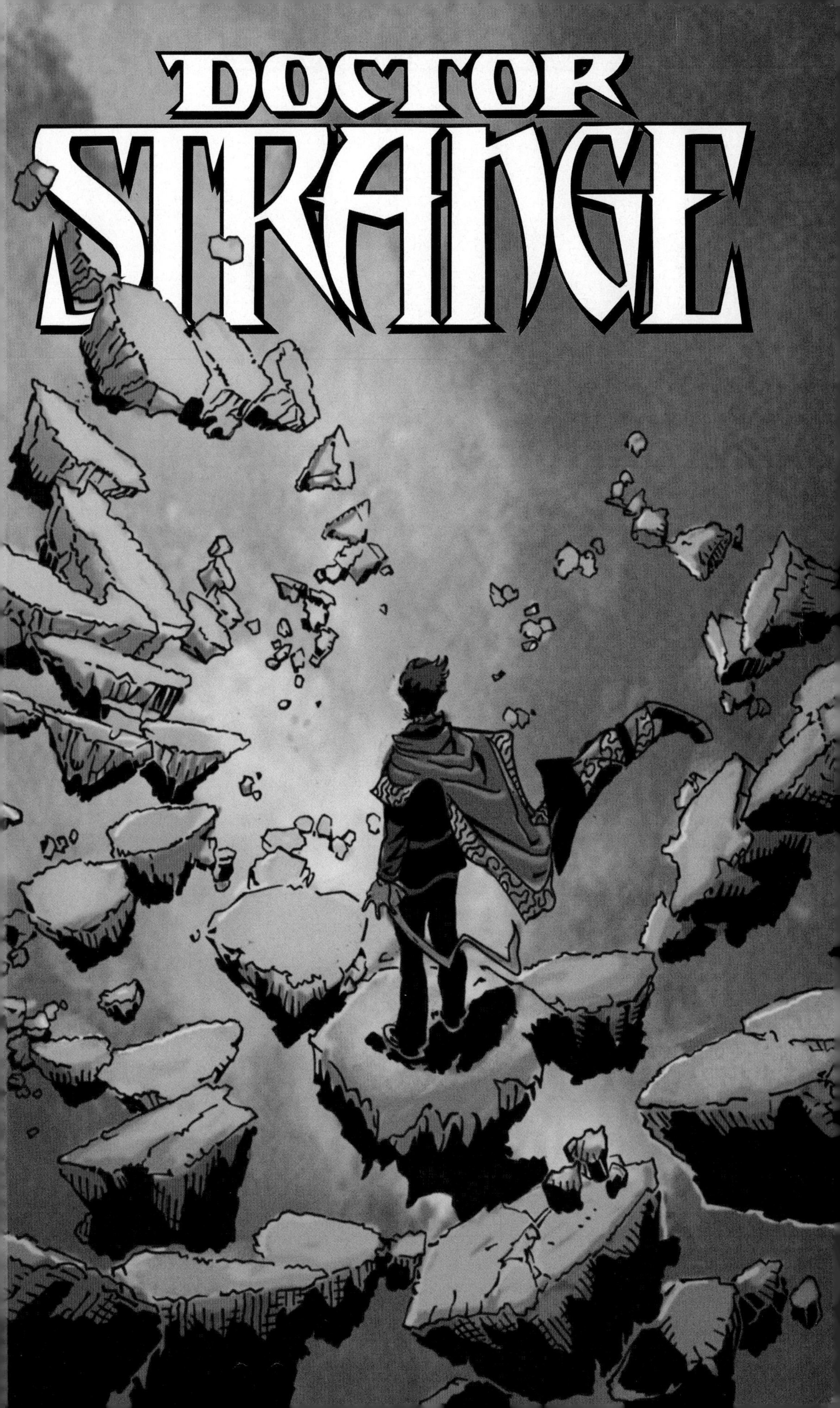
DOCTOR
STRANGE

COLLECTION EDITOR: **JENNIFER GRÜNWALD**
ASSOCIATE EDITOR: **SARAH BRUNSTAD**
ASSOCIATE MANAGING EDITOR: **ALEX STARBUCK**
EDITOR, SPECIAL PROJECTS: **MARK D. BEAZLEY**
VP, PRODUCTION & SPECIAL PROJECTS: **JEFF YOUNGQUIST**
SVP PRINT, SALES & MARKETING: **DAVID GABRIEL**
BOOK DESIGNER: **JAY BOWEN**

EDITOR IN CHIEF: **AXEL ALONSO**
CHIEF CREATIVE OFFICER: **JOE QUESADA**
PUBLISHER: **DAN BUCKLEY**
EXECUTIVE PRODUCER: **ALAN FINE**

DOCTOR STRANGE VOL. 1: THE WAY OF THE WEIRD. Contains material originally published in magazine form as DOCTOR STRANGE #1-5. First printing 2016. ISBN# 978-0-7851-9516-0. Published by MARVEL WORLDWIDE, INC., a subsid
of MARVEL ENTERTAINMENT, LLC. OFFICE OF PUBLICATION: 135 West 50th Street, New York, NY 10020. Copyright © 2016 MARVEL No similarity between any of the names, characters, persons, and/or institutions in this magazine v
those of any living or dead person or institution is intended, and any such similarity which may exist is purely coincidental. **Printed in the U.S.A.** ALAN FINE, President, Marvel Entertainment; DAN BUCKLEY, President, TV, Publishing & Br
Management; JOE QUESADA, Chief Creative Officer; TOM BREVOORT, SVP of Publishing; DAVID BOGART, SVP of Business Affairs & Operations, Publishing & Partnership; C.B. CEBULSKI, VP of Brand Management & Development, Asia; DA
GABRIEL, SVP of Sales & Marketing, Publishing; JEFF YOUNGQUIST, VP of Production & Special Projects; DAN CARR, Executive Director of Publishing Technology; ALEX MORALES, Director of Publishing Operations; SUSAN CRESPI, Produc
Manager; STAN LEE, Chairman Emeritus. For information regarding advertising in Marvel Comics or on Marvel.com, please contact Vit DeBellis, Integrated Sales Manager, at vdebellis@marvel.com. For Marvel subscription inquiries, ple

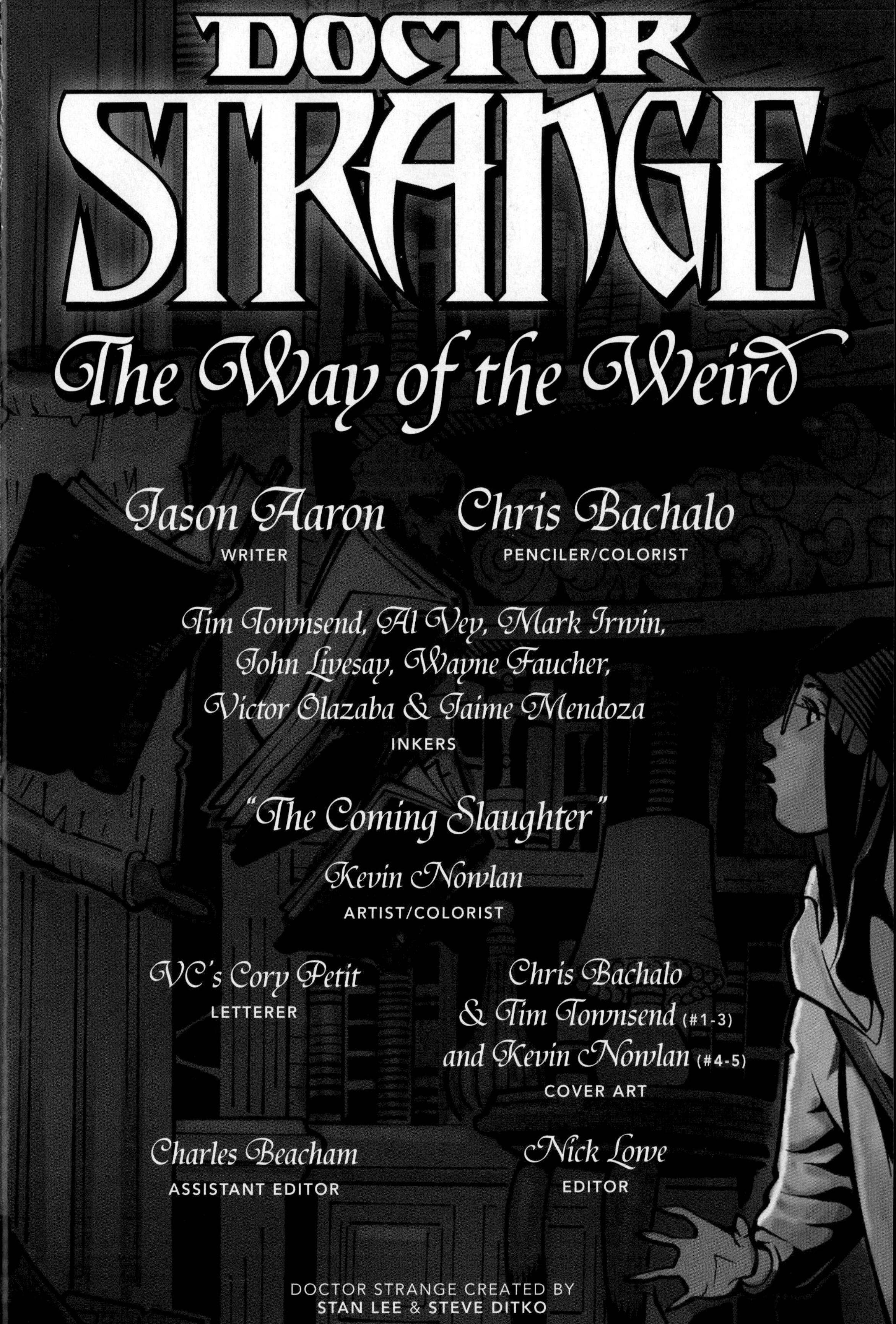

DOCTOR STRANGE

The Way of the Weird

Jason Aaron
WRITER

Chris Bachalo
PENCILER/COLORIST

Tim Townsend, Al Vey, Mark Irwin, John Livesay, Wayne Faucher, Victor Olazaba & Jaime Mendoza
INKERS

"The Coming Slaughter"

Kevin Nowlan
ARTIST/COLORIST

VC's Cory Petit
LETTERER

Chris Bachalo & Tim Townsend (#1-3) **and Kevin Nowlan** (#4-5)
COVER ART

Charles Beacham
ASSISTANT EDITOR

Nick Lowe
EDITOR

DOCTOR STRANGE CREATED BY
STAN LEE & STEVE DITKO

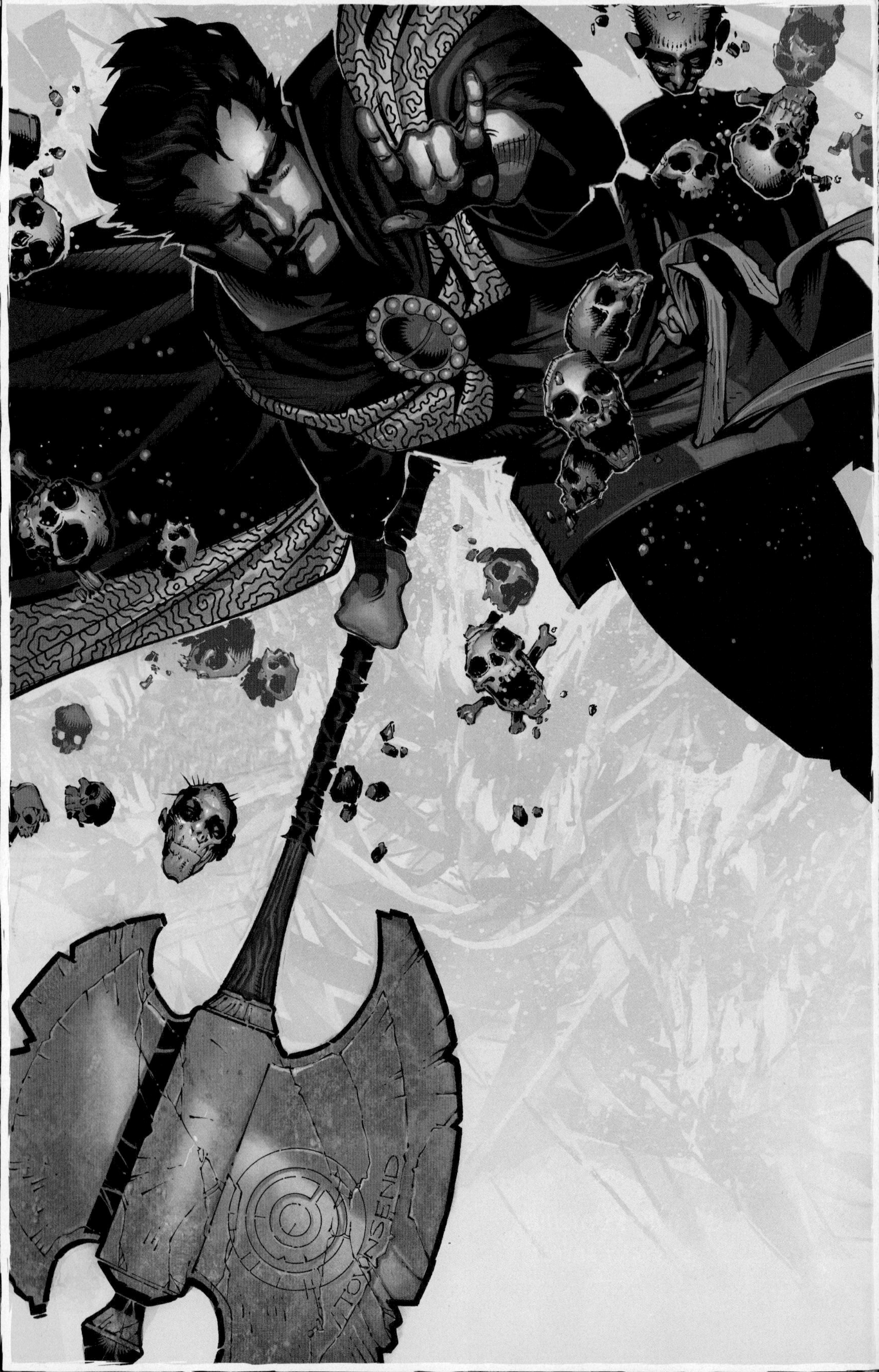
TOWNSEND

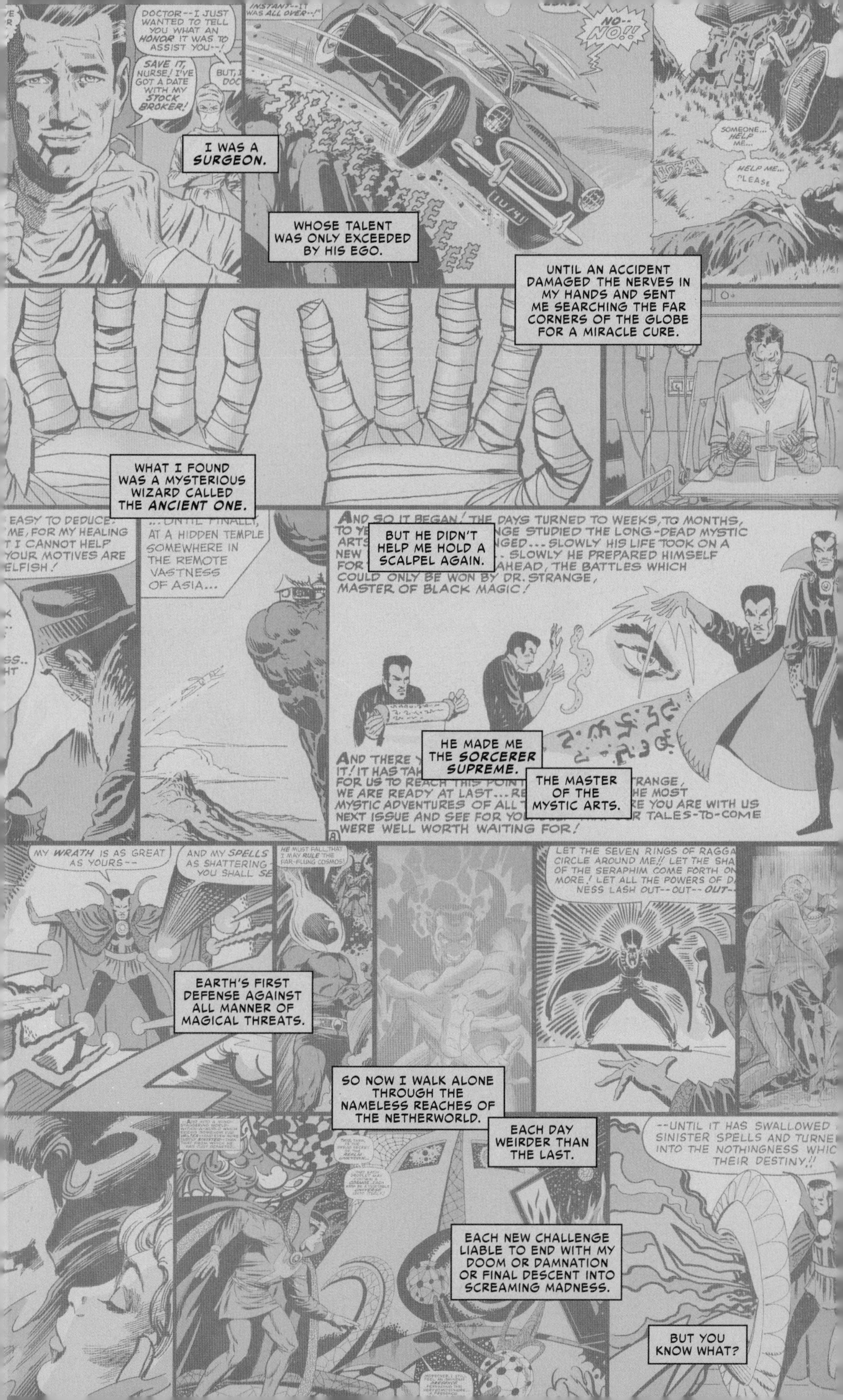
DOCTOR--I JUST WANTED TO TELL YOU WHAT AN HONOR IT WAS TO ASSIST YOU--!
SAVE IT, NURSE! I'VE GOT A DATE WITH MY STOCK BROKER!
I WAS A SURGEON.
NO-- NO!!
WHOSE TALENT WAS ONLY EXCEEDED BY HIS EGO.
SOMEONE... HELP ME...
HELP ME... PLEASE
UNTIL AN ACCIDENT DAMAGED THE NERVES IN MY HANDS AND SENT ME SEARCHING THE FAR CORNERS OF THE GLOBE FOR A MIRACLE CURE.
WHAT I FOUND WAS A MYSTERIOUS WIZARD CALLED THE ANCIENT ONE.
...UNTIL FINALLY, AT A HIDDEN TEMPLE SOMEWHERE IN THE REMOTE VASTNESS OF ASIA...
BUT HE DIDN'T HELP ME HOLD A SCALPEL AGAIN.
MASTER OF BLACK MAGIC!
HE MADE ME THE SORCERER SUPREME.
THE MASTER OF THE MYSTIC ARTS.
WE ARE READY AT LAST...
NEXT ISSUE AND SEE FOR YO
WERE WELL WORTH WAITING FOR!
MY WRATH IS AS GREAT AS YOURS--
EARTH'S FIRST DEFENSE AGAINST ALL MANNER OF MAGICAL THREATS.
SO NOW I WALK ALONE THROUGH THE NAMELESS REACHES OF THE NETHERWORLD.
EACH DAY WEIRDER THAN THE LAST.
EACH NEW CHALLENGE LIABLE TO END WITH MY DOOM OR DAMNATION OR FINAL DESCENT INTO SCREAMING MADNESS.
BUT YOU KNOW WHAT?

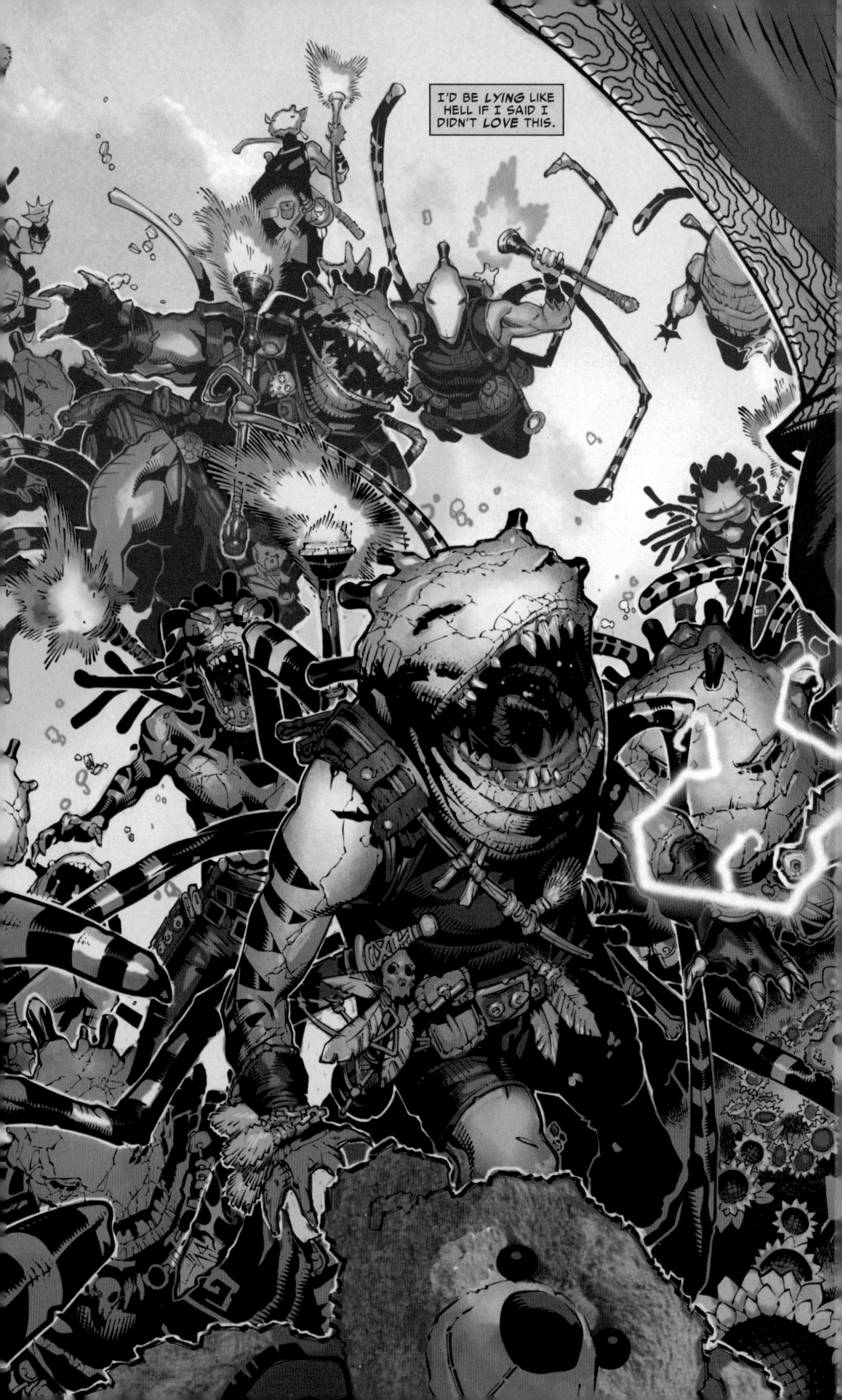
I'D BE LYING LIKE HELL IF I SAID I DIDN'T LOVE THIS.

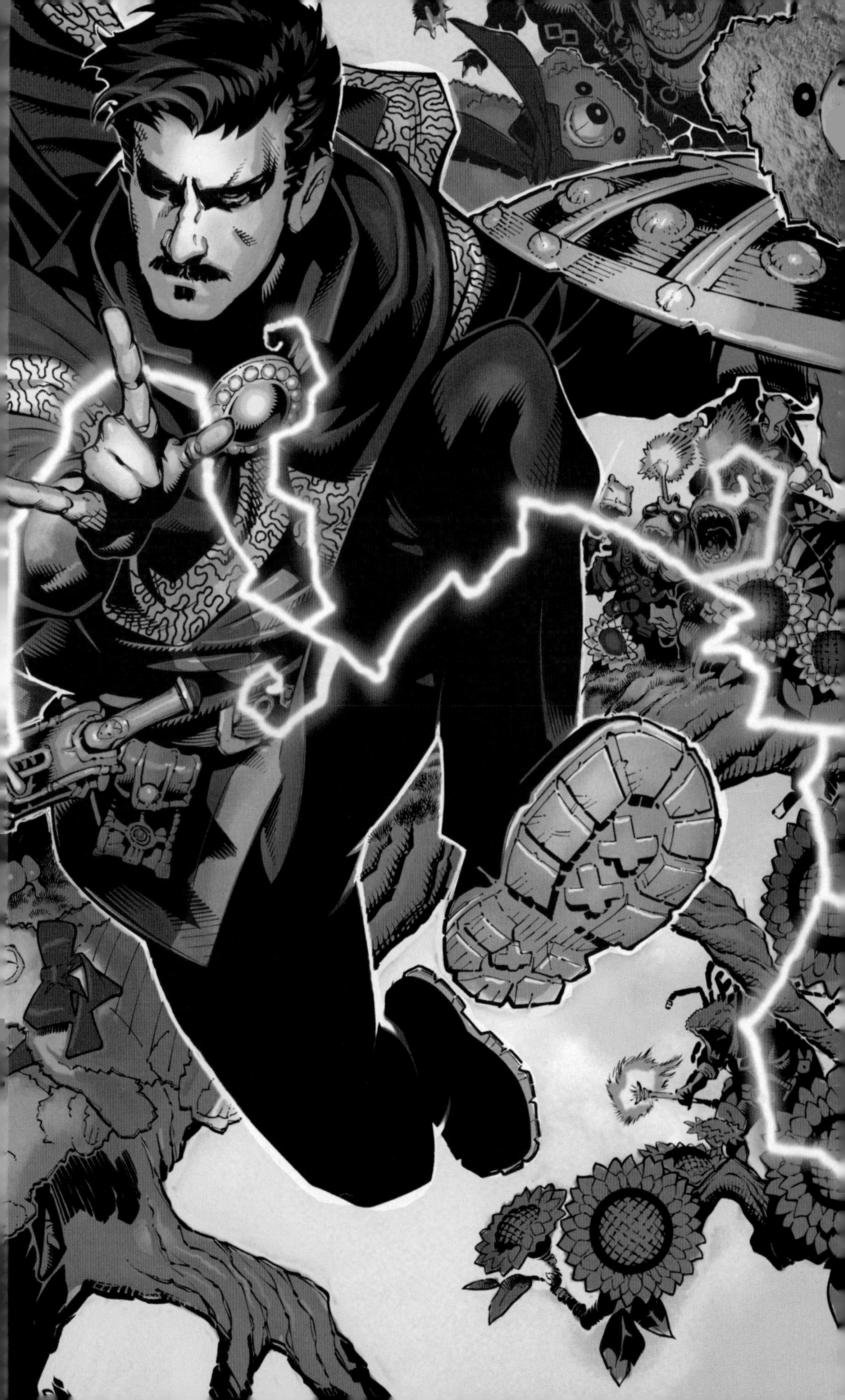

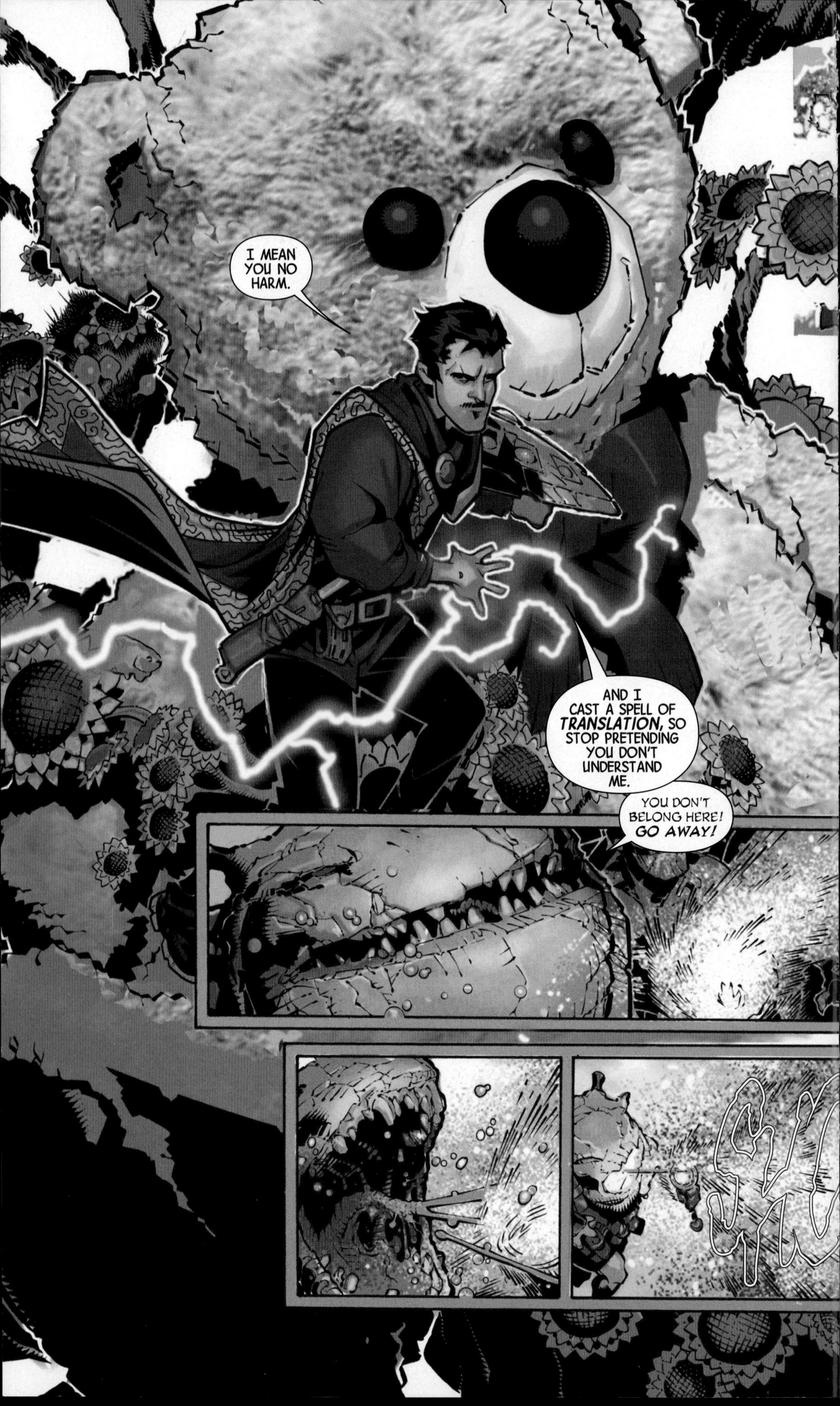

I MEAN YOU NO HARM.
AND I CAST A SPELL OF *TRANSLATION*, SO STOP PRETENDING YOU DON'T UNDERSTAND ME.
YOU DON'T BELONG HERE! *GO AWAY!*

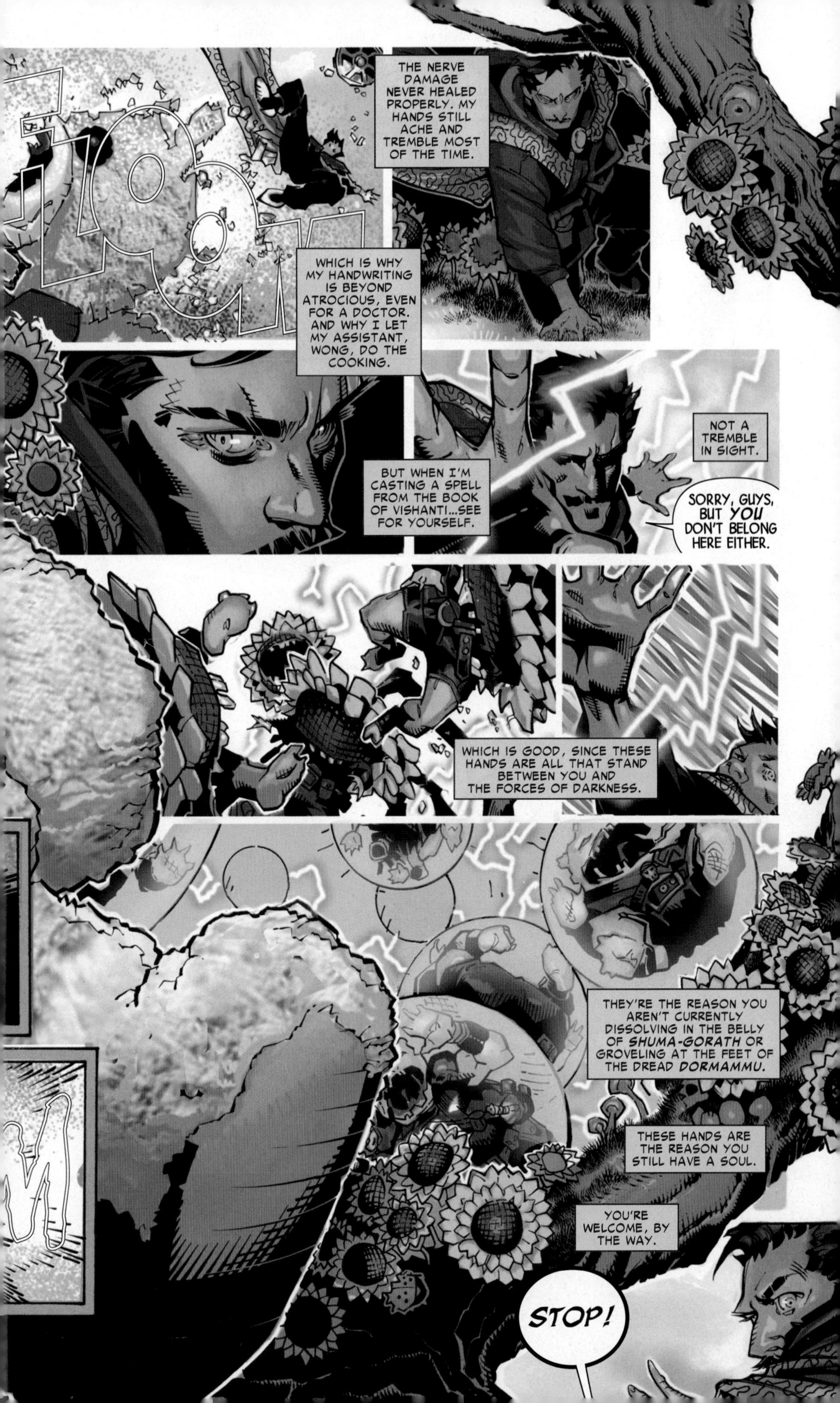
THE NERVE DAMAGE NEVER HEALED PROPERLY. MY HANDS STILL ACHE AND TREMBLE MOST OF THE TIME.
WHICH IS WHY MY HANDWRITING IS BEYOND ATROCIOUS, EVEN FOR A DOCTOR. AND WHY I LET MY ASSISTANT, WONG, DO THE COOKING.
BUT WHEN I'M CASTING A SPELL FROM THE BOOK OF VISHANTI...SEE FOR YOURSELF.
NOT A TREMBLE IN SIGHT.
SORRY, GUYS, BUT YOU DON'T BELONG HERE EITHER.
WHICH IS GOOD, SINCE THESE HANDS ARE ALL THAT STAND BETWEEN YOU AND THE FORCES OF DARKNESS.
THEY'RE THE REASON YOU AREN'T CURRENTLY DISSOLVING IN THE BELLY OF SHUMA-GORATH OR GROVELING AT THE FEET OF THE DREAD DORMAMMU.
THESE HANDS ARE THE REASON YOU STILL HAVE A SOUL.
YOU'RE WELCOME, BY THE WAY.
STOP!

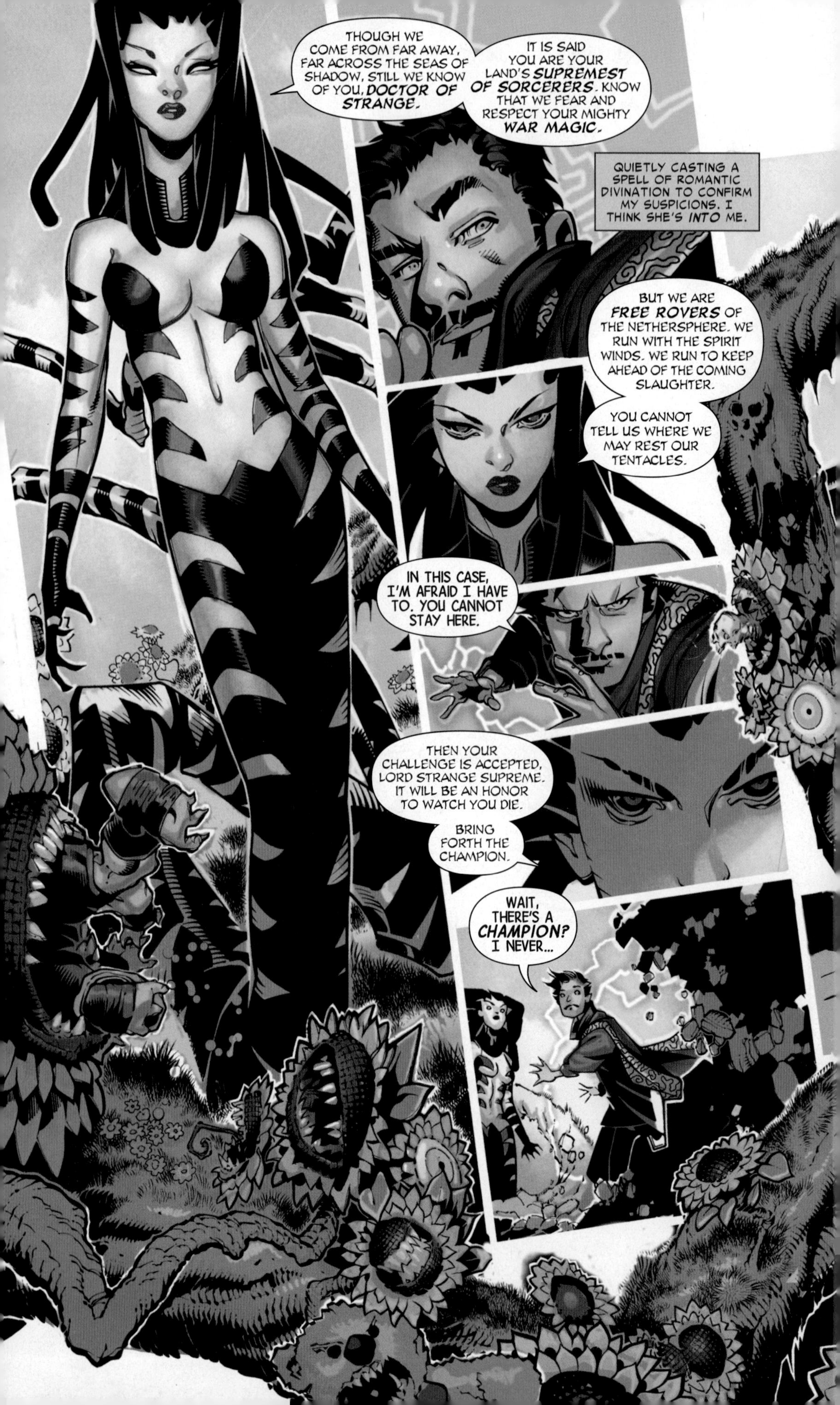

THOUGH WE COME FROM FAR AWAY, FAR ACROSS THE SEAS OF SHADOW, STILL WE KNOW OF YOU, DOCTOR OF STRANGE.
IT IS SAID YOU ARE YOUR LAND'S SUPREMEST OF SORCERERS. KNOW THAT WE FEAR AND RESPECT YOUR MIGHTY WAR MAGIC.
QUIETLY CASTING A SPELL OF ROMANTIC DIVINATION TO CONFIRM MY SUSPICIONS. I THINK SHE'S INTO ME.
BUT WE ARE FREE ROVERS OF THE NETHERSPHERE. WE RUN WITH THE SPIRIT WINDS. WE RUN TO KEEP AHEAD OF THE COMING SLAUGHTER.
YOU CANNOT TELL US WHERE WE MAY REST OUR TENTACLES.
IN THIS CASE, I'M AFRAID I HAVE TO. YOU CANNOT STAY HERE.
THEN YOUR CHALLENGE IS ACCEPTED, LORD STRANGE SUPREME. IT WILL BE AN HONOR TO WATCH YOU DIE.
BRING FORTH THE CHAMPION.
WAIT, THERE'S A CHAMPION? I NEVER...

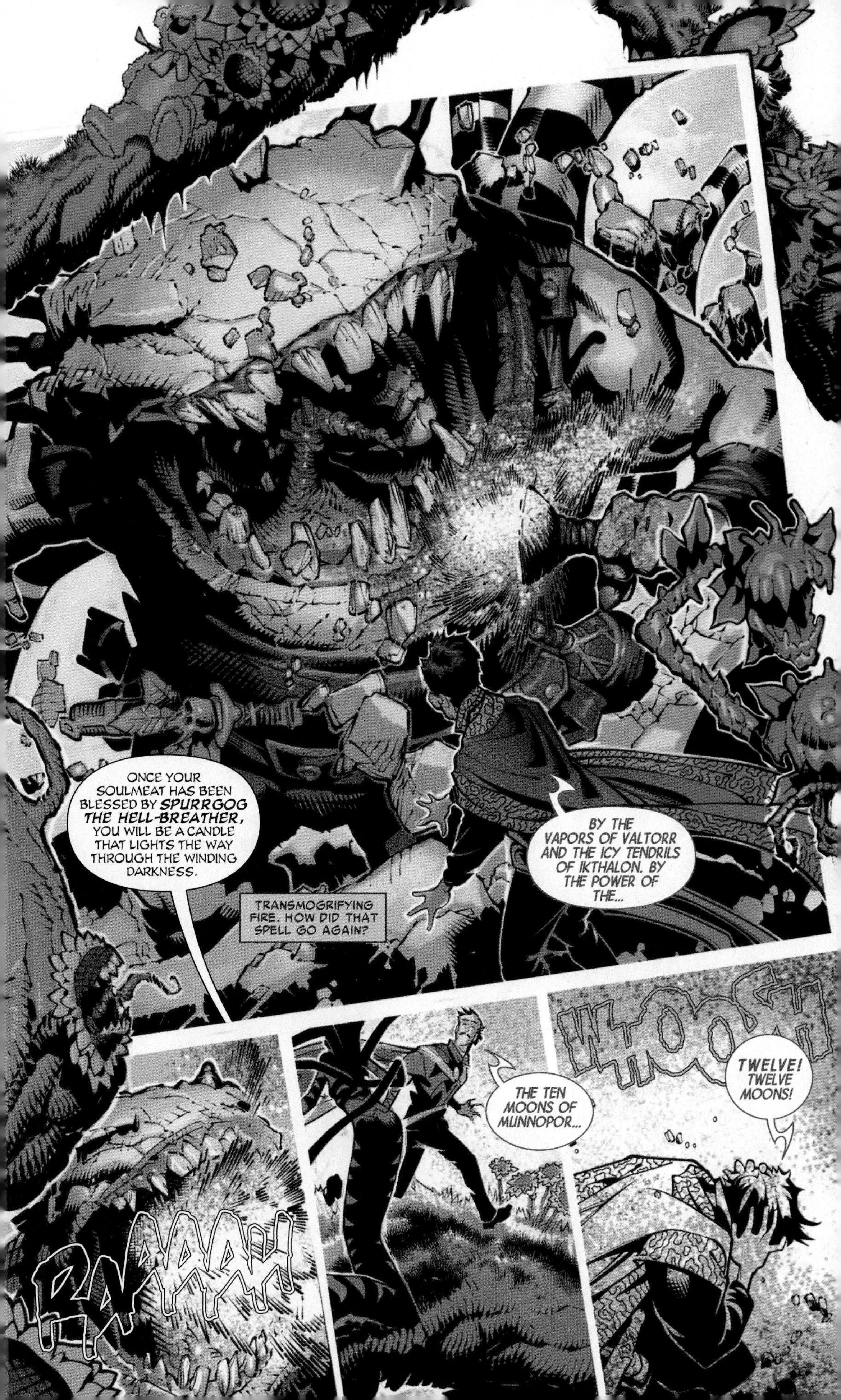
ONCE YOUR SOULMEAT HAS BEEN BLESSED BY ***SPURRGOG THE HELL-BREATHER,*** YOU WILL BE A CANDLE THAT LIGHTS THE WAY THROUGH THE WINDING DARKNESS.
BY THE *VAPORS OF VALTORR AND THE ICY TENDRILS OF IKTHALON. BY THE POWER OF THE...*
TRANSMOGRIFYING FIRE. HOW DID THAT SPELL GO AGAIN?
RAAAAH
THE TEN MOONS OF MUNNOPOR...
WHOOSH
TWELVE! TWELVE MOONS!

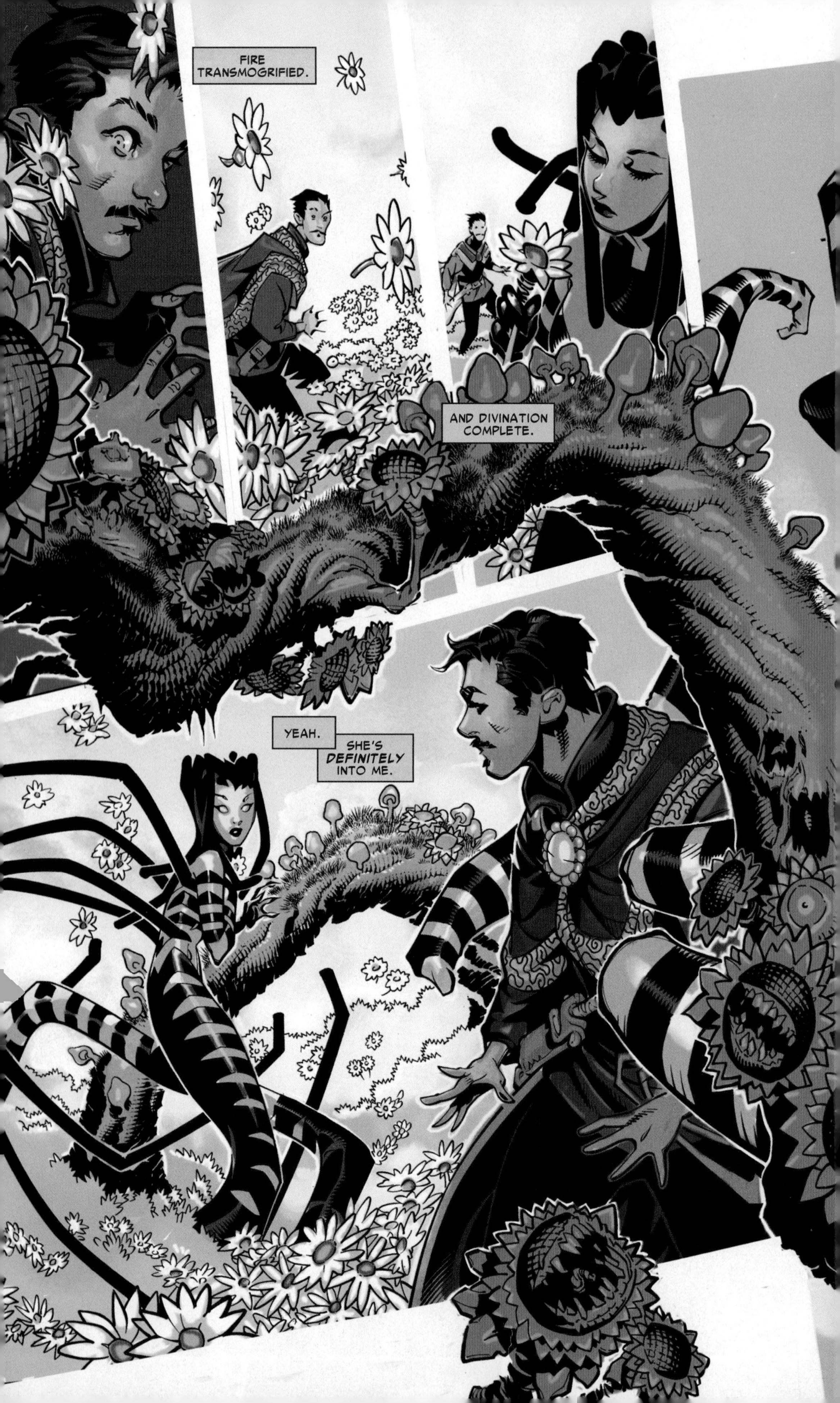
FIRE TRANSMOGRIFIED.
AND DIVINATION COMPLETE.
YEAH.
SHE'S *DEFINITELY* INTO ME.

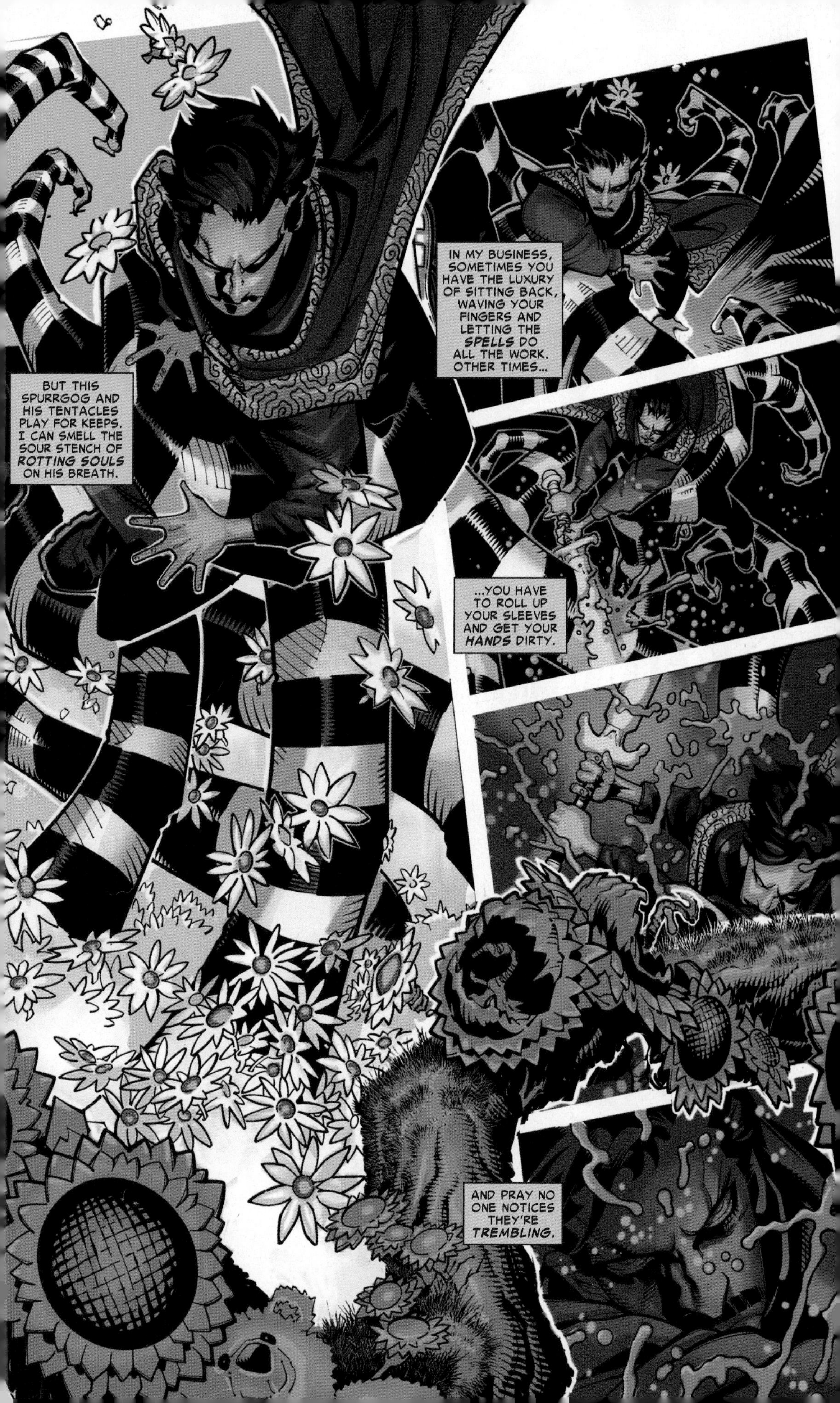
BUT THIS SPURRGOG AND HIS TENTACLES PLAY FOR KEEPS. I CAN SMELL THE SOUR STENCH OF ROTTING SOULS ON HIS BREATH.
IN MY BUSINESS, SOMETIMES YOU HAVE THE LUXURY OF SITTING BACK, WAVING YOUR FINGERS AND LETTING THE SPELLS DO ALL THE WORK. OTHER TIMES...
...YOU HAVE TO ROLL UP YOUR SLEEVES AND GET YOUR HANDS DIRTY.
AND PRAY NO ONE NOTICES THEY'RE TREMBLING.

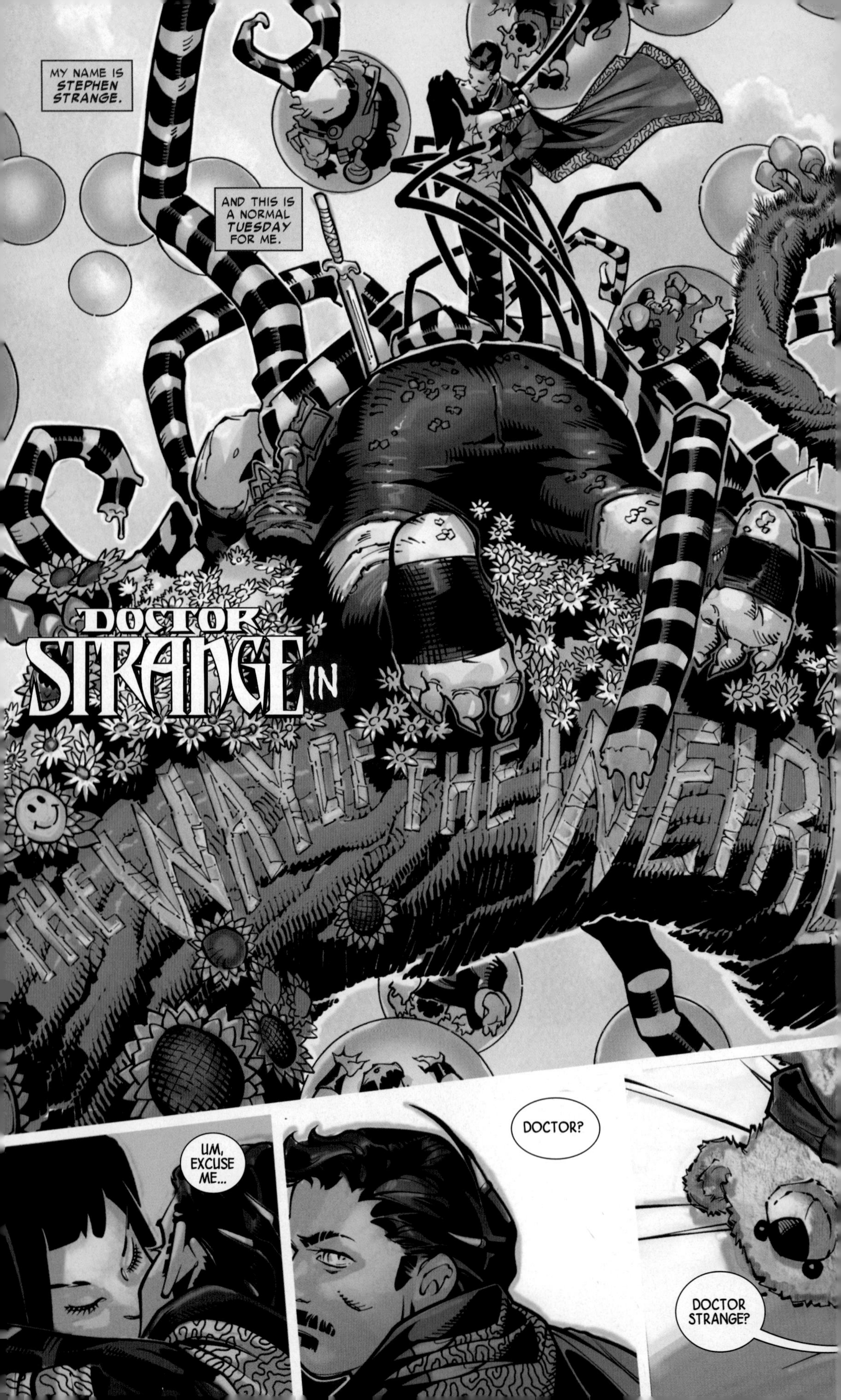

MY NAME IS *STEPHEN STRANGE.*
AND THIS IS A NORMAL *TUESDAY* FOR ME.
DOCTOR STRANGE IN
THE WAY OF THE WEIRD
UM, EXCUSE ME...
DOCTOR?
DOCTOR STRANGE?

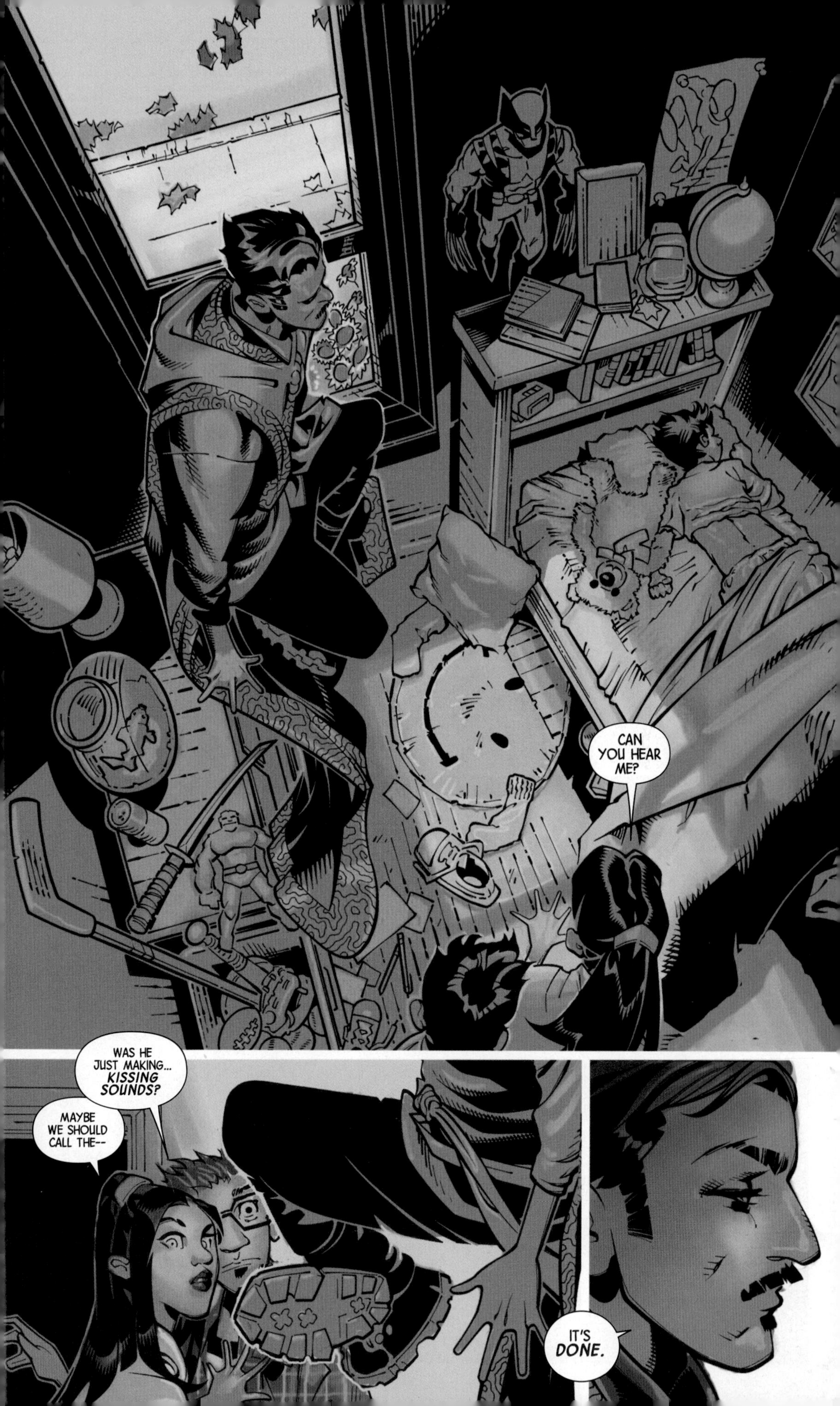

CAN YOU HEAR ME?
WAS HE JUST MAKING... KISSING SOUNDS?
MAYBE WE SHOULD CALL THE--
IT'S DONE.

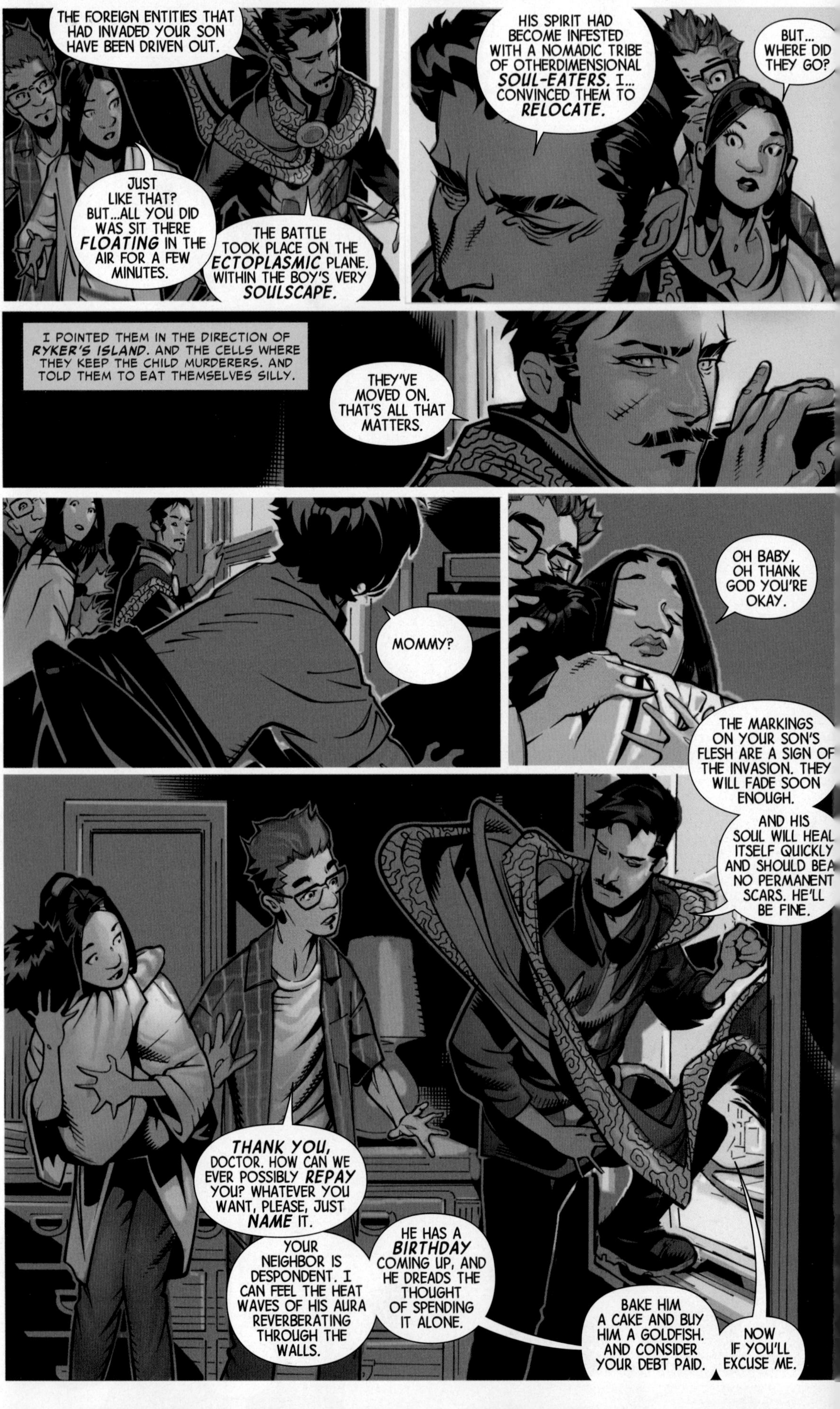
THE FOREIGN ENTITIES THAT HAD INVADED YOUR SON HAVE BEEN DRIVEN OUT.
JUST LIKE THAT? BUT...ALL YOU DID WAS SIT THERE FLOATING IN THE AIR FOR A FEW MINUTES.
THE BATTLE TOOK PLACE ON THE ECTOPLASMIC PLANE. WITHIN THE BOY'S VERY SOULSCAPE.
HIS SPIRIT HAD BECOME INFESTED WITH A NOMADIC TRIBE OF OTHERDIMENSIONAL SOUL-EATERS. I... CONVINCED THEM TO RELOCATE.
BUT... WHERE DID THEY GO?
I POINTED THEM IN THE DIRECTION OF RYKER'S ISLAND. AND THE CELLS WHERE THEY KEEP THE CHILD MURDERERS. AND TOLD THEM TO EAT THEMSELVES SILLY.
THEY'VE MOVED ON. THAT'S ALL THAT MATTERS.
MOMMY?
OH BABY. OH THANK GOD YOU'RE OKAY.
THE MARKINGS ON YOUR SON'S FLESH ARE A SIGN OF THE INVASION. THEY WILL FADE SOON ENOUGH.
AND HIS SOUL WILL HEAL ITSELF QUICKLY AND SHOULD BEA NO PERMANENT SCARS. HE'LL BE FINE.
THANK YOU, DOCTOR. HOW CAN WE EVER POSSIBLY REPAY YOU? WHATEVER YOU WANT, PLEASE, JUST NAME IT.
YOUR NEIGHBOR IS DESPONDENT. I CAN FEEL THE HEAT WAVES OF HIS AURA REVERBERATING THROUGH THE WALLS.
HE HAS A BIRTHDAY COMING UP, AND HE DREADS THE THOUGHT OF SPENDING IT ALONE.
BAKE HIM A CAKE AND BUY HIM A GOLDFISH. AND CONSIDER YOUR DEBT PAID.
NOW IF YOU'LL EXCUSE ME.

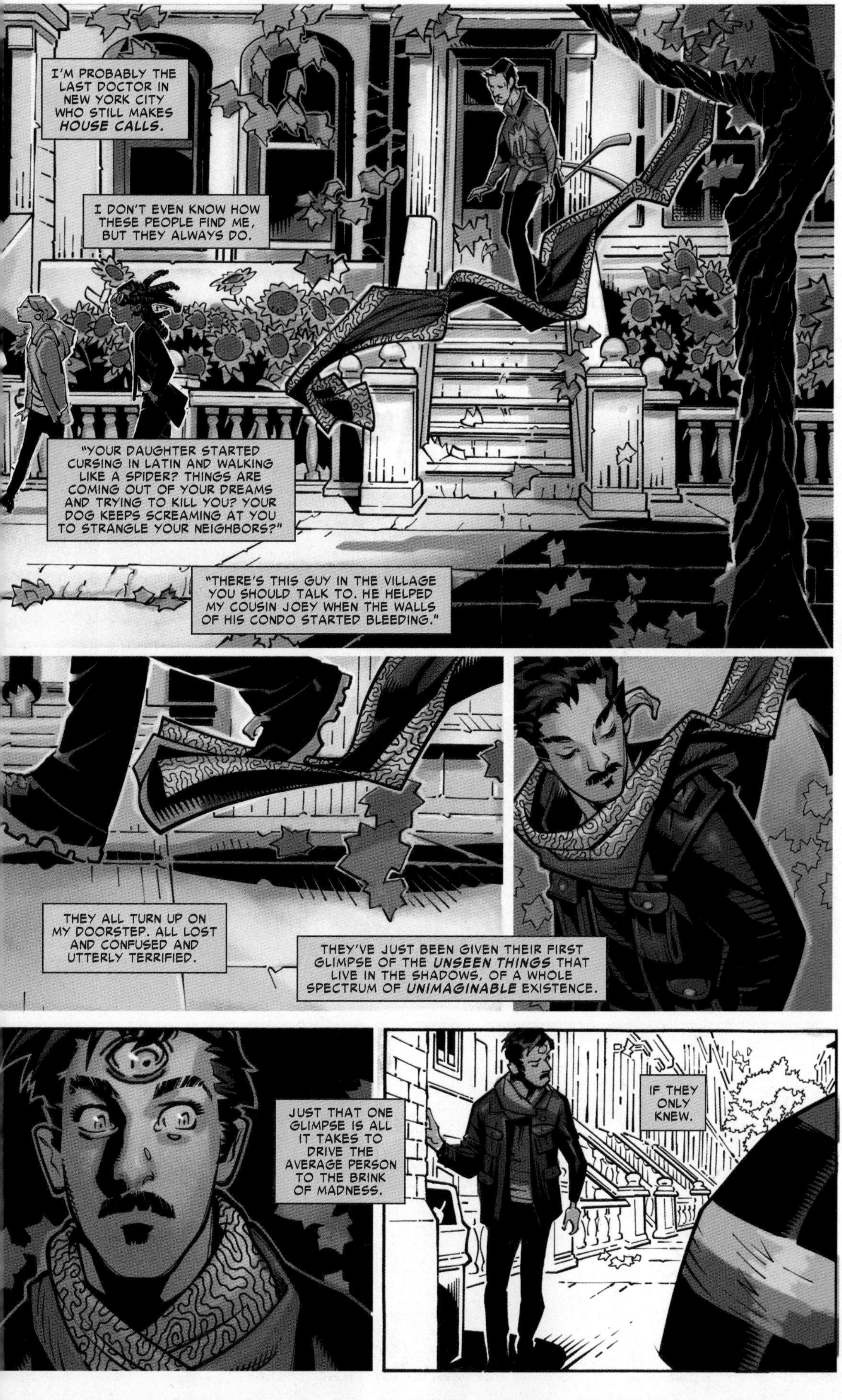
I'M PROBABLY THE LAST DOCTOR IN NEW YORK CITY WHO STILL MAKES *HOUSE CALLS.*
I DON'T EVEN KNOW HOW THESE PEOPLE FIND ME, BUT THEY ALWAYS DO.
"YOUR DAUGHTER STARTED CURSING IN LATIN AND WALKING LIKE A SPIDER? THINGS ARE COMING OUT OF YOUR DREAMS AND TRYING TO KILL YOU? YOUR DOG KEEPS SCREAMING AT YOU TO STRANGLE YOUR NEIGHBORS?"
"THERE'S THIS GUY IN THE VILLAGE YOU SHOULD TALK TO. HE HELPED MY COUSIN JOEY WHEN THE WALLS OF HIS CONDO STARTED BLEEDING."
THEY ALL TURN UP ON MY DOORSTEP. ALL LOST AND CONFUSED AND UTTERLY TERRIFIED.
THEY'VE JUST BEEN GIVEN THEIR FIRST GLIMPSE OF THE *UNSEEN THINGS* THAT LIVE IN THE SHADOWS, OF A WHOLE SPECTRUM OF *UNIMAGINABLE* EXISTENCE.
JUST THAT ONE GLIMPSE IS ALL IT TAKES TO DRIVE THE AVERAGE PERSON TO THE BRINK OF MADNESS.
IF THEY ONLY KNEW.

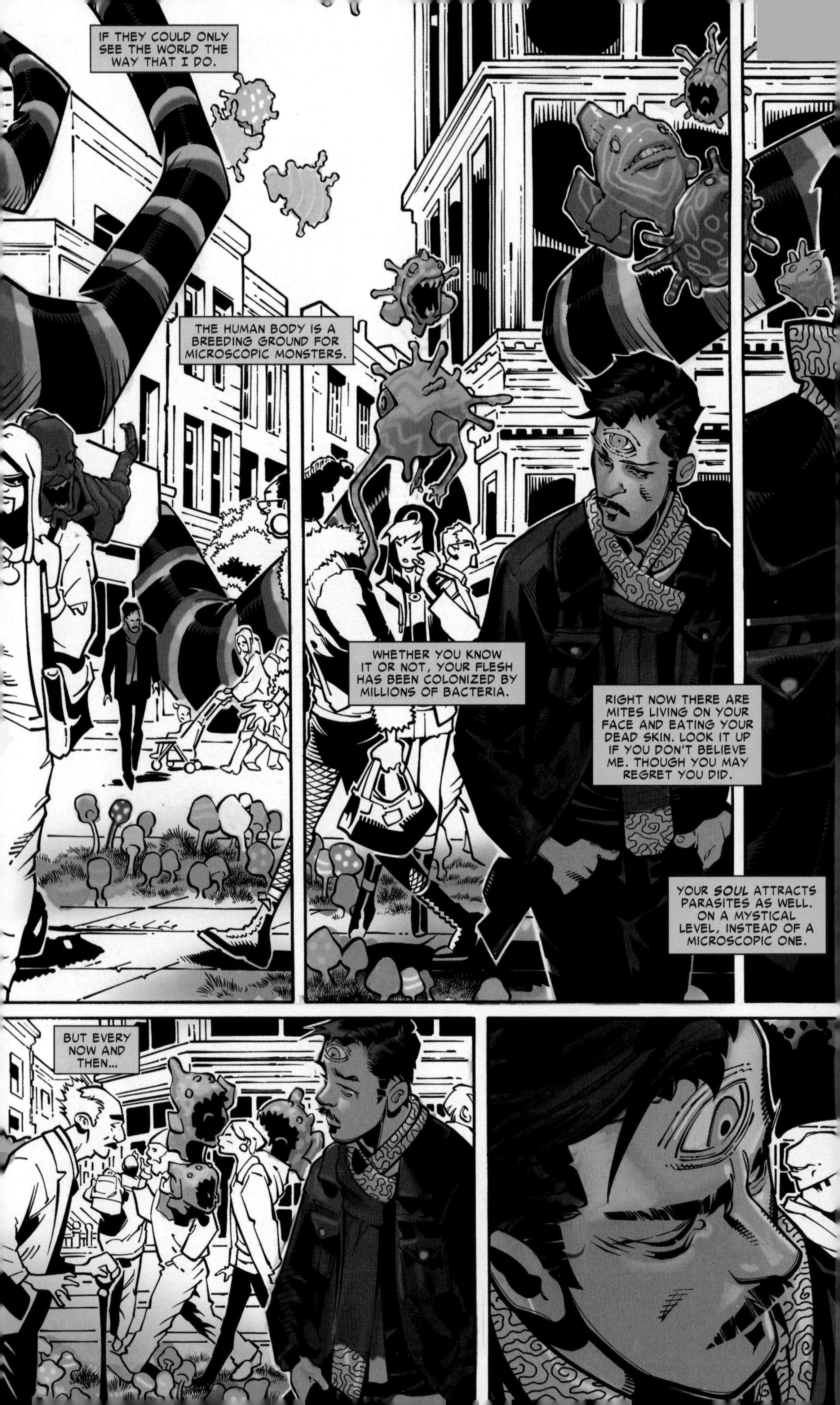
IF THEY COULD ONLY SEE THE WORLD THE WAY THAT I DO.
THE HUMAN BODY IS A BREEDING GROUND FOR MICROSCOPIC MONSTERS.
WHETHER YOU KNOW IT OR NOT, YOUR FLESH HAS BEEN COLONIZED BY MILLIONS OF BACTERIA.
RIGHT NOW THERE ARE MITES LIVING ON YOUR FACE AND EATING YOUR DEAD SKIN. LOOK IT UP IF YOU DON'T BELIEVE ME. THOUGH YOU MAY REGRET YOU DID.
YOUR *SOUL* ATTRACTS PARASITES AS WELL. ON A MYSTICAL LEVEL, INSTEAD OF A MICROSCOPIC ONE.
BUT EVERY NOW AND THEN...

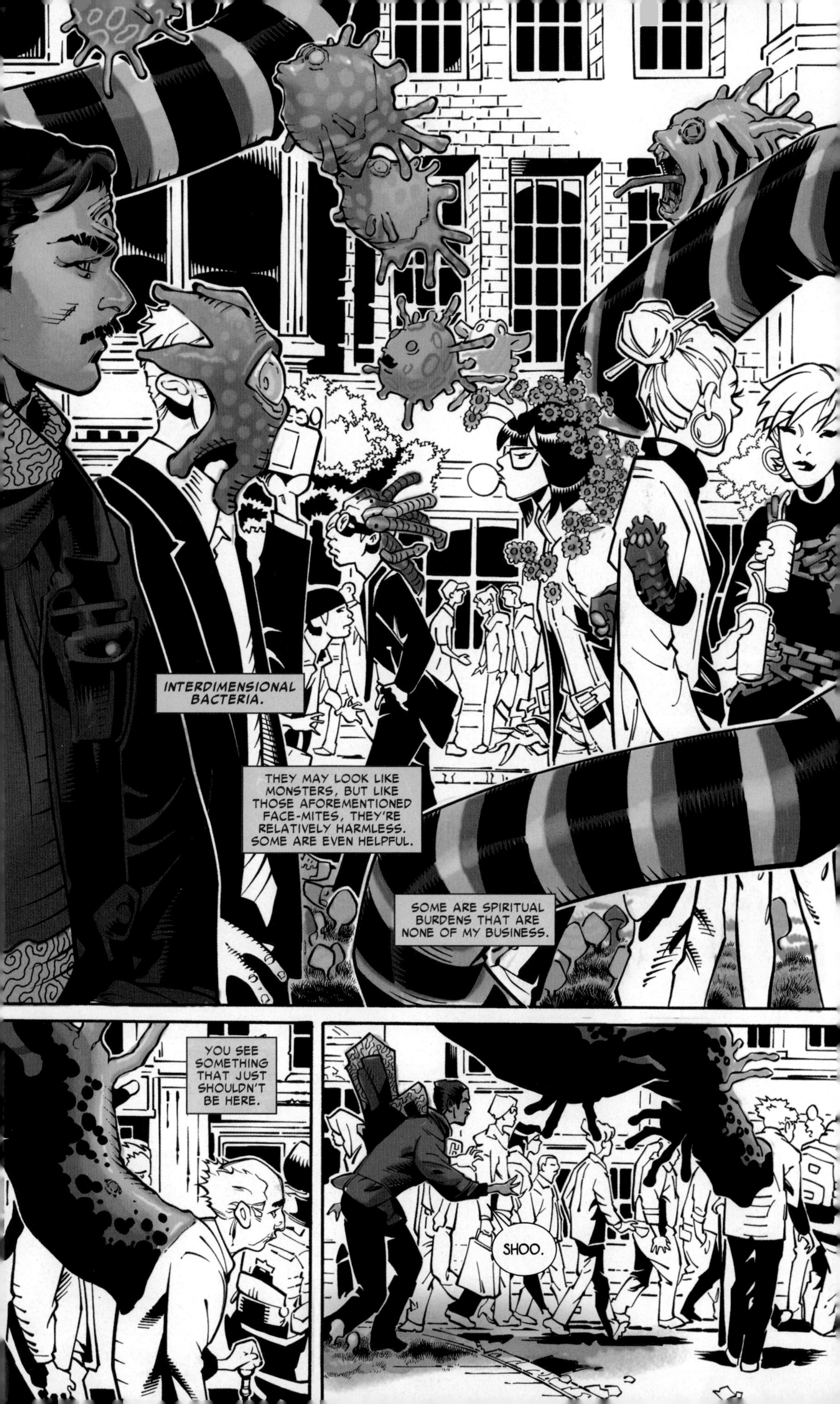
INTERDIMENSIONAL BACTERIA.
THEY MAY LOOK LIKE MONSTERS, BUT LIKE THOSE AFOREMENTIONED FACE-MITES, THEY'RE RELATIVELY HARMLESS. SOME ARE EVEN HELPFUL.
SOME ARE SPIRITUAL BURDENS THAT ARE NONE OF MY BUSINESS.
YOU SEE SOMETHING THAT JUST SHOULDN'T BE HERE.
SHOO.

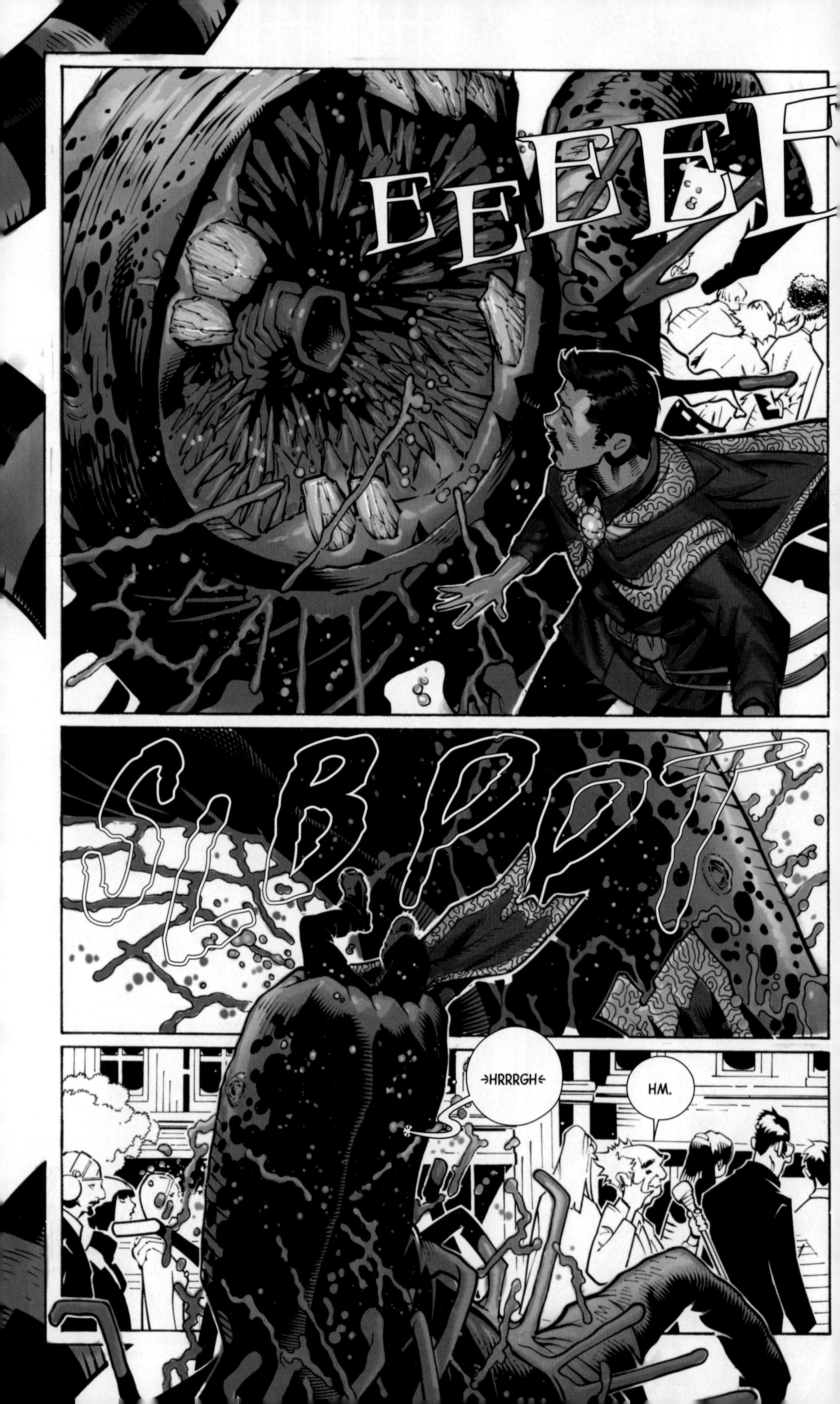
EEEEE
SLRPPT
HRRRGH
HM.

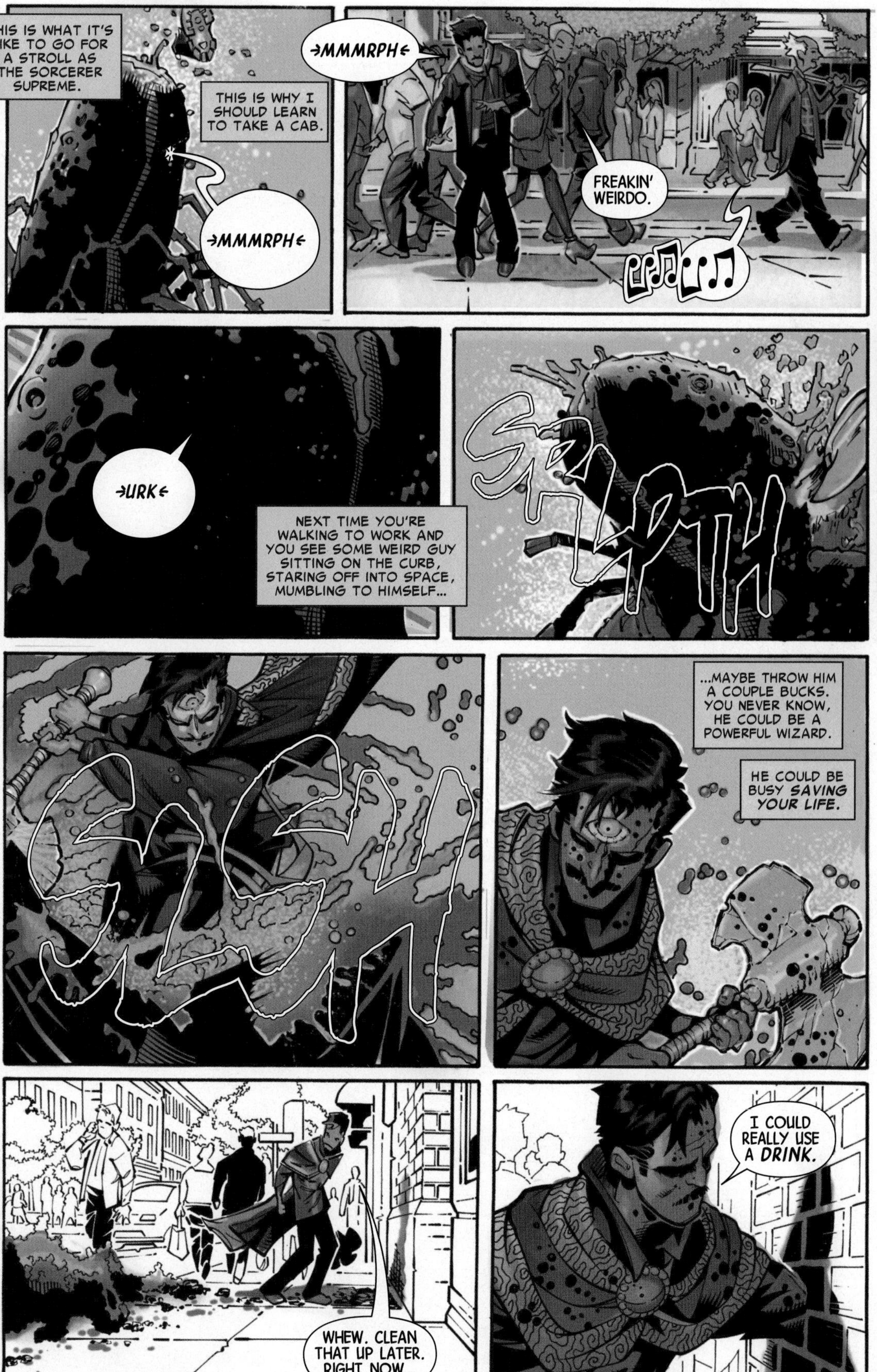
HIS IS WHAT IT'S IKE TO GO FOR A STROLL AS THE SORCERER SUPREME.
THIS IS WHY I SHOULD LEARN TO TAKE A CAB.
MMMRPH
MMMRPH
FREAKIN' WEIRDO.
URK
NEXT TIME YOU'RE WALKING TO WORK AND YOU SEE SOME WEIRD GUY SITTING ON THE CURB, STARING OFF INTO SPACE, MUMBLING TO HIMSELF...
...MAYBE THROW HIM A COUPLE BUCKS. YOU NEVER KNOW, HE COULD BE A POWERFUL WIZARD.
HE COULD BE BUSY SAVING YOUR LIFE.
WHEW. CLEAN THAT UP LATER. RIGHT NOW...
I COULD REALLY USE A DRINK.

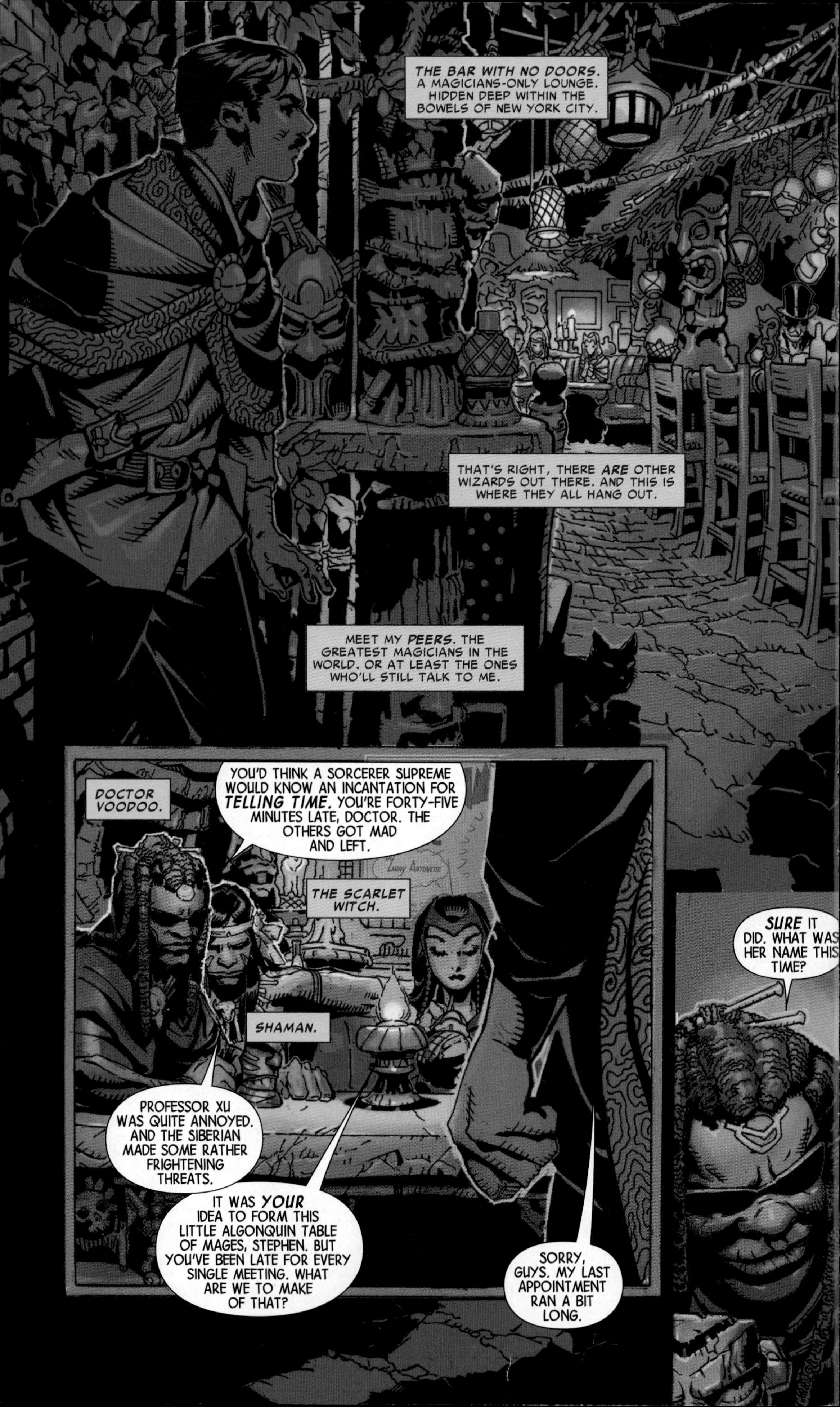

THE BAR WITH NO DOORS. A MAGICIANS-ONLY LOUNGE. HIDDEN DEEP WITHIN THE BOWELS OF NEW YORK CITY.
THAT'S RIGHT, THERE ARE OTHER WIZARDS OUT THERE. AND THIS IS WHERE THEY ALL HANG OUT.
MEET MY PEERS. THE GREATEST MAGICIANS IN THE WORLD. OR AT LEAST THE ONES WHO'LL STILL TALK TO ME.
DOCTOR VOODOO.
YOU'D THINK A SORCERER SUPREME WOULD KNOW AN INCANTATION FOR TELLING TIME. YOU'RE FORTY-FIVE MINUTES LATE, DOCTOR. THE OTHERS GOT MAD AND LEFT.
THE SCARLET WITCH.
SHAMAN.
PROFESSOR XU WAS QUITE ANNOYED. AND THE SIBERIAN MADE SOME RATHER FRIGHTENING THREATS.
IT WAS YOUR IDEA TO FORM THIS LITTLE ALGONQUIN TABLE OF MAGES, STEPHEN. BUT YOU'VE BEEN LATE FOR EVERY SINGLE MEETING. WHAT ARE WE TO MAKE OF THAT?
SORRY, GUYS. MY LAST APPOINTMENT RAN A BIT LONG.
SURE IT DID. WHAT WAS HER NAME THIS TIME?

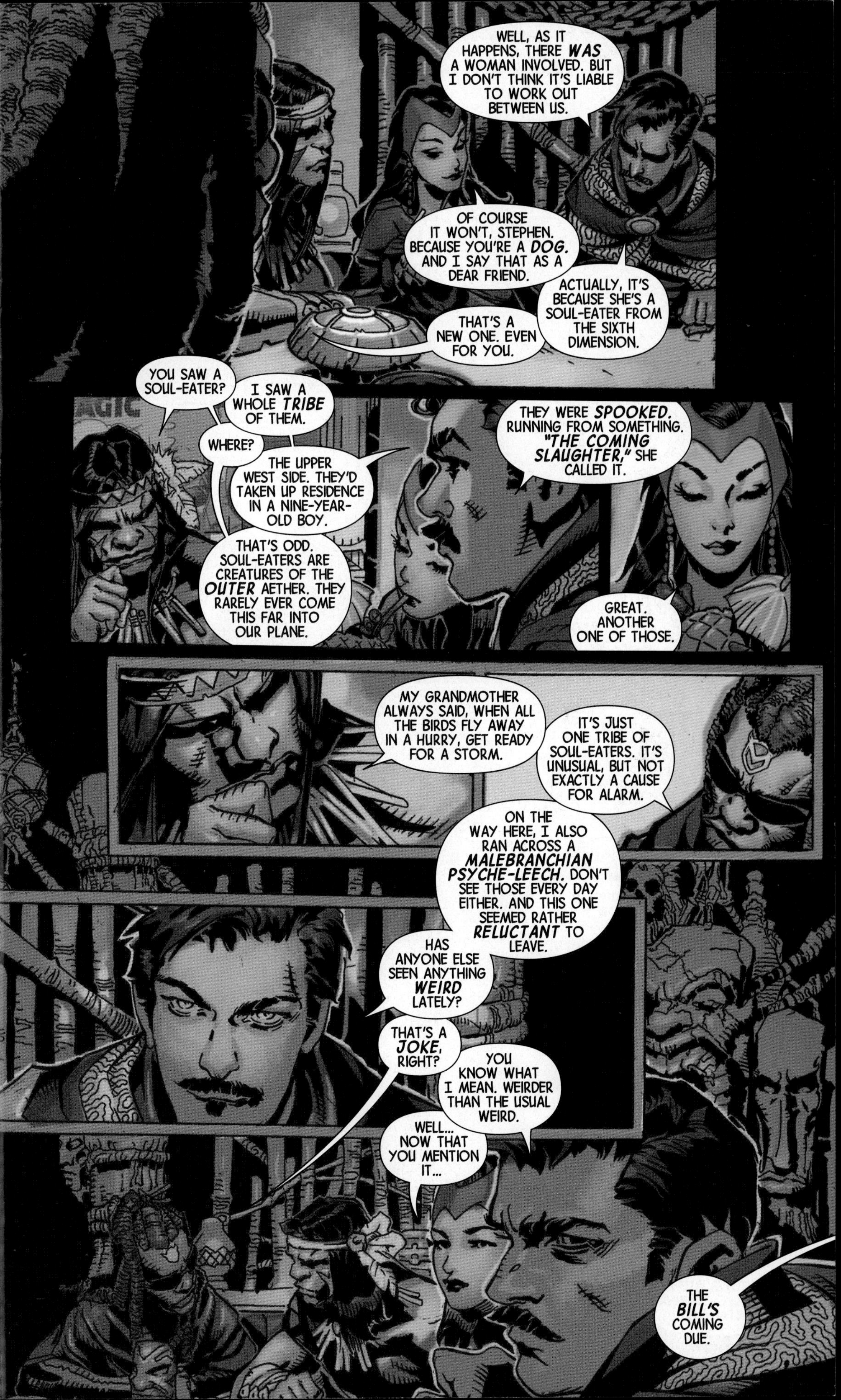
WELL, AS IT HAPPENS, THERE WAS A WOMAN INVOLVED. BUT I DON'T THINK IT'S LIABLE TO WORK OUT BETWEEN US.
OF COURSE IT WON'T, STEPHEN. BECAUSE YOU'RE A DOG. AND I SAY THAT AS A DEAR FRIEND.
ACTUALLY, IT'S BECAUSE SHE'S A SOUL-EATER FROM THE SIXTH DIMENSION.
THAT'S A NEW ONE. EVEN FOR YOU.
YOU SAW A SOUL-EATER?
I SAW A WHOLE TRIBE OF THEM.
WHERE?
THE UPPER WEST SIDE. THEY'D TAKEN UP RESIDENCE IN A NINE-YEAR-OLD BOY.
THEY WERE SPOOKED. RUNNING FROM SOMETHING. "THE COMING SLAUGHTER," SHE CALLED IT.
THAT'S ODD. SOUL-EATERS ARE CREATURES OF THE OUTER AETHER. THEY RARELY EVER COME THIS FAR INTO OUR PLANE.
GREAT. ANOTHER ONE OF THOSE.
MY GRANDMOTHER ALWAYS SAID, WHEN ALL THE BIRDS FLY AWAY IN A HURRY, GET READY FOR A STORM.
IT'S JUST ONE TRIBE OF SOUL-EATERS. IT'S UNUSUAL, BUT NOT EXACTLY A CAUSE FOR ALARM.
ON THE WAY HERE, I ALSO RAN ACROSS A MALEBRANCHIAN PSYCHE-LEECH. DON'T SEE THOSE EVERY DAY EITHER. AND THIS ONE SEEMED RATHER RELUCTANT TO LEAVE.
HAS ANYONE ELSE SEEN ANYTHING WEIRD LATELY?
THAT'S A JOKE, RIGHT?
YOU KNOW WHAT I MEAN. WEIRDER THAN THE USUAL WEIRD.
WELL... NOW THAT YOU MENTION IT...
THE BILL'S COMING DUE.

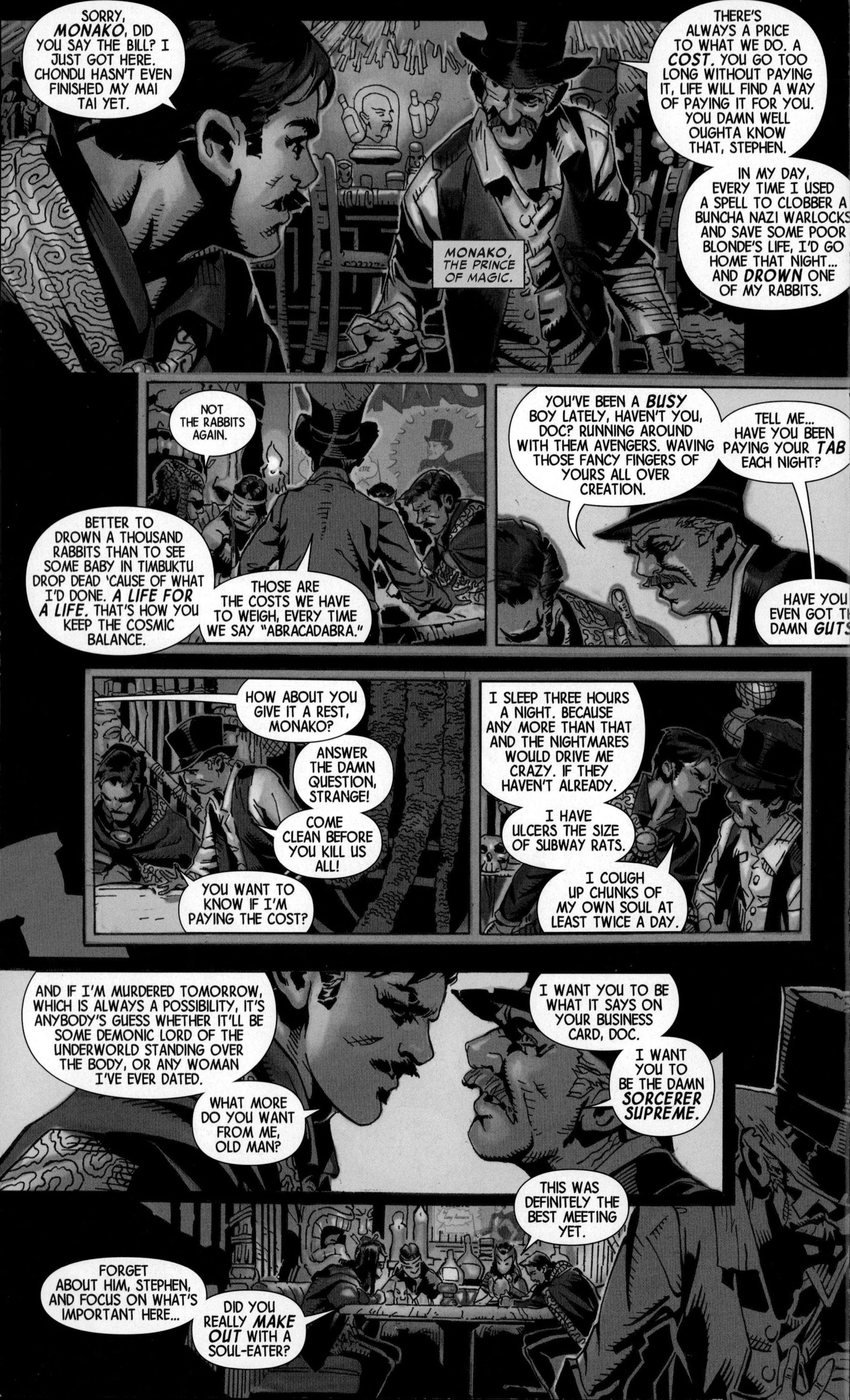
SORRY, MONAKO, DID YOU SAY THE BILL? I JUST GOT HERE. CHONDU HASN'T EVEN FINISHED MY MAI TAI YET.
THERE'S ALWAYS A PRICE TO WHAT WE DO. A COST. YOU GO TOO LONG WITHOUT PAYING IT, LIFE WILL FIND A WAY OF PAYING IT FOR YOU. YOU DAMN WELL OUGHTA KNOW THAT, STEPHEN.
MONAKO, THE PRINCE OF MAGIC.
IN MY DAY, EVERY TIME I USED A SPELL TO CLOBBER A BUNCHA NAZI WARLOCKS AND SAVE SOME POOR BLONDE'S LIFE, I'D GO HOME THAT NIGHT... AND DROWN ONE OF MY RABBITS.
NOT THE RABBITS AGAIN.
BETTER TO DROWN A THOUSAND RABBITS THAN TO SEE SOME BABY IN TIMBUKTU DROP DEAD 'CAUSE OF WHAT I'D DONE. A LIFE FOR A LIFE. THAT'S HOW YOU KEEP THE COSMIC BALANCE.
THOSE ARE THE COSTS WE HAVE TO WEIGH, EVERY TIME WE SAY "ABRACADABRA."
YOU'VE BEEN A BUSY BOY LATELY, HAVEN'T YOU, DOC? RUNNING AROUND WITH THEM AVENGERS. WAVING THOSE FANCY FINGERS OF YOURS ALL OVER CREATION.
TELL ME... HAVE YOU BEEN PAYING YOUR TAB EACH NIGHT?
HAVE YOU EVEN GOT TH DAMN GUTS
HOW ABOUT YOU GIVE IT A REST, MONAKO?
ANSWER THE DAMN QUESTION, STRANGE!
COME CLEAN BEFORE YOU KILL US ALL!
YOU WANT TO KNOW IF I'M PAYING THE COST?
I SLEEP THREE HOURS A NIGHT. BECAUSE ANY MORE THAN THAT AND THE NIGHTMARES WOULD DRIVE ME CRAZY. IF THEY HAVEN'T ALREADY.
I HAVE ULCERS THE SIZE OF SUBWAY RATS.
I COUGH UP CHUNKS OF MY OWN SOUL AT LEAST TWICE A DAY.
AND IF I'M MURDERED TOMORROW, WHICH IS ALWAYS A POSSIBILITY, IT'S ANYBODY'S GUESS WHETHER IT'LL BE SOME DEMONIC LORD OF THE UNDERWORLD STANDING OVER THE BODY, OR ANY WOMAN I'VE EVER DATED.
WHAT MORE DO YOU WANT FROM ME, OLD MAN?
I WANT YOU TO BE WHAT IT SAYS ON YOUR BUSINESS CARD, DOC.
I WANT YOU TO BE THE DAMN SORCERER SUPREME.
THIS WAS DEFINITELY THE BEST MEETING YET.
FORGET ABOUT HIM, STEPHEN, AND FOCUS ON WHAT'S IMPORTANT HERE...
DID YOU REALLY MAKE OUT WITH A SOUL-EATER?

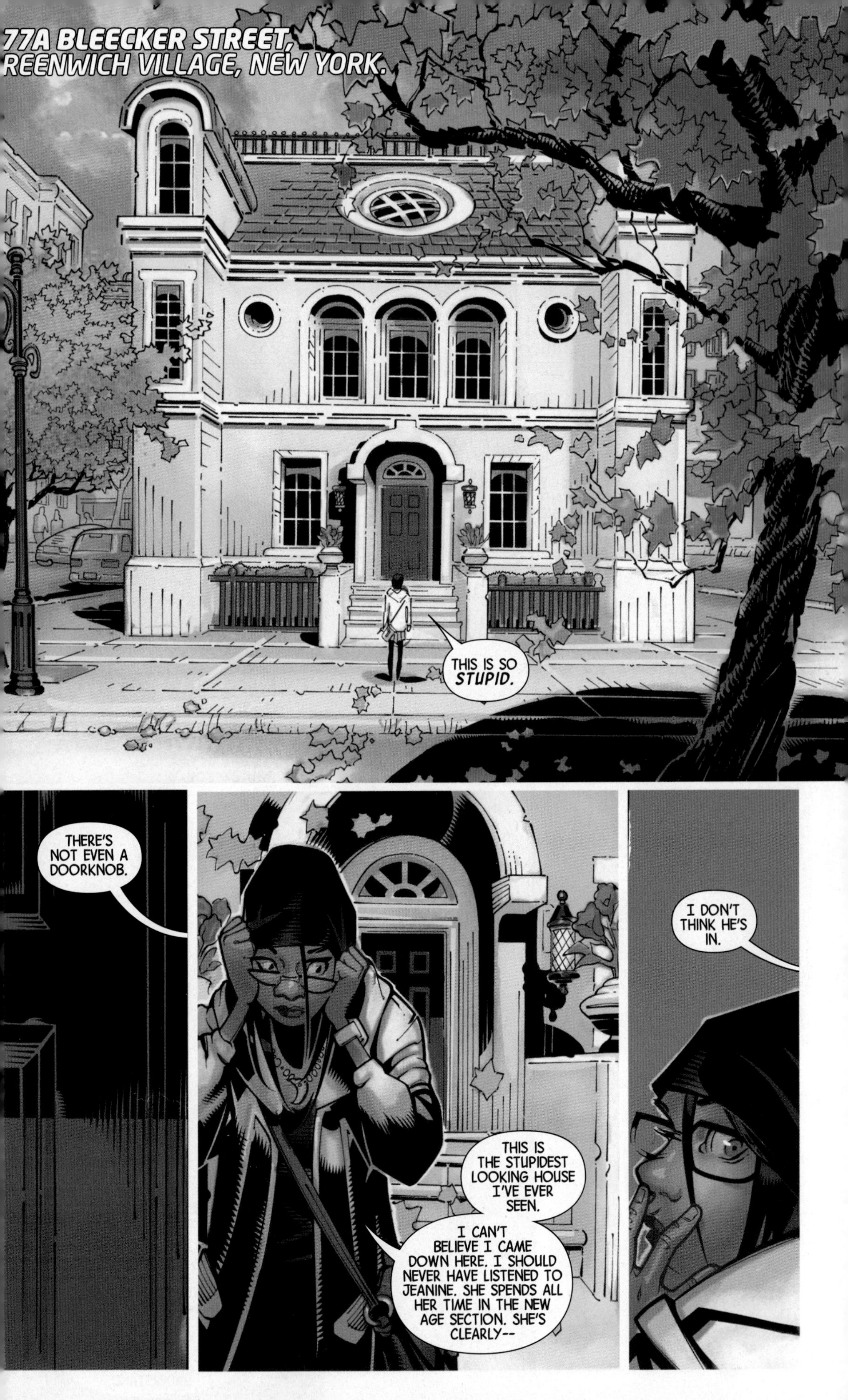
77A BLEECKER STREET,
REENWICH VILLAGE, NEW YORK.
THIS IS SO STUPID.
THERE'S NOT EVEN A DOORKNOB.
THIS IS THE STUPIDEST LOOKING HOUSE I'VE EVER SEEN.
I CAN'T BELIEVE I CAME DOWN HERE. I SHOULD NEVER HAVE LISTENED TO JEANINE. SHE SPENDS ALL HER TIME IN THE NEW AGE SECTION. SHE'S CLEARLY--
I DON'T THINK HE'S IN.

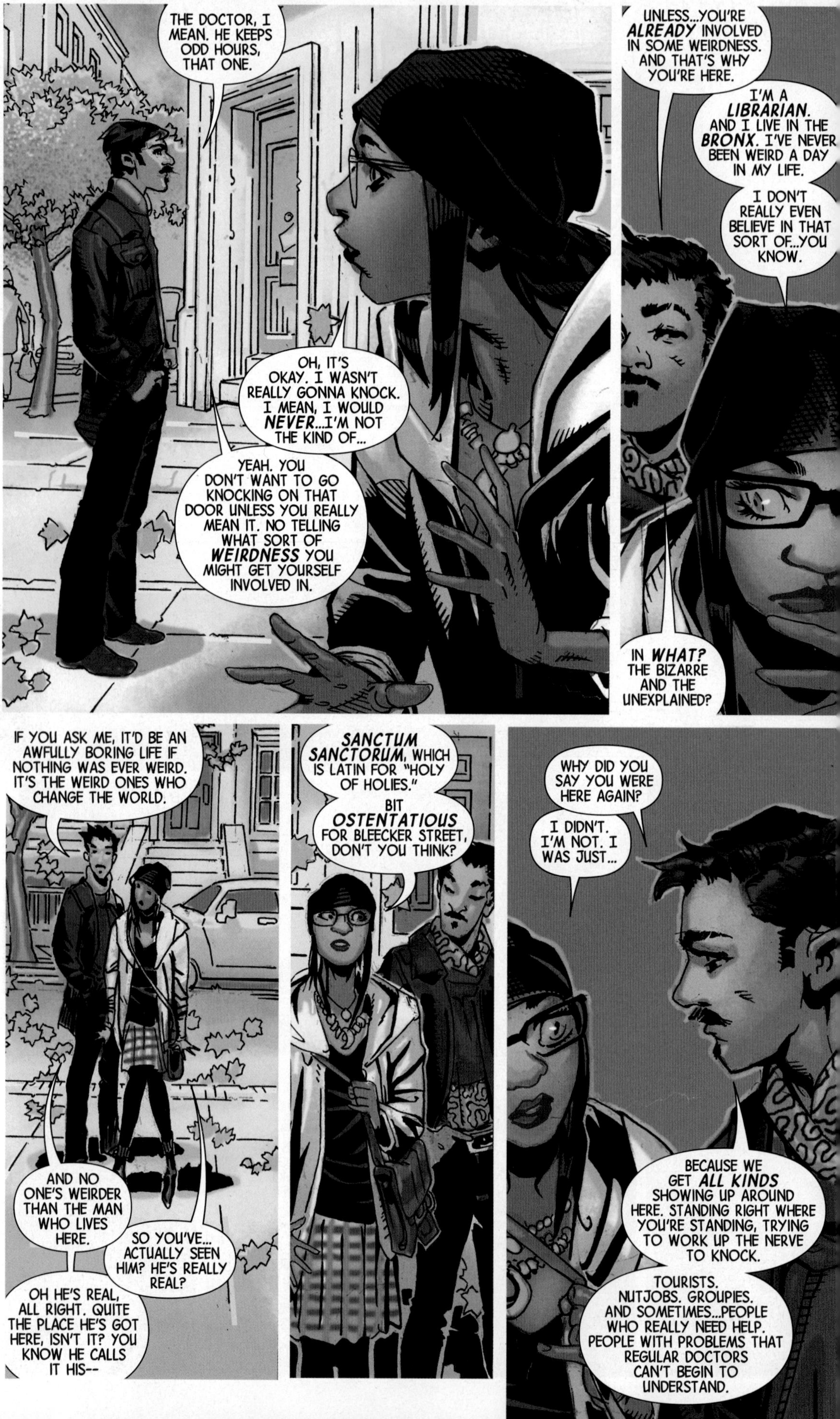
THE DOCTOR, I MEAN. HE KEEPS ODD HOURS, THAT ONE.
OH, IT'S OKAY. I WASN'T REALLY GONNA KNOCK. I MEAN, I WOULD NEVER...I'M NOT THE KIND OF...
YEAH. YOU DON'T WANT TO GO KNOCKING ON THAT DOOR UNLESS YOU REALLY MEAN IT. NO TELLING WHAT SORT OF WEIRDNESS YOU MIGHT GET YOURSELF INVOLVED IN.
UNLESS...YOU'RE ALREADY INVOLVED IN SOME WEIRDNESS. AND THAT'S WHY YOU'RE HERE.
I'M A LIBRARIAN. AND I LIVE IN THE BRONX. I'VE NEVER BEEN WEIRD A DAY IN MY LIFE.
I DON'T REALLY EVEN BELIEVE IN THAT SORT OF...YOU KNOW.
IN WHAT? THE BIZARRE AND THE UNEXPLAINED?
IF YOU ASK ME, IT'D BE AN AWFULLY BORING LIFE IF NOTHING WAS EVER WEIRD. IT'S THE WEIRD ONES WHO CHANGE THE WORLD.
AND NO ONE'S WEIRDER THAN THE MAN WHO LIVES HERE.
SO YOU'VE... ACTUALLY SEEN HIM? HE'S REALLY REAL?
OH HE'S REAL, ALL RIGHT. QUITE THE PLACE HE'S GOT HERE, ISN'T IT? YOU KNOW HE CALLS IT HIS--
SANCTUM SANCTORUM, WHICH IS LATIN FOR "HOLY OF HOLIES."
BIT OSTENTATIOUS FOR BLEECKER STREET, DON'T YOU THINK?
WHY DID YOU SAY YOU WERE HERE AGAIN?
I DIDN'T. I'M NOT. I WAS JUST...
BECAUSE WE GET ALL KINDS SHOWING UP AROUND HERE. STANDING RIGHT WHERE YOU'RE STANDING, TRYING TO WORK UP THE NERVE TO KNOCK.
TOURISTS. NUTJOBS. GROUPIES. AND SOMETIMES...PEOPLE WHO REALLY NEED HELP. PEOPLE WITH PROBLEMS THAT REGULAR DOCTORS CAN'T BEGIN TO UNDERSTAND.

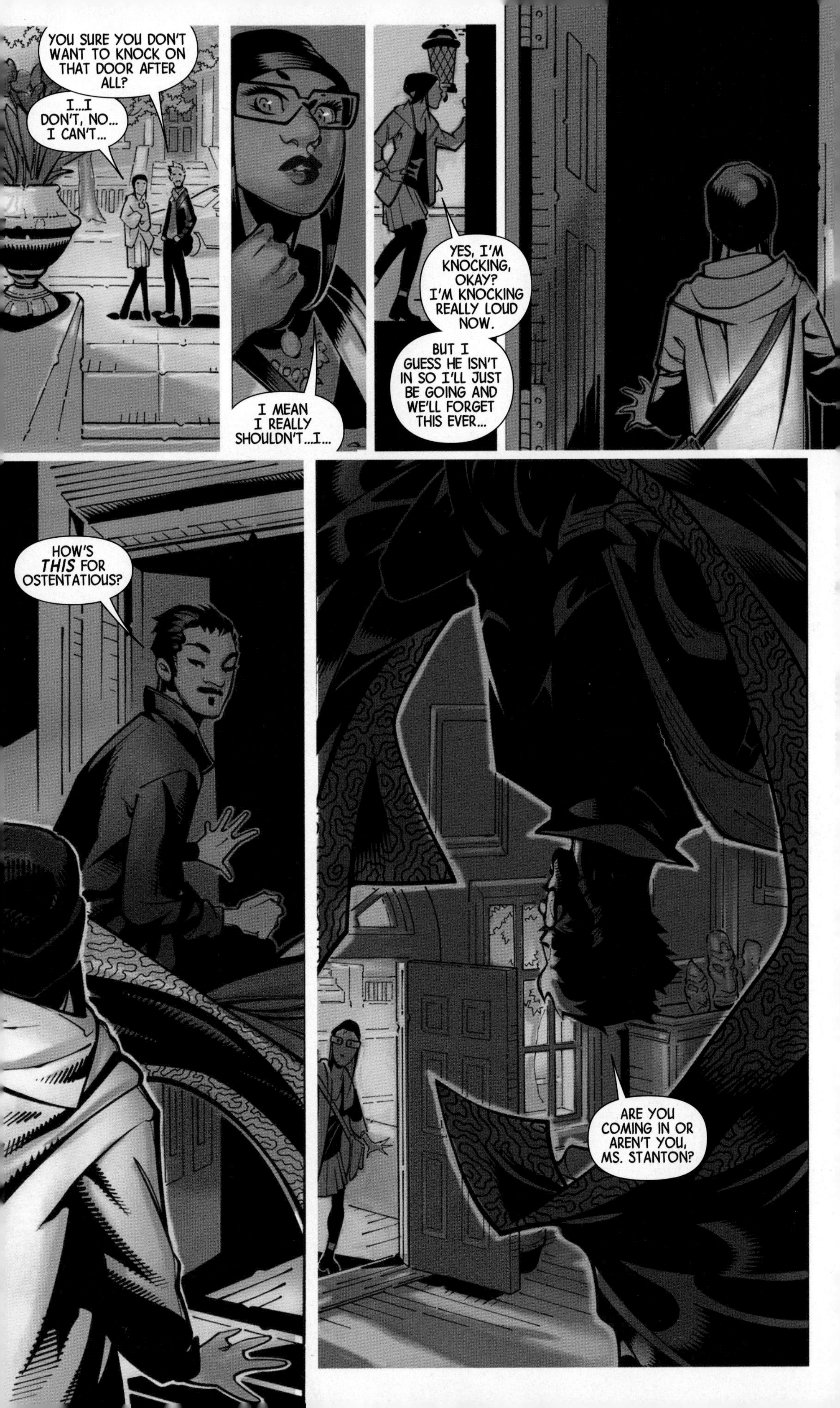

YOU SURE YOU DON'T WANT TO KNOCK ON THAT DOOR AFTER ALL?
I...I DON'T, NO... I CAN'T...
I MEAN I REALLY SHOULDN'T...I...
YES, I'M KNOCKING, OKAY? I'M KNOCKING REALLY LOUD NOW.
BUT I GUESS HE ISN'T IN SO I'LL JUST BE GOING AND WE'LL FORGET THIS EVER...
HOW'S *THIS* FOR OSTENTATIOUS?
ARE YOU COMING IN OR AREN'T YOU, MS. STANTON?

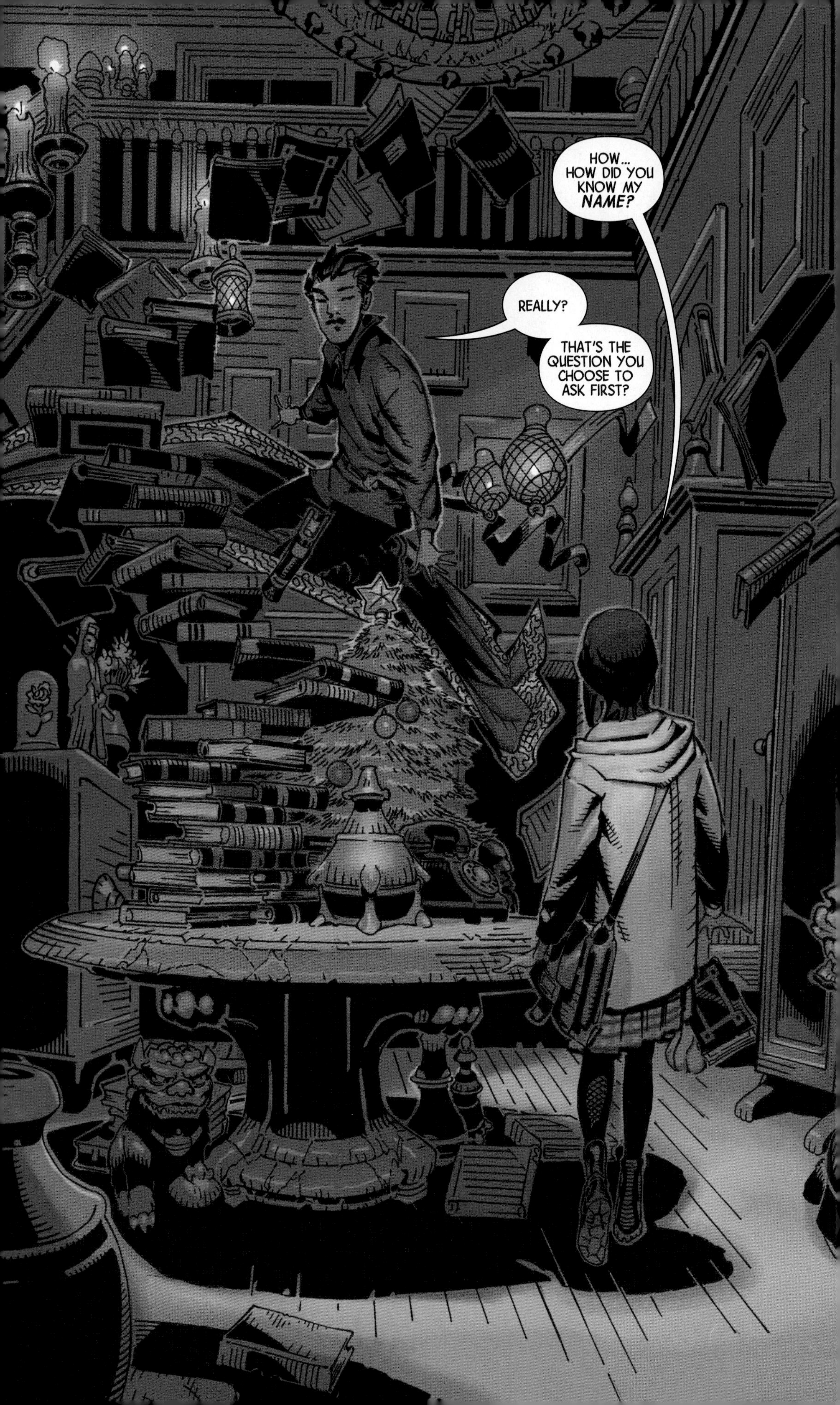
HOW... HOW DID YOU KNOW MY NAME?
REALLY?
THAT'S THE QUESTION YOU CHOOSE TO ASK FIRST?

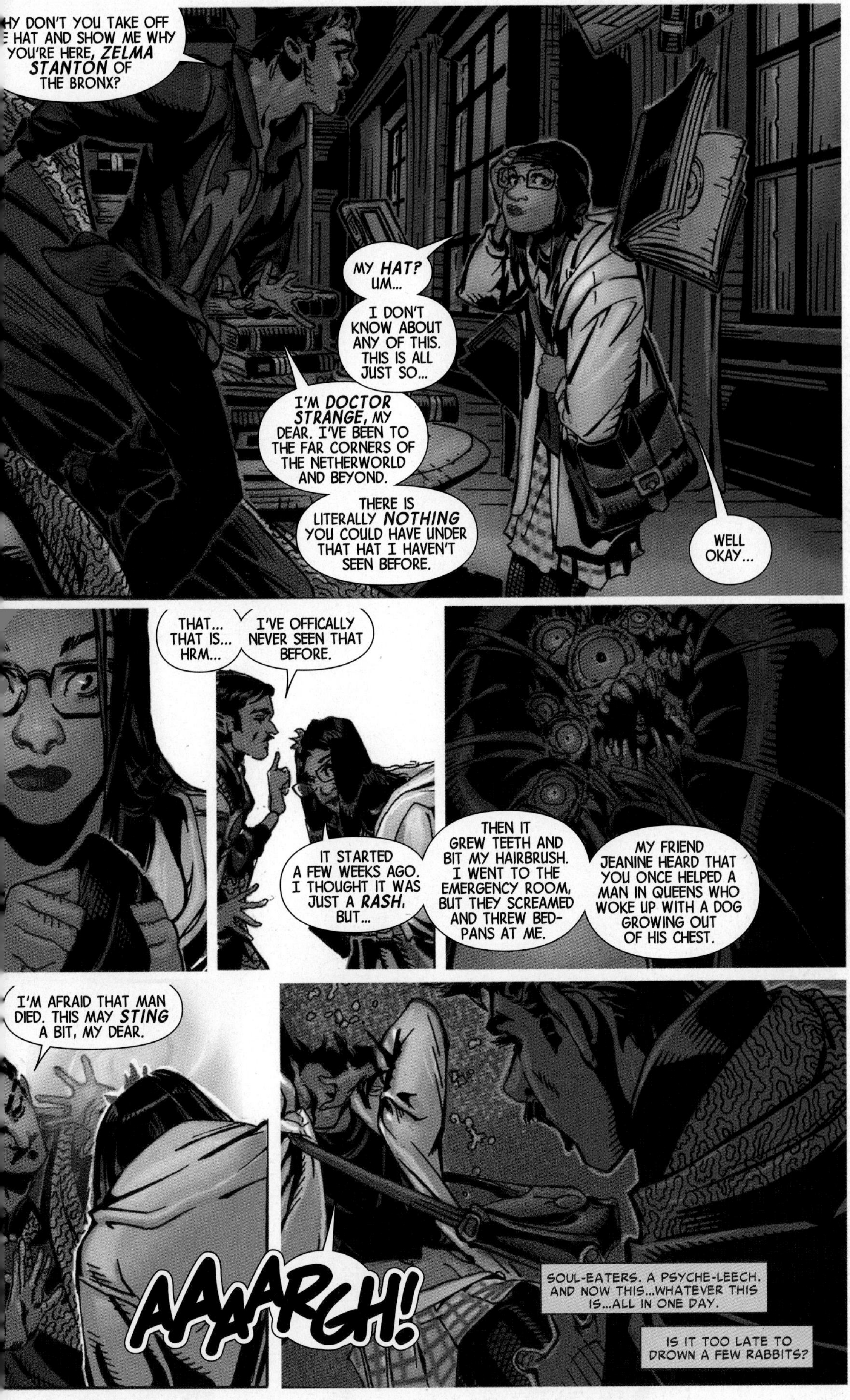
HY DON'T YOU TAKE OFF E HAT AND SHOW ME WHY YOU'RE HERE, ZELMA STANTON OF THE BRONX?
MY HAT? UM...
I DON'T KNOW ABOUT ANY OF THIS. THIS IS ALL JUST SO...
I'M DOCTOR STRANGE, MY DEAR. I'VE BEEN TO THE FAR CORNERS OF THE NETHERWORLD AND BEYOND.
THERE IS LITERALLY NOTHING YOU COULD HAVE UNDER THAT HAT I HAVEN'T SEEN BEFORE.
WELL OKAY...
THAT... THAT IS... HRM...
I'VE OFFICALLY NEVER SEEN THAT BEFORE.
IT STARTED A FEW WEEKS AGO. I THOUGHT IT WAS JUST A RASH, BUT...
THEN IT GREW TEETH AND BIT MY HAIRBRUSH. I WENT TO THE EMERGENCY ROOM, BUT THEY SCREAMED AND THREW BED-PANS AT ME.
MY FRIEND JEANINE HEARD THAT YOU ONCE HELPED A MAN IN QUEENS WHO WOKE UP WITH A DOG GROWING OUT OF HIS CHEST.
I'M AFRAID THAT MAN DIED. THIS MAY STING A BIT, MY DEAR.
AAAARGH!
SOUL-EATERS. A PSYCHE-LEECH. AND NOW THIS...WHATEVER THIS IS...ALL IN ONE DAY.
IS IT TOO LATE TO DROWN A FEW RABBITS?

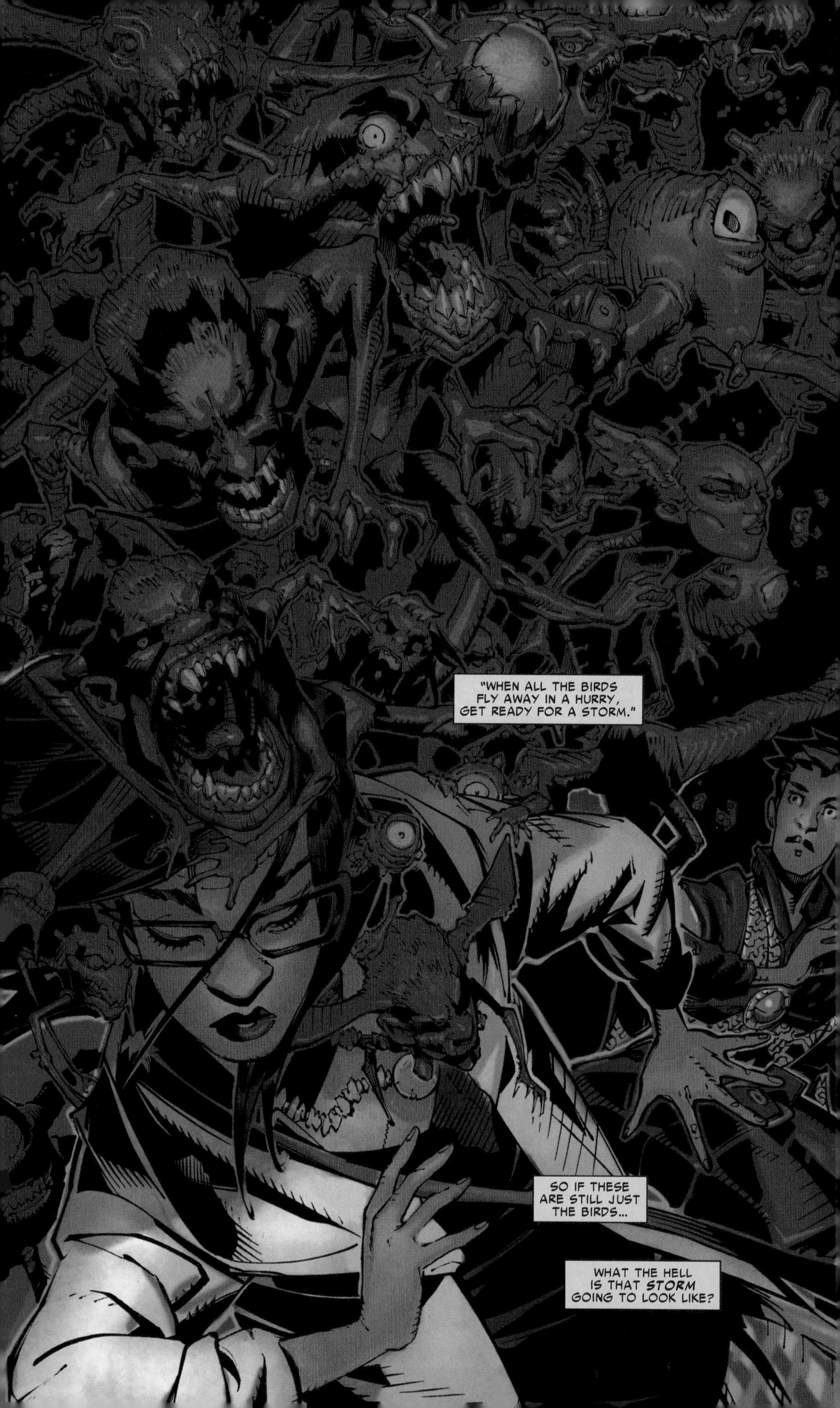
"WHEN ALL THE BIRDS FLY AWAY IN A HURRY, GET READY FOR A STORM."
SO IF THESE ARE STILL JUST THE BIRDS...
WHAT THE HELL IS THAT *STORM* GOING TO LOOK LIKE?

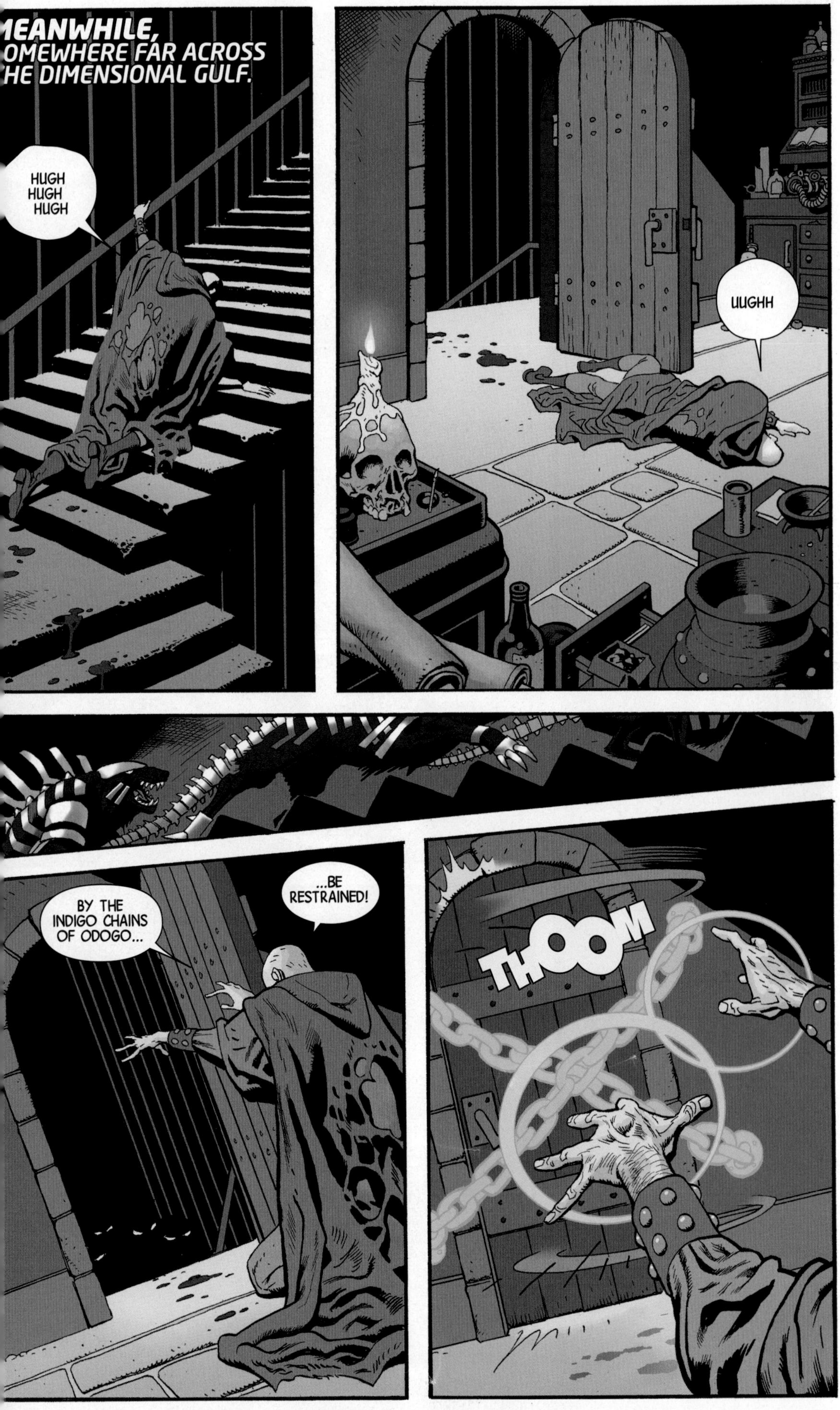
MEANWHILE,
SOMEWHERE FAR ACROSS
THE DIMENSIONAL GULF.
HUGH
HUGH
HUGH
UUGHH
BY THE
INDIGO CHAINS
OF ODOGO...
...BE
RESTRAINED!
THOOM

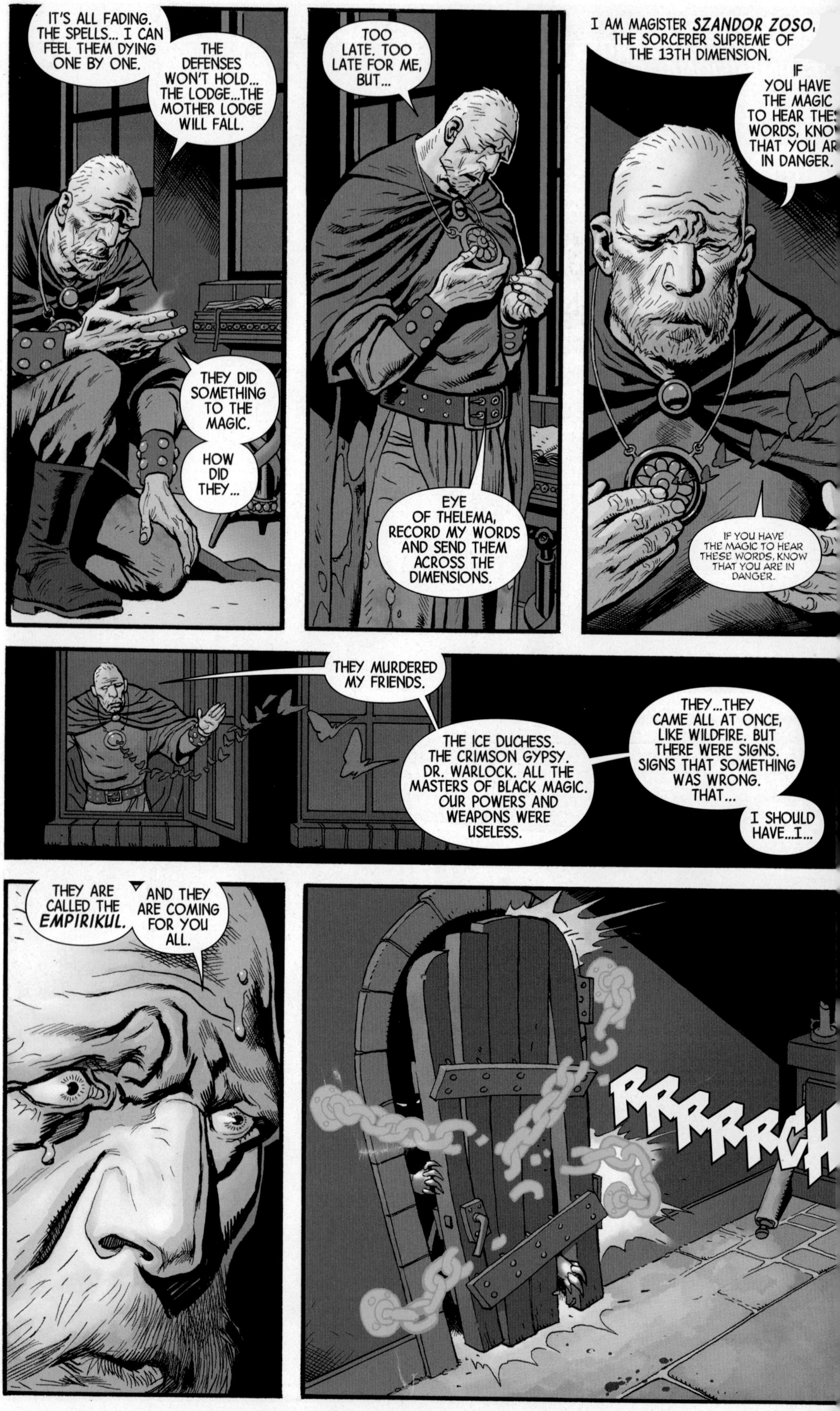
IT'S ALL FADING. THE SPELLS... I CAN FEEL THEM DYING ONE BY ONE.
THE DEFENSES WON'T HOLD... THE LODGE...THE MOTHER LODGE WILL FALL.
THEY DID SOMETHING TO THE MAGIC.
HOW DID THEY...
TOO LATE. TOO LATE FOR ME, BUT...
EYE OF THELEMA, RECORD MY WORDS AND SEND THEM ACROSS THE DIMENSIONS.
I AM MAGISTER SZANDOR ZOSO, THE SORCERER SUPREME OF THE 13TH DIMENSION.
IF YOU HAVE THE MAGIC TO HEAR THE WORDS, KNO THAT YOU AR IN DANGER.
IF YOU HAVE THE MAGIC TO HEAR THESE WORDS, KNOW THAT YOU ARE IN DANGER.
THEY MURDERED MY FRIENDS.
THE ICE DUCHESS. THE CRIMSON GYPSY. DR. WARLOCK. ALL THE MASTERS OF BLACK MAGIC. OUR POWERS AND WEAPONS WERE USELESS.
THEY...THEY CAME ALL AT ONCE, LIKE WILDFIRE. BUT THERE WERE SIGNS. SIGNS THAT SOMETHING WAS WRONG. THAT...
I SHOULD HAVE...I...
THEY ARE CALLED THE EMPIRIKUL.
AND THEY ARE COMING FOR YOU ALL.
RRRRRCH

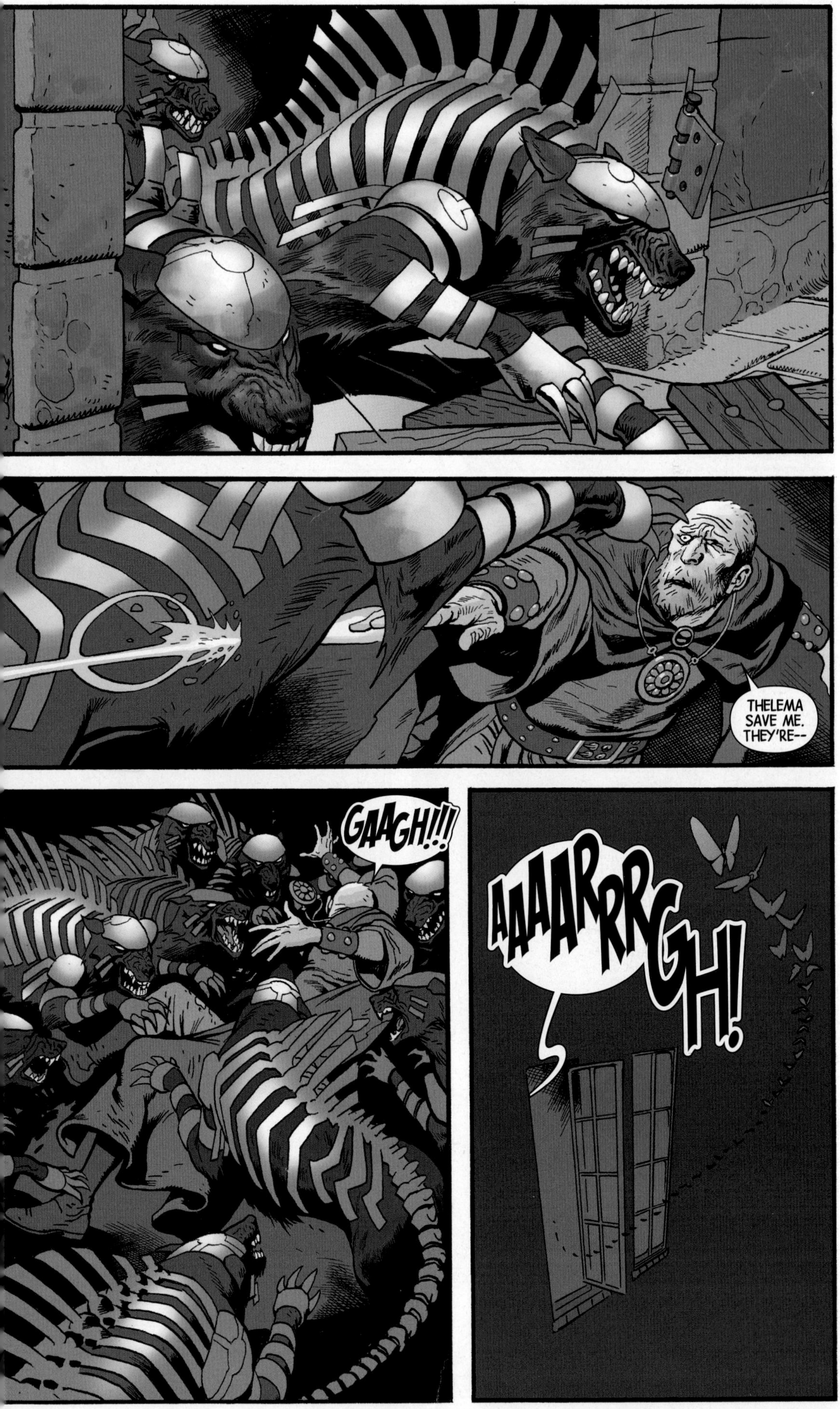
THELEMA SAVE ME. THEY'RE--
GAAGH!!!
AAAARRRGH!

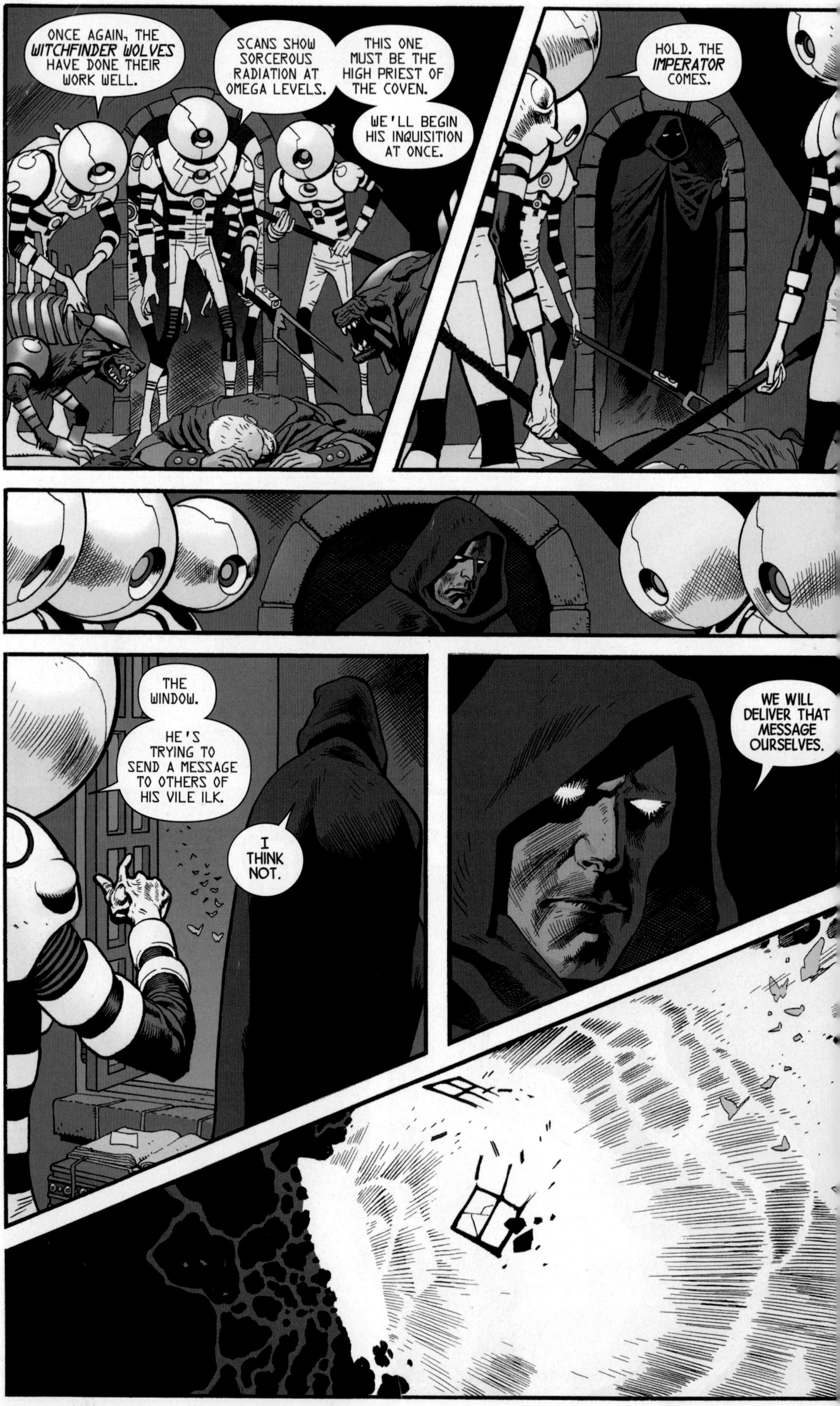

ONCE AGAIN, THE WITCHFINDER WOLVES HAVE DONE THEIR WORK WELL.
SCANS SHOW SORCEROUS RADIATION AT OMEGA LEVELS.
THIS ONE MUST BE THE HIGH PRIEST OF THE COVEN.
WE'LL BEGIN HIS INQUISITION AT ONCE.
HOLD. THE IMPERATOR COMES.
THE WINDOW.
HE'S TRYING TO SEND A MESSAGE TO OTHERS OF HIS VILE ILK.
I THINK NOT.
WE WILL DELIVER THAT MESSAGE OURSELVES.

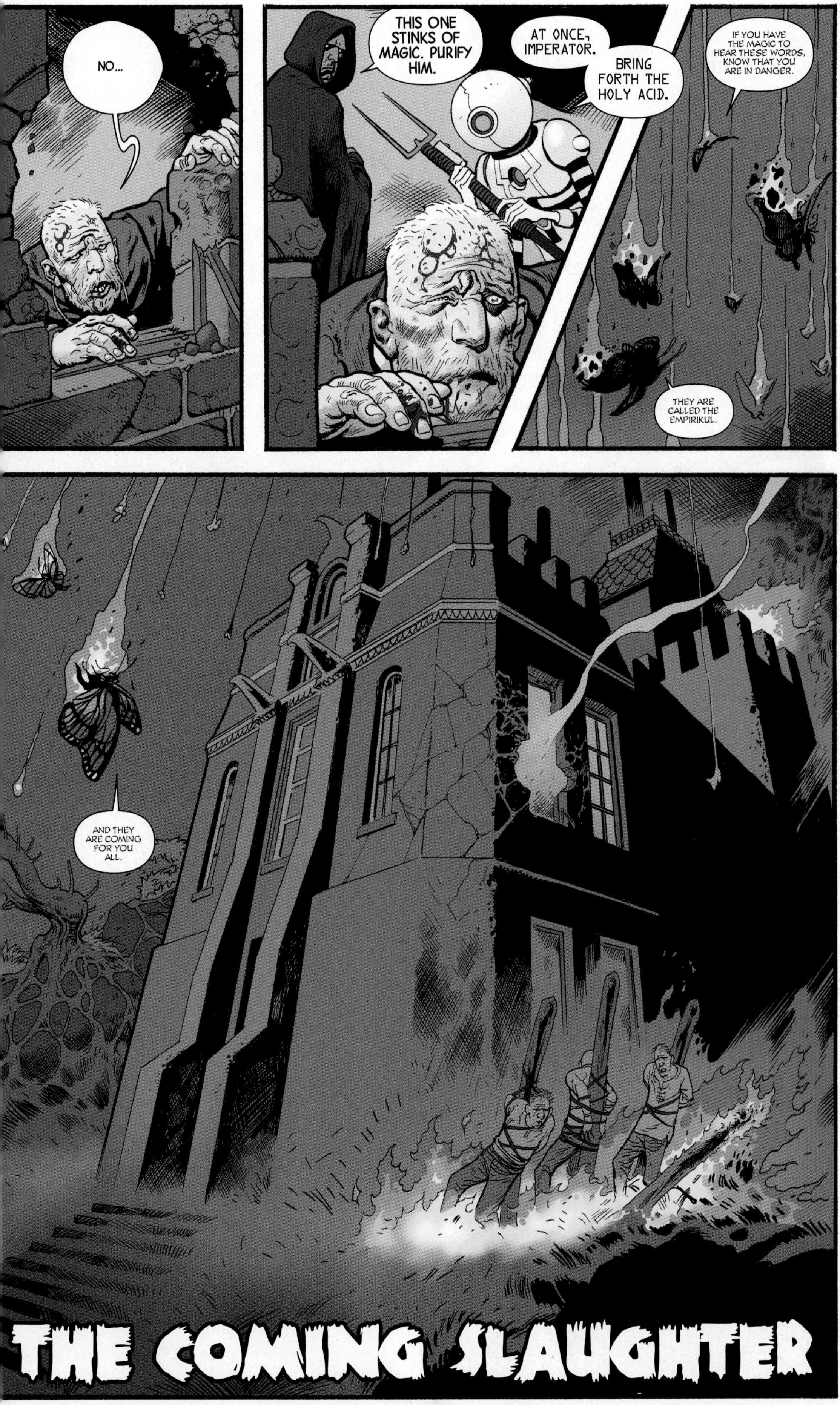
NO...
THIS ONE STINKS OF MAGIC. PURIFY HIM.
AT ONCE, IMPERATOR.
BRING FORTH THE HOLY ACID.
IF YOU HAVE THE MAGIC TO HEAR THESE WORDS, KNOW THAT YOU ARE IN DANGER.
THEY ARE CALLED THE EMPIRIKUL.
AND THEY ARE COMING FOR YOU ALL.
THE COMING SLAUGHTER

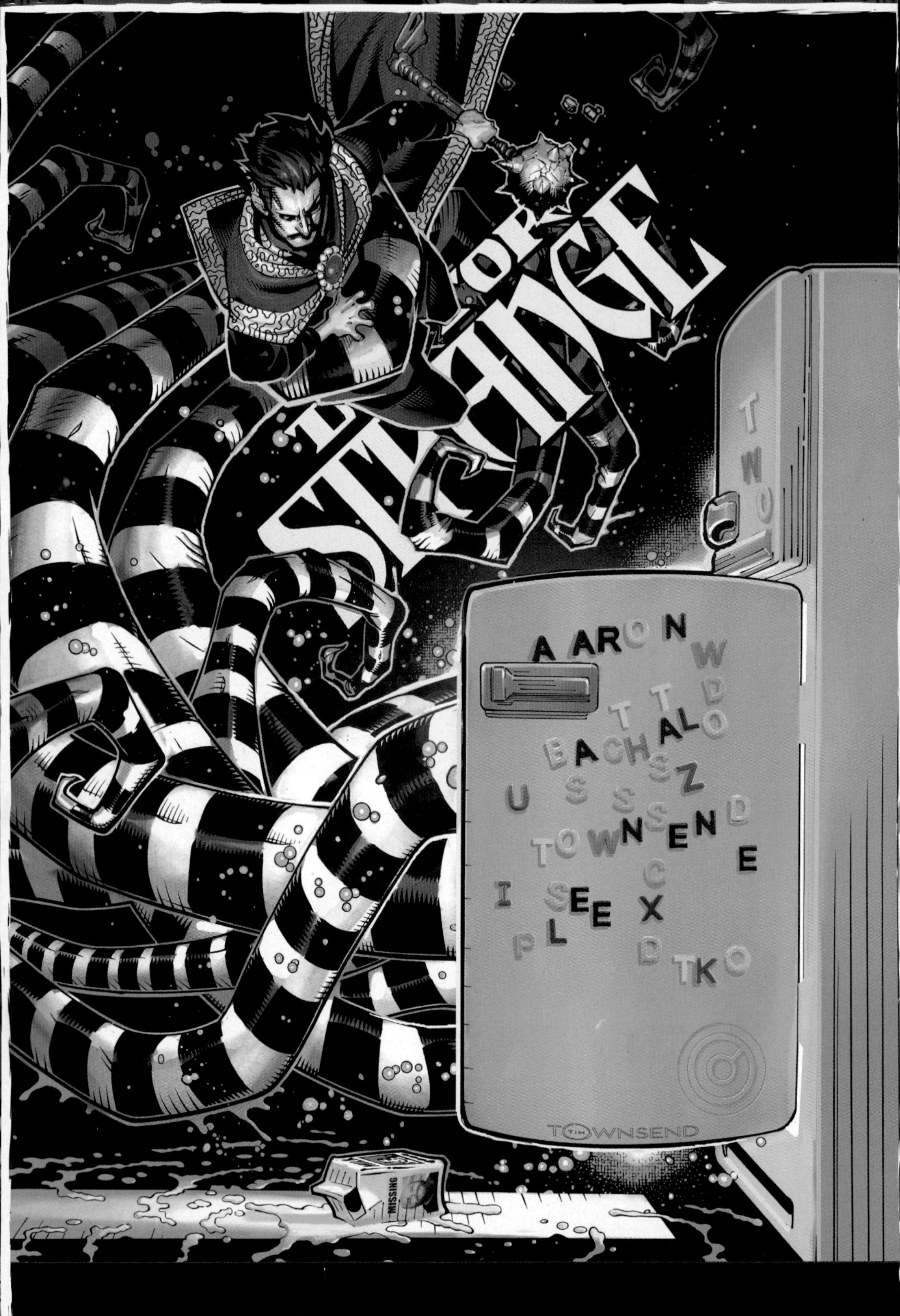
AARON
BACHALO
TOWNSEND
TIM TOWNSEND
MISSING

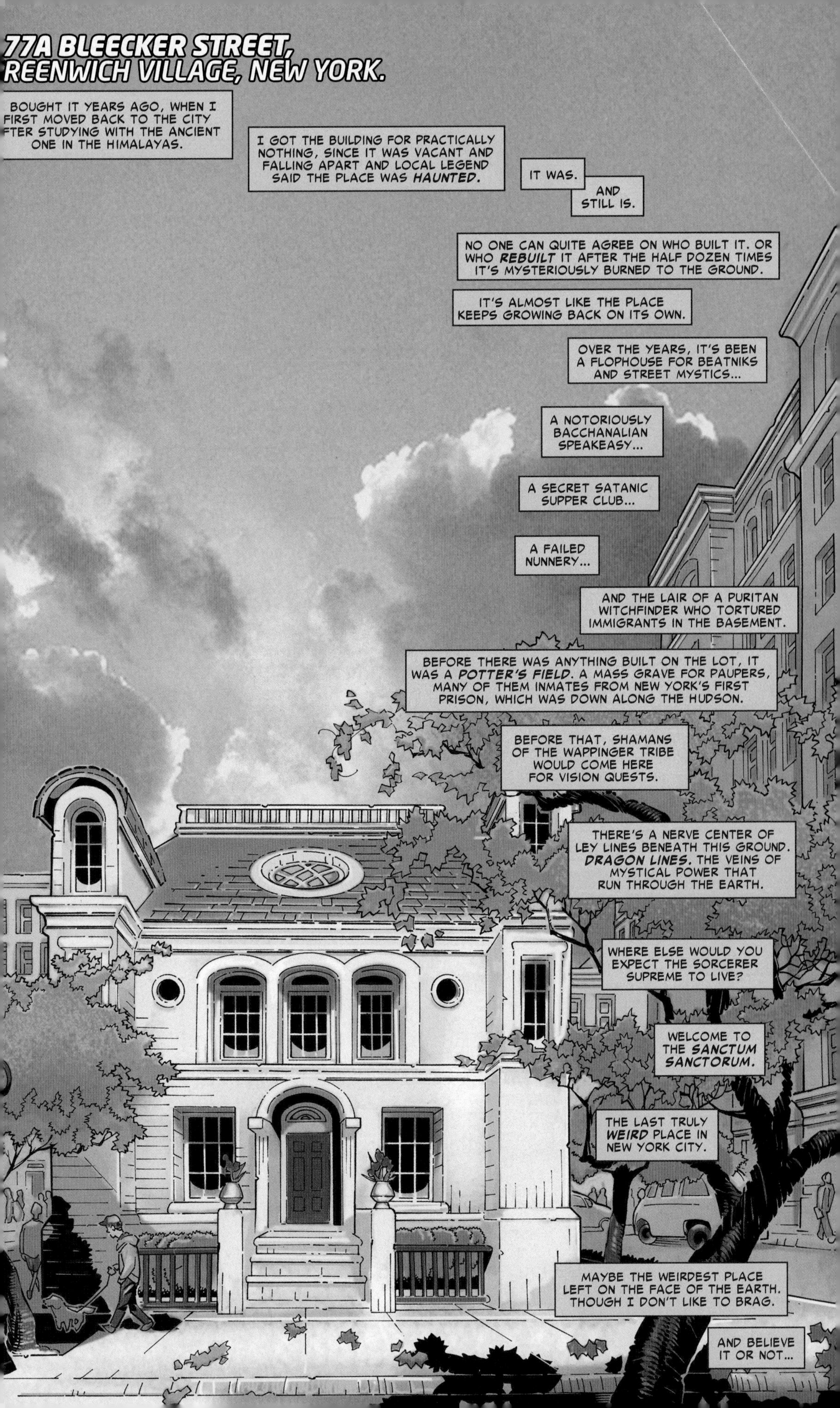

77A BLEECKER STREET, REENWICH VILLAGE, NEW YORK.
BOUGHT IT YEARS AGO, WHEN I FIRST MOVED BACK TO THE CITY FTER STUDYING WITH THE ANCIENT ONE IN THE HIMALAYAS.
I GOT THE BUILDING FOR PRACTICALLY NOTHING, SINCE IT WAS VACANT AND FALLING APART AND LOCAL LEGEND SAID THE PLACE WAS HAUNTED.
IT WAS.
AND STILL IS.
NO ONE CAN QUITE AGREE ON WHO BUILT IT. OR WHO REBUILT IT AFTER THE HALF DOZEN TIMES IT'S MYSTERIOUSLY BURNED TO THE GROUND.
IT'S ALMOST LIKE THE PLACE KEEPS GROWING BACK ON ITS OWN.
OVER THE YEARS, IT'S BEEN A FLOPHOUSE FOR BEATNIKS AND STREET MYSTICS...
A NOTORIOUSLY BACCHANALIAN SPEAKEASY...
A SECRET SATANIC SUPPER CLUB...
A FAILED NUNNERY...
AND THE LAIR OF A PURITAN WITCHFINDER WHO TORTURED IMMIGRANTS IN THE BASEMENT.
BEFORE THERE WAS ANYTHING BUILT ON THE LOT, IT WAS A POTTER'S FIELD. A MASS GRAVE FOR PAUPERS, MANY OF THEM INMATES FROM NEW YORK'S FIRST PRISON, WHICH WAS DOWN ALONG THE HUDSON.
BEFORE THAT, SHAMANS OF THE WAPPINGER TRIBE WOULD COME HERE FOR VISION QUESTS.
THERE'S A NERVE CENTER OF LEY LINES BENEATH THIS GROUND. DRAGON LINES. THE VEINS OF MYSTICAL POWER THAT RUN THROUGH THE EARTH.
WHERE ELSE WOULD YOU EXPECT THE SORCERER SUPREME TO LIVE?
WELCOME TO THE SANCTUM SANCTORUM.
THE LAST TRULY WEIRD PLACE IN NEW YORK CITY.
MAYBE THE WEIRDEST PLACE LEFT ON THE FACE OF THE EARTH. THOUGH I DON'T LIKE TO BRAG.
AND BELIEVE IT OR NOT...

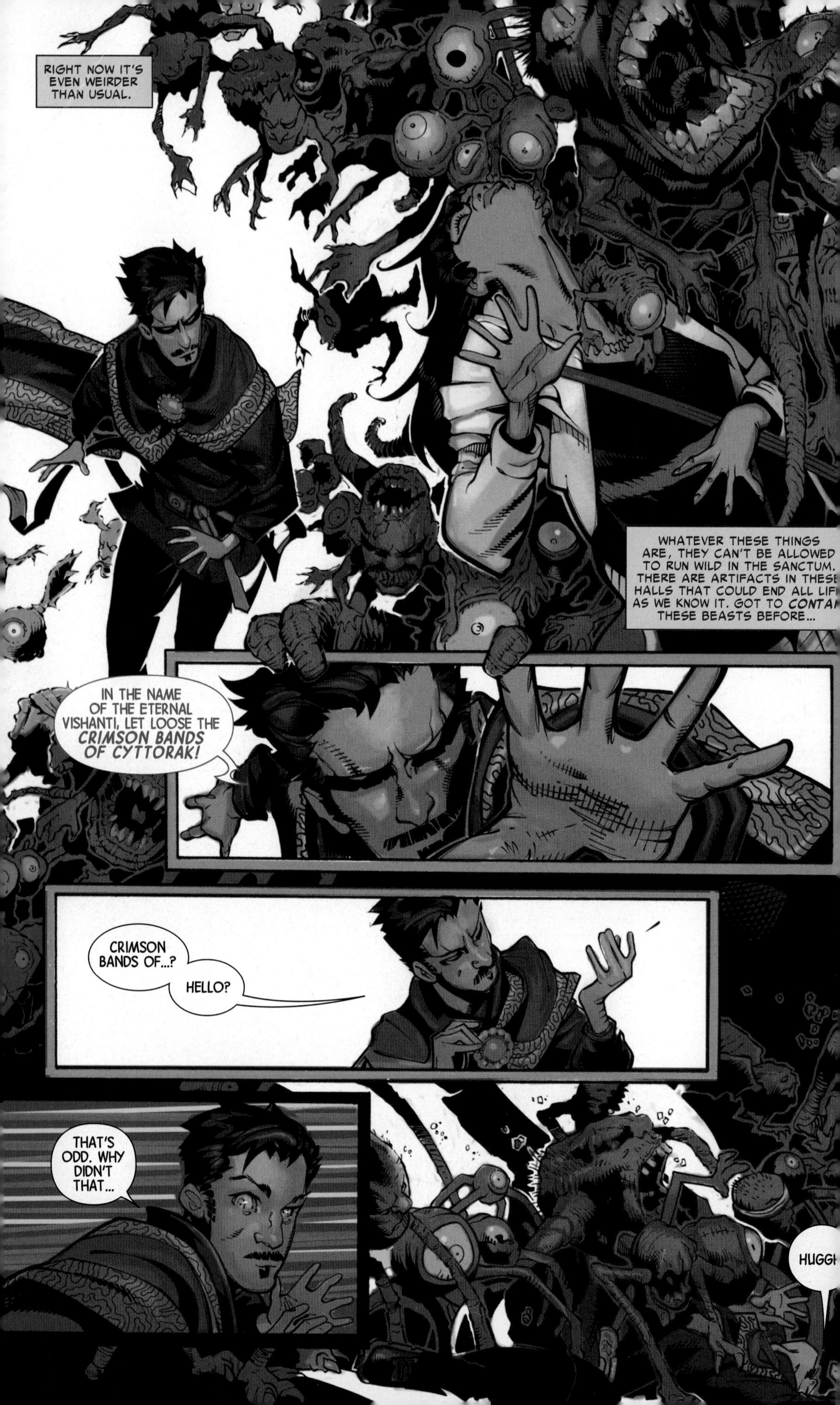
RIGHT NOW IT'S EVEN WEIRDER THAN USUAL.
WHATEVER THESE THINGS ARE, THEY CAN'T BE ALLOWED TO RUN WILD IN THE SANCTUM. THERE ARE ARTIFACTS IN THESE HALLS THAT COULD END ALL LIFE AS WE KNOW IT. GOT TO CONTAIN THESE BEASTS BEFORE...
IN THE NAME OF THE ETERNAL VISHANTI, LET LOOSE THE CRIMSON BANDS OF CYTTORAK!
CRIMSON BANDS OF...?
HELLO?
THAT'S ODD. WHY DIDN'T THAT...
HUGG

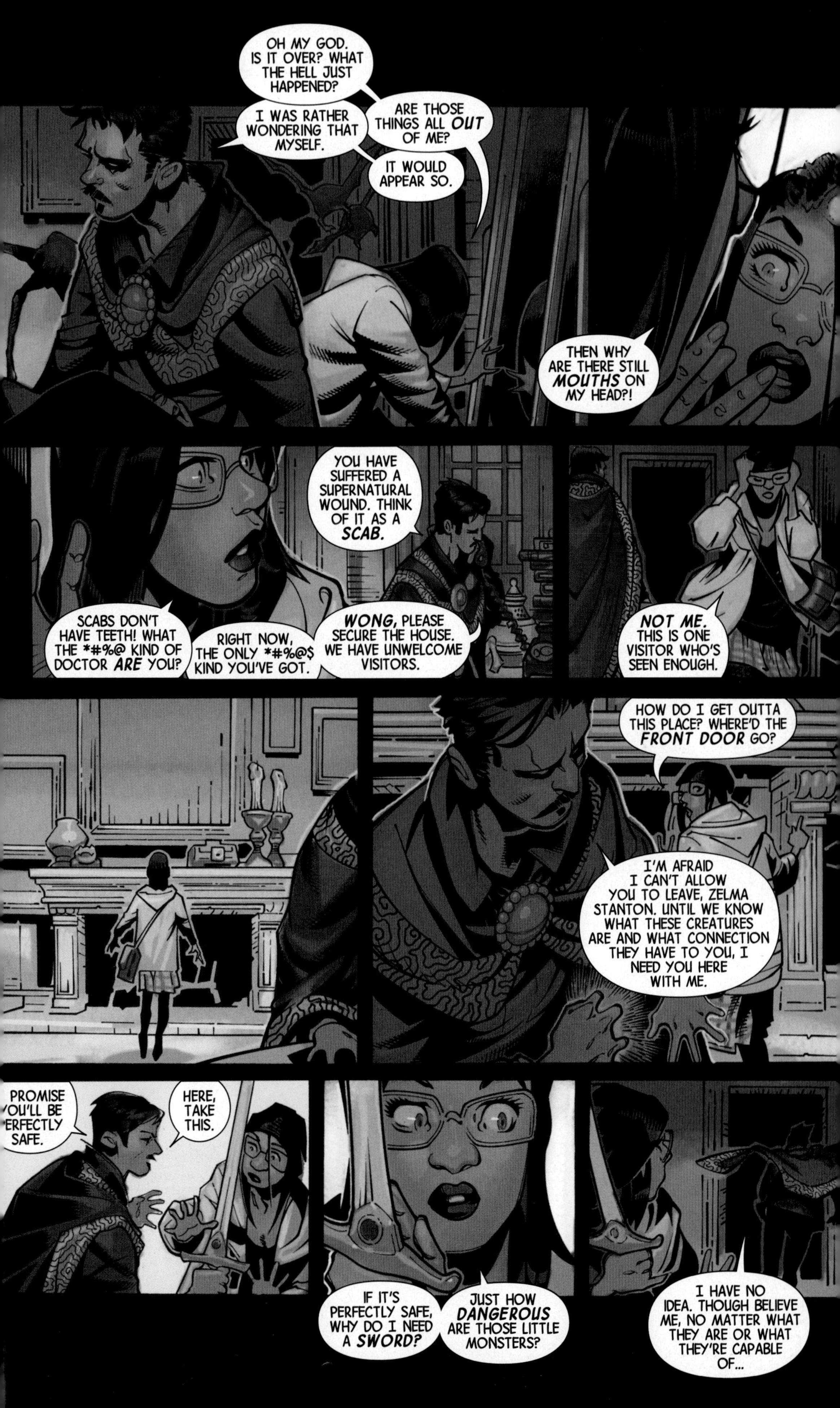
OH MY GOD. IS IT OVER? WHAT THE HELL JUST HAPPENED?
I WAS RATHER WONDERING THAT MYSELF.
ARE THOSE THINGS ALL OUT OF ME?
IT WOULD APPEAR SO.
THEN WHY ARE THERE STILL MOUTHS ON MY HEAD?!
YOU HAVE SUFFERED A SUPERNATURAL WOUND. THINK OF IT AS A SCAB.
SCABS DON'T HAVE TEETH! WHAT THE *#%@ KIND OF DOCTOR ARE YOU?
RIGHT NOW, THE ONLY *#%@$ KIND YOU'VE GOT.
WONG, PLEASE SECURE THE HOUSE. WE HAVE UNWELCOME VISITORS.
NOT ME. THIS IS ONE VISITOR WHO'S SEEN ENOUGH.
HOW DO I GET OUTTA THIS PLACE? WHERE'D THE FRONT DOOR GO?
I'M AFRAID I CAN'T ALLOW YOU TO LEAVE, ZELMA STANTON. UNTIL WE KNOW WHAT THESE CREATURES ARE AND WHAT CONNECTION THEY HAVE TO YOU, I NEED YOU HERE WITH ME.
PROMISE OU'LL BE ERFECTLY SAFE.
HERE, TAKE THIS.
IF IT'S PERFECTLY SAFE, WHY DO I NEED A SWORD?
JUST HOW DANGEROUS ARE THOSE LITTLE MONSTERS?
I HAVE NO IDEA. THOUGH BELIEVE ME, NO MATTER WHAT THEY ARE OR WHAT THEY'RE CAPABLE OF...

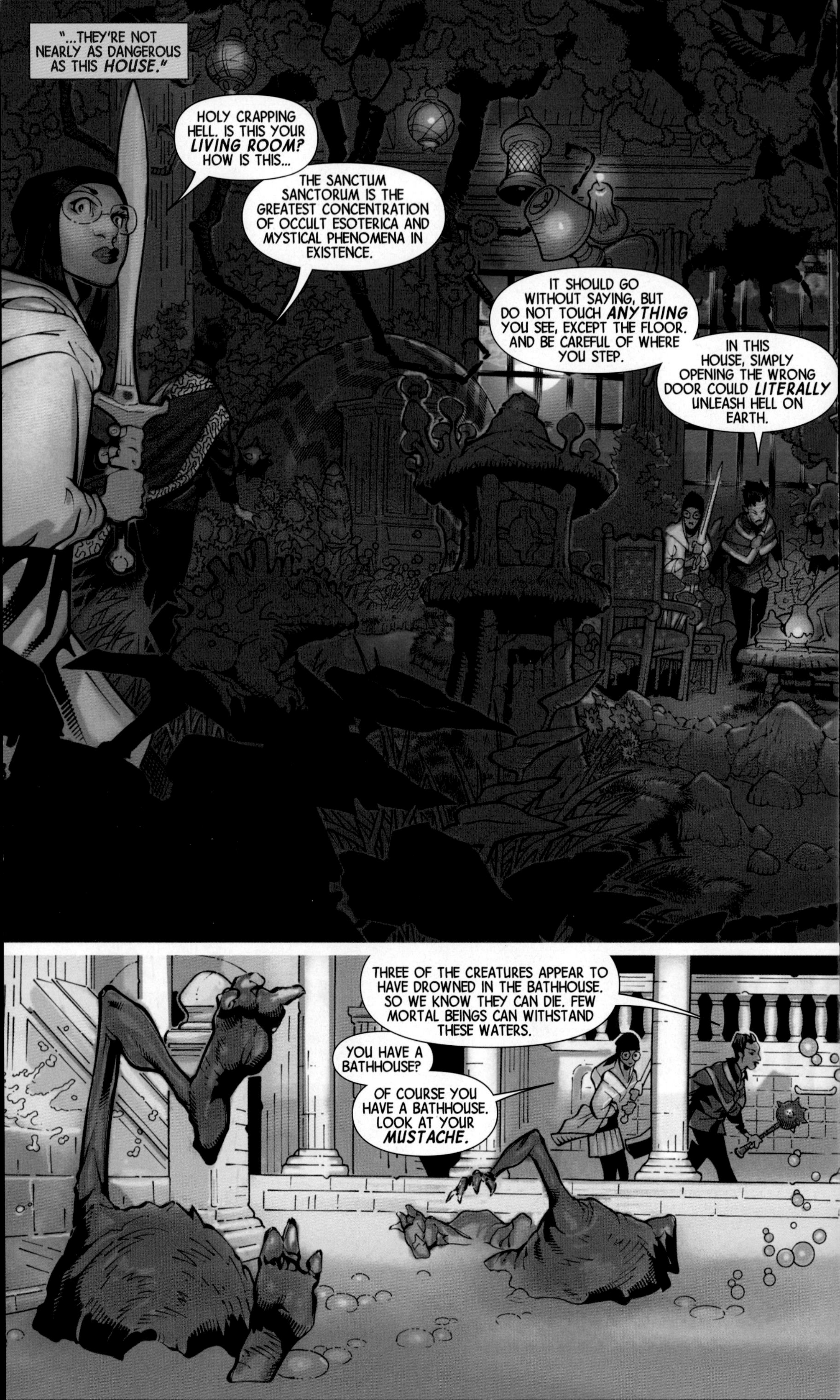
"...THEY'RE NOT NEARLY AS DANGEROUS AS THIS *HOUSE*."
HOLY CRAPPING HELL. IS THIS YOUR *LIVING ROOM?* HOW IS THIS...
THE SANCTUM SANCTORUM IS THE GREATEST CONCENTRATION OF OCCULT ESOTERICA AND MYSTICAL PHENOMENA IN EXISTENCE.
IT SHOULD GO WITHOUT SAYING, BUT DO NOT TOUCH *ANYTHING* YOU SEE, EXCEPT THE FLOOR. AND BE CAREFUL OF WHERE YOU STEP.
IN THIS HOUSE, SIMPLY OPENING THE WRONG DOOR COULD *LITERALLY* UNLEASH HELL ON EARTH.
THREE OF THE CREATURES APPEAR TO HAVE DROWNED IN THE BATHHOUSE. SO WE KNOW THEY CAN DIE. FEW MORTAL BEINGS CAN WITHSTAND THESE WATERS.
YOU HAVE A BATHHOUSE?
OF COURSE YOU HAVE A BATHHOUSE. LOOK AT YOUR *MUSTACHE.*

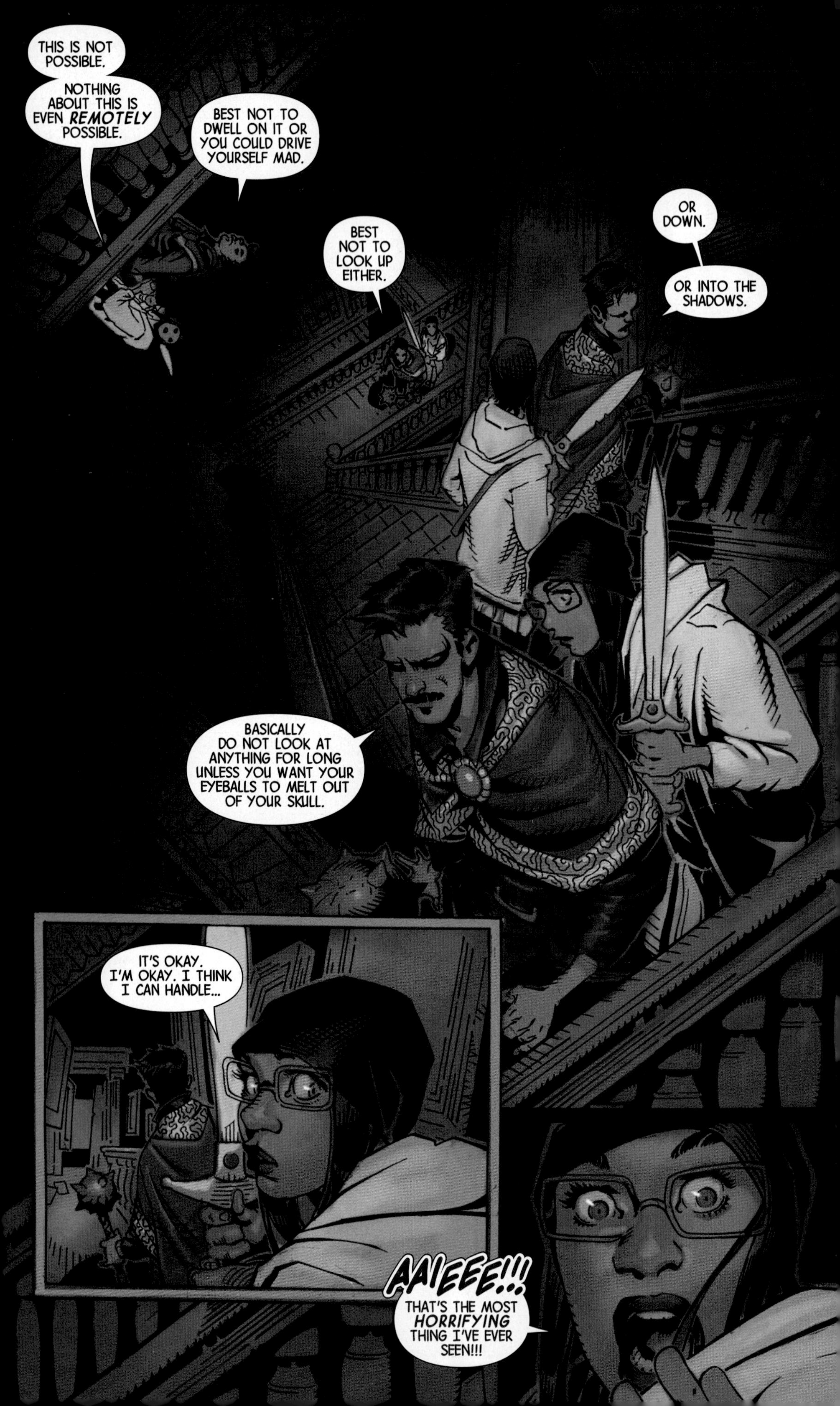
THIS IS NOT POSSIBLE.
NOTHING ABOUT THIS IS EVEN *REMOTELY* POSSIBLE.
BEST NOT TO DWELL ON IT OR YOU COULD DRIVE YOURSELF MAD.
BEST NOT TO LOOK UP EITHER.
OR DOWN.
OR INTO THE SHADOWS.
BASICALLY DO NOT LOOK AT ANYTHING FOR LONG UNLESS YOU WANT YOUR EYEBALLS TO MELT OUT OF YOUR SKULL.
IT'S OKAY. I'M OKAY. I THINK I CAN HANDLE...
AAIEEE!!!
THAT'S THE MOST *HORRIFYING* THING I'VE EVER SEEN!!!

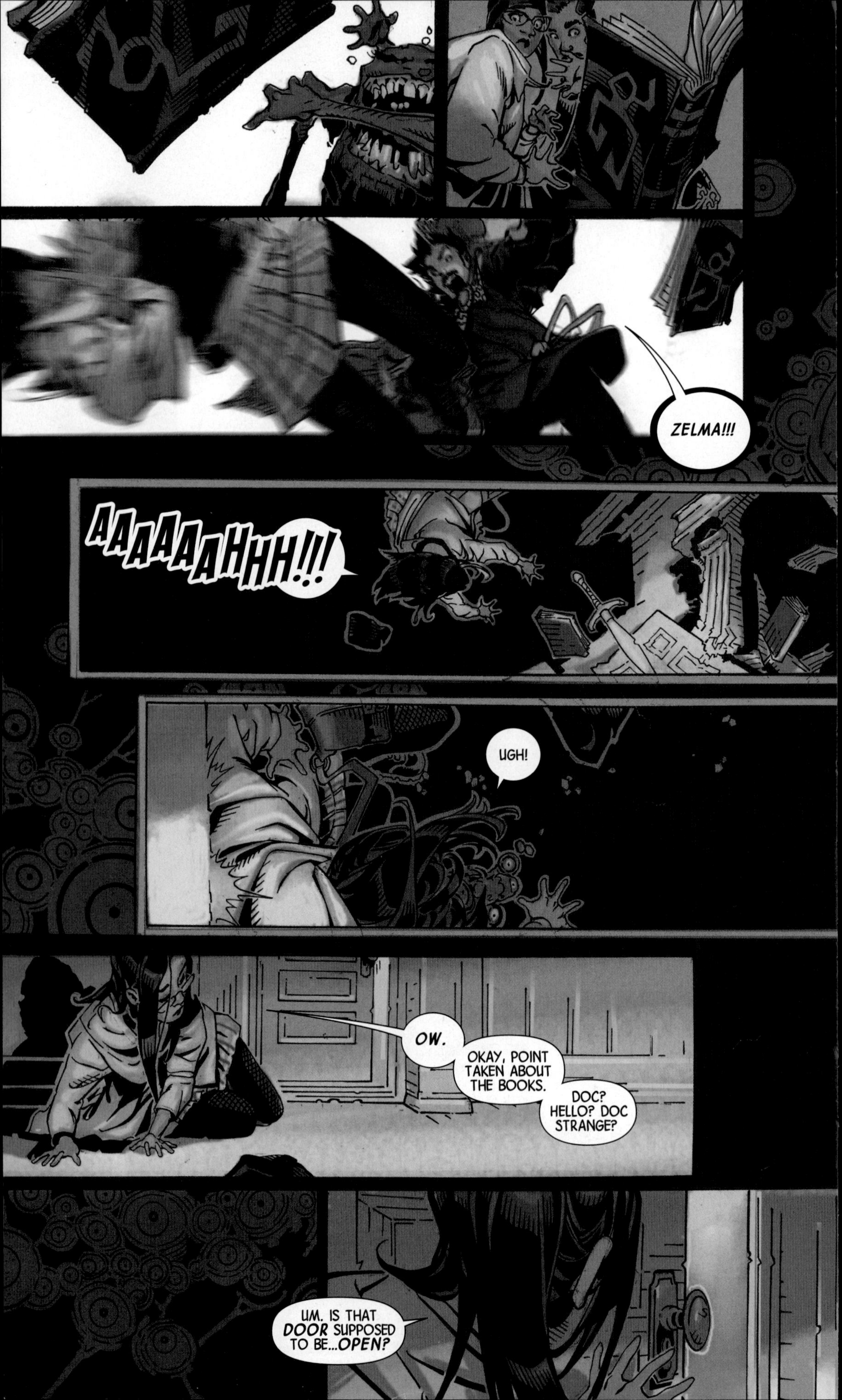
ZELMA!!!
AAAAAAHHH!!!
UGH!
OW.
OKAY, POINT TAKEN ABOUT THE BOOKS.
DOC? HELLO? DOC STRANGE?
UM. IS THAT DOOR SUPPOSED TO BE...OPEN?

THE KITCHEN...THAT MEANS...

NO! GET AWAY FROM THE...!

CHK

NOOOO!!!

AAAAAGGH!

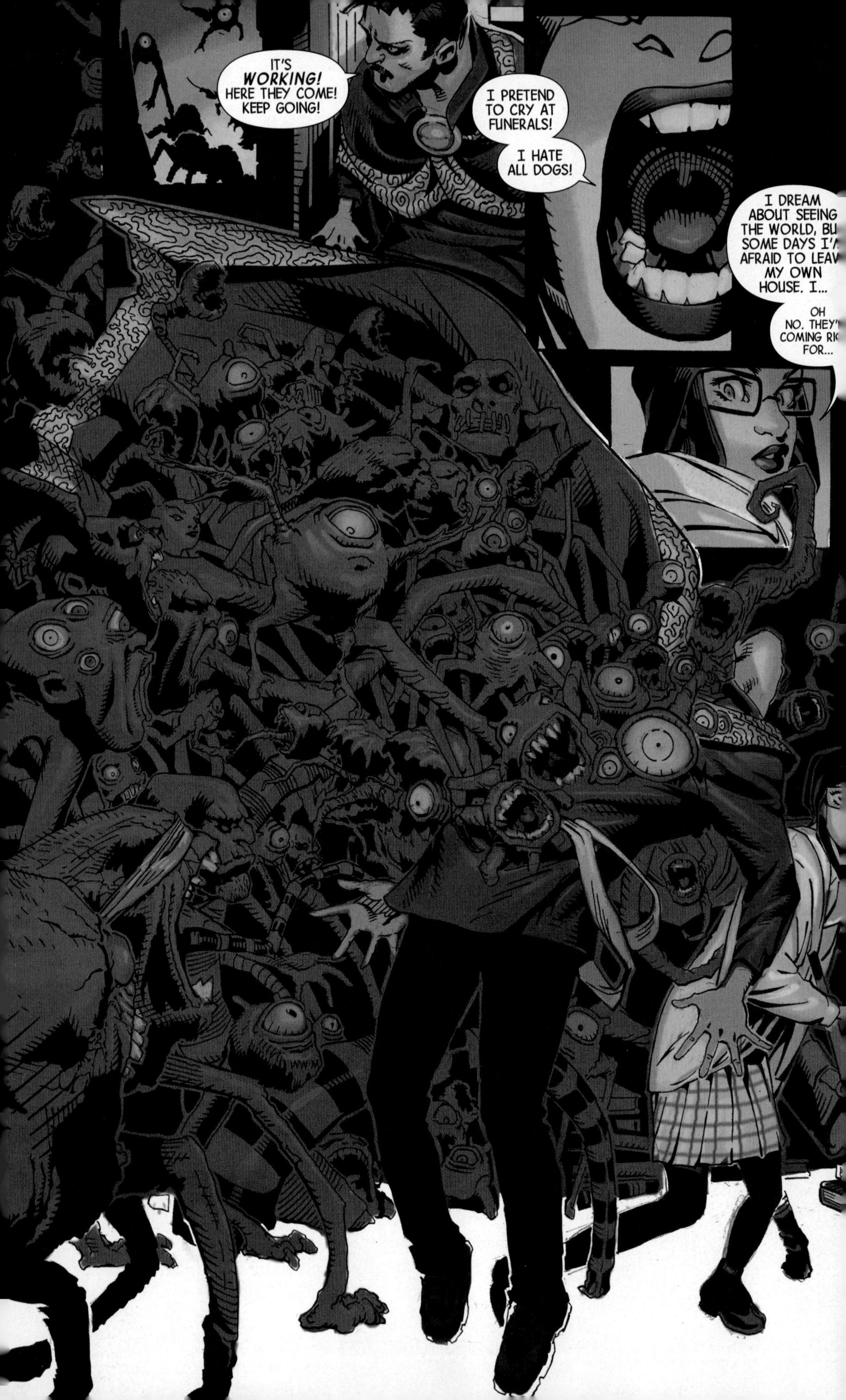
IT'S *WORKING!* HERE THEY COME! KEEP GOING!
I PRETEND TO CRY AT FUNERALS!
I HATE ALL DOGS!
I DREAM ABOUT SEEING THE WORLD, BU SOME DAYS I' AFRAID TO LEAV MY OWN HOUSE. I...
OH NO. THEY' COMING RI FOR...

AND ON *THAT* NOTE...I THINK IT'S TIME I HEAD BACK TO THE BRONX. THANK YOU FOR EVERYTHING, DOC. IT'S BEEN... AN INTERESTING DAY.

INDEED, IT HAS. AND PLEASE, CALL ME *STEPHEN*.

CHMP

OW.

SORRY.

OKAY. WELL. I GUESS I'LL SEE YOU AROUND MAYBE. OR NOT. PROBABLY NOT. BUT ANYWAY...

WOULD YOU LIKE TO COME *SORT MY BOOKS* SOMETIME?

I...

WAIT, IT THAT A *EUPHEMISM?*

NO, I MEAN *LITERALLY* SORT MY BOOKS. MY LIBRARY IS A *DISASTER*, AS YOU'VE SEEN. SOMETIMES LIVES DEPEND ON ME FINDING THE RIGHT BOOK, SO I SUPPOSE I REALLY SHOULD SEEK PROFESSIONAL HELP.

THIS ISN'T LIKE...YOUR WEIRD WAY OF ASKING ME ON A *DATE*, IS IT?

ONE DISASTER AT A TIME, ZELMA. TRUST ME, MY LIBRARY IS *NOTHING* COMPARED TO MY LOVE LIFE.

THOUGH IF MY LIFE AND HOUSE AND KUNG FU MANSERVANT AND THE MIND-STAGGERING SECRETS OF MY REFRIGERATOR ARE ENTIRELY TOO WEIRD FOR YOU AND YOU WISH *NEVER* TO RETURN...

BELIEVE ME, I'LL UNDERSTAND.

I'M FREE ON SATURDAYS. SEE YA THEN, DOC.

I CAN BE WEIRD FOR ONE DAY A WEEK.

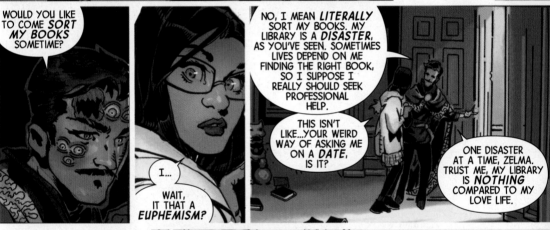

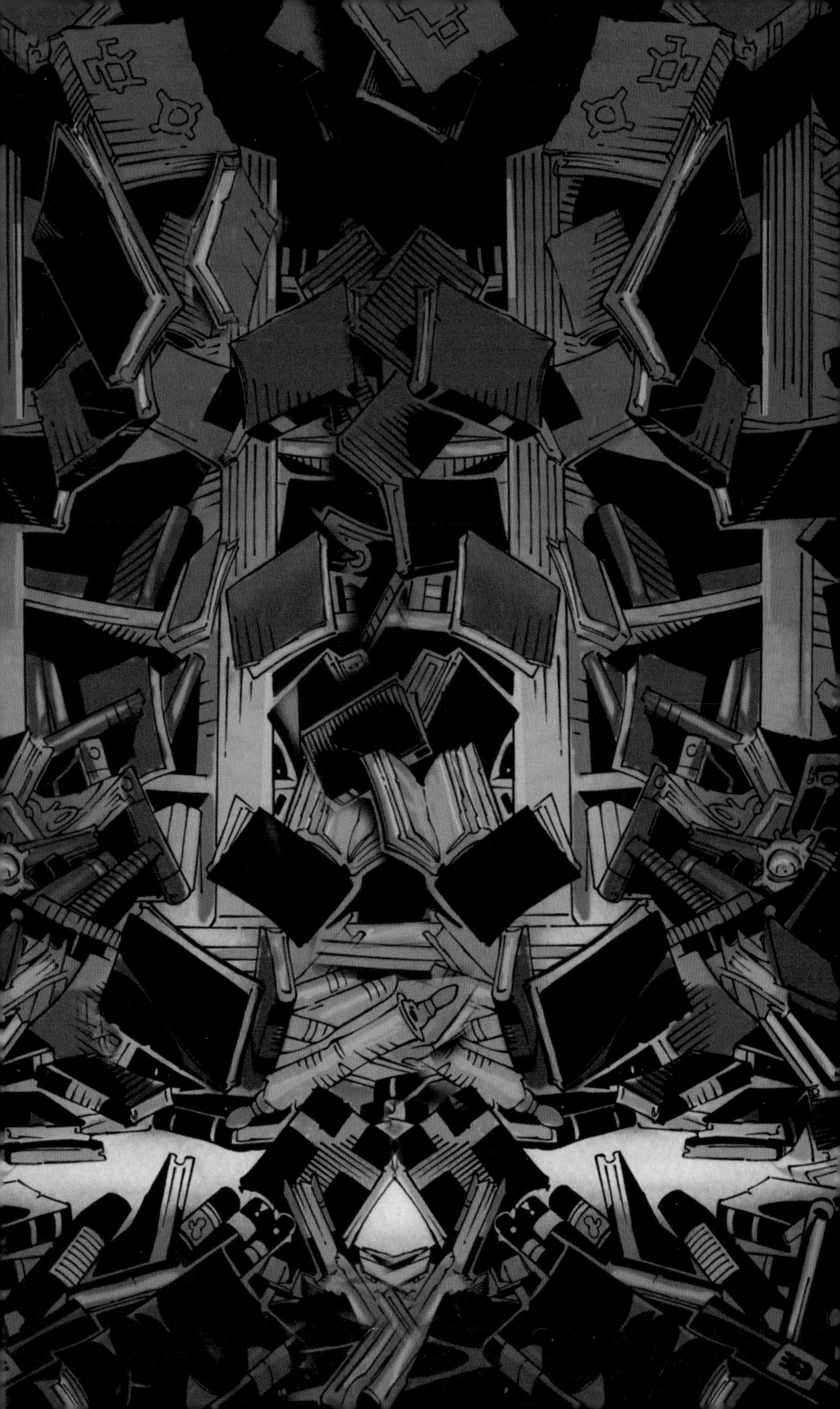

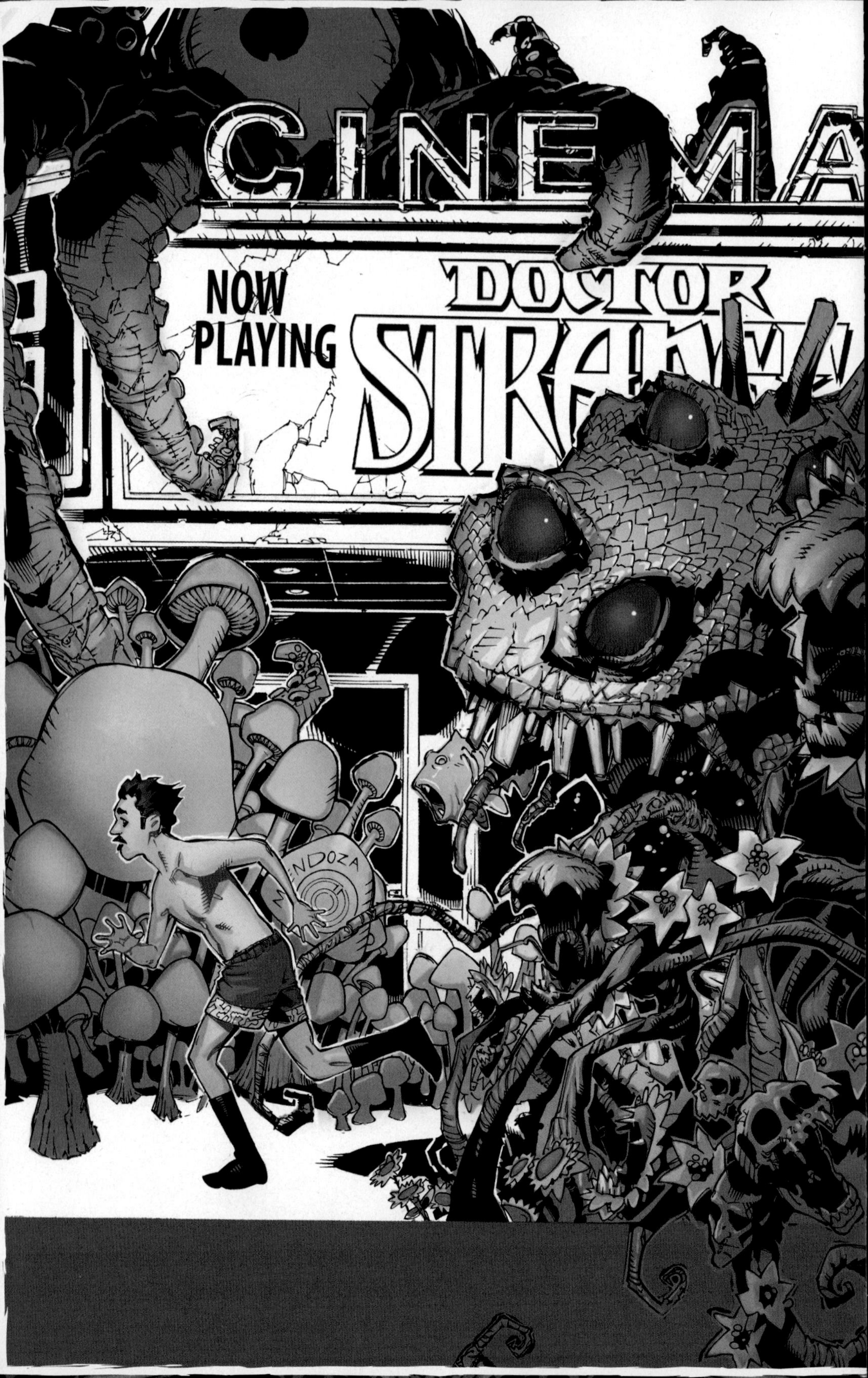
CINEMA
NOW PLAYING
DOCTOR

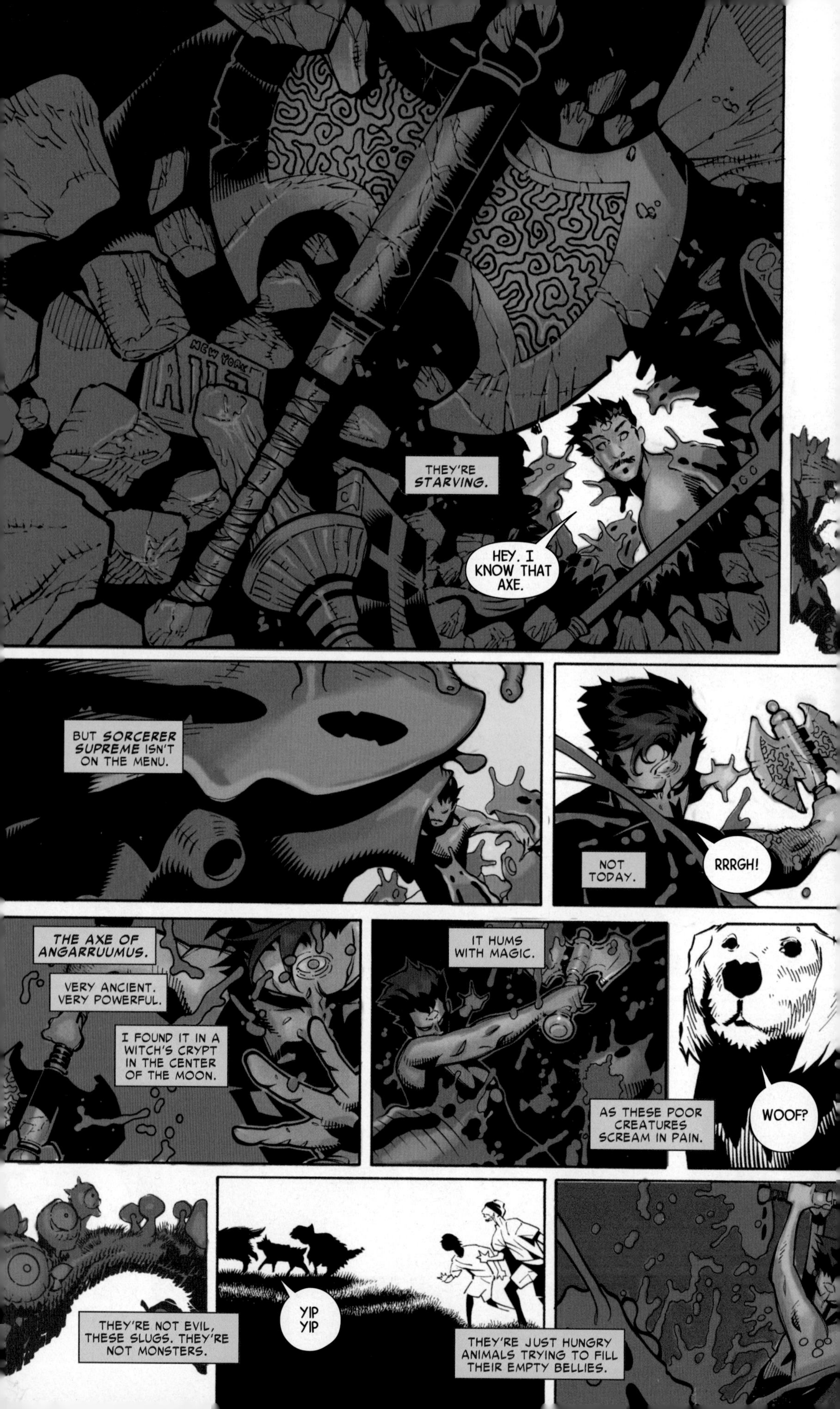

THEY'RE *STARVING.*
HEY. I KNOW THAT AXE.
BUT *SORCERER SUPREME* ISN'T ON THE MENU.
NOT TODAY.
RRRGH!
THE AXE OF ANGARRUUMUS.
VERY ANCIENT. VERY POWERFUL.
I FOUND IT IN A WITCH'S CRYPT IN THE CENTER OF THE MOON.
IT HUMS WITH MAGIC.
AS THESE POOR CREATURES SCREAM IN PAIN.
WOOF?
THEY'RE NOT EVIL, THESE SLUGS. THEY'RE NOT MONSTERS.
YIP YIP
THEY'RE JUST HUNGRY ANIMALS TRYING TO FILL THEIR EMPTY BELLIES.

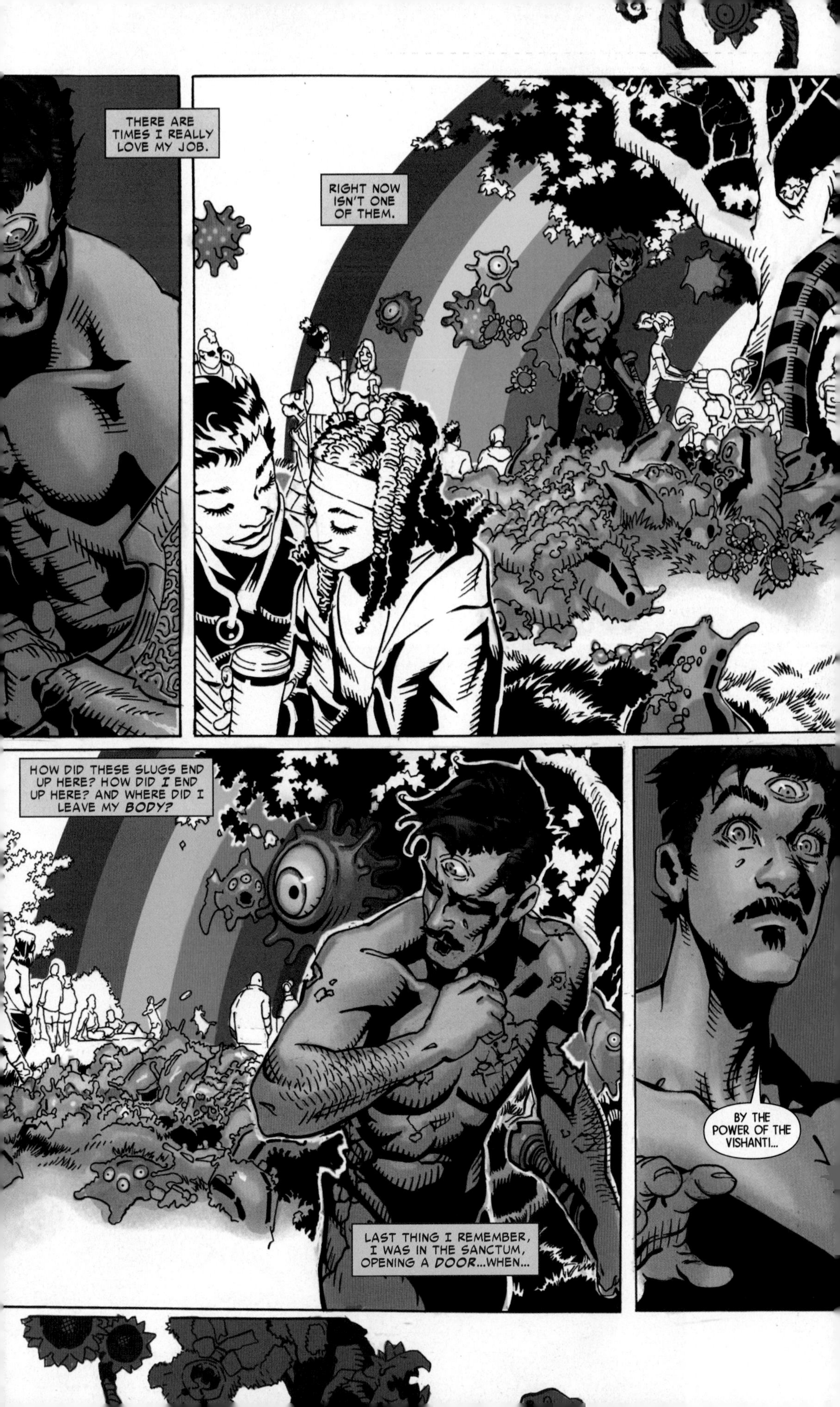
THERE ARE TIMES I REALLY LOVE MY JOB.
RIGHT NOW ISN'T ONE OF THEM.
HOW DID THESE SLUGS END UP HERE? HOW DID *I* END UP HERE? AND WHERE DID I LEAVE MY *BODY?*
LAST THING I REMEMBER, I WAS IN THE SANCTUM, OPENING A *DOOR*...WHEN...
BY THE POWER OF THE VISHANTI...

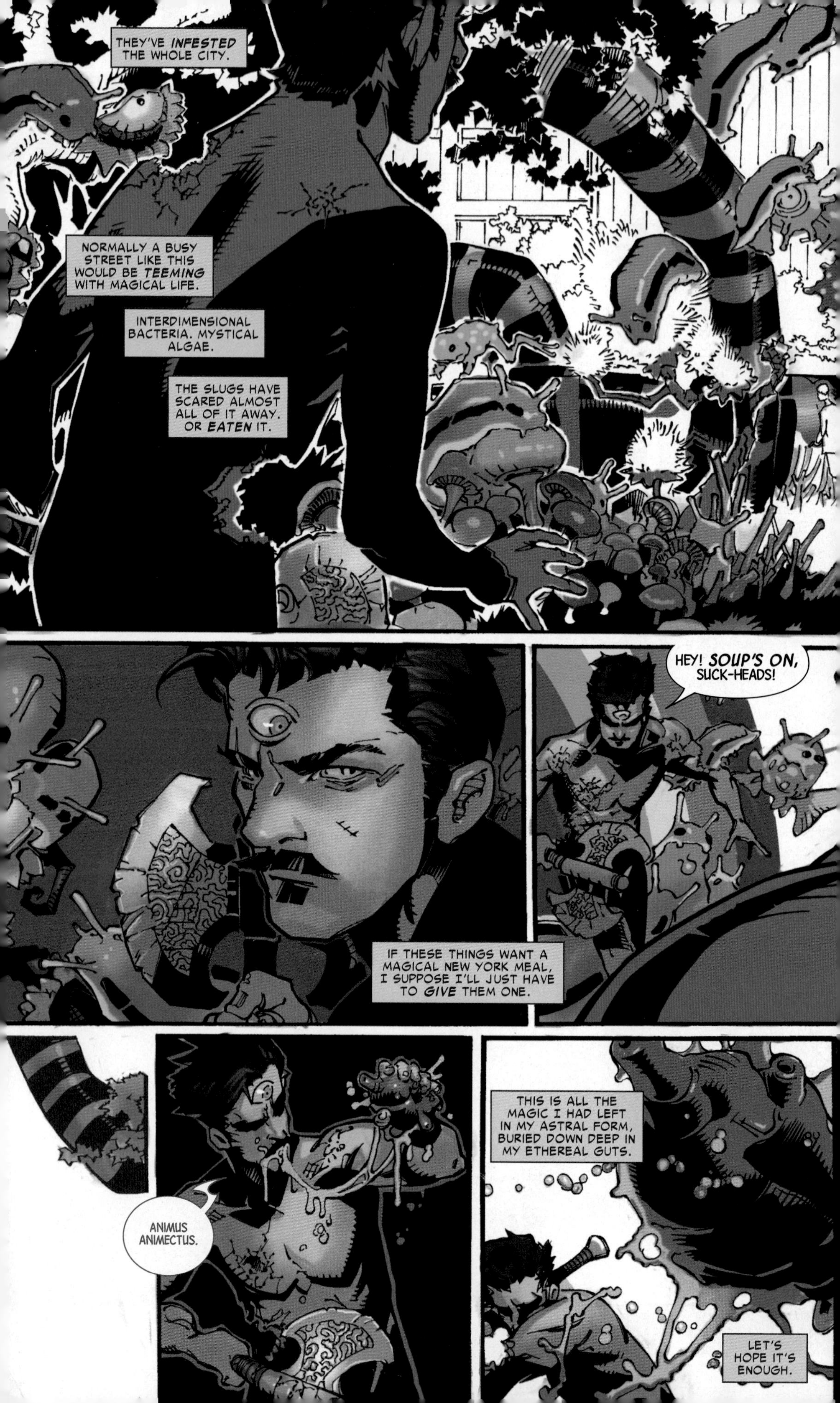
THEY'VE INFESTED THE WHOLE CITY.
NORMALLY A BUSY STREET LIKE THIS WOULD BE TEEMING WITH MAGICAL LIFE.
INTERDIMENSIONAL BACTERIA. MYSTICAL ALGAE.
THE SLUGS HAVE SCARED ALMOST ALL OF IT AWAY. OR EATEN IT.
IF THESE THINGS WANT A MAGICAL NEW YORK MEAL, I SUPPOSE I'LL JUST HAVE TO GIVE THEM ONE.
HEY! SOUP'S ON, SUCK-HEADS!
ANIMUS ANIMECTUS.
THIS IS ALL THE MAGIC I HAD LEFT IN MY ASTRAL FORM, BURIED DOWN DEEP IN MY ETHEREAL GUTS.
LET'S HOPE IT'S ENOUGH.

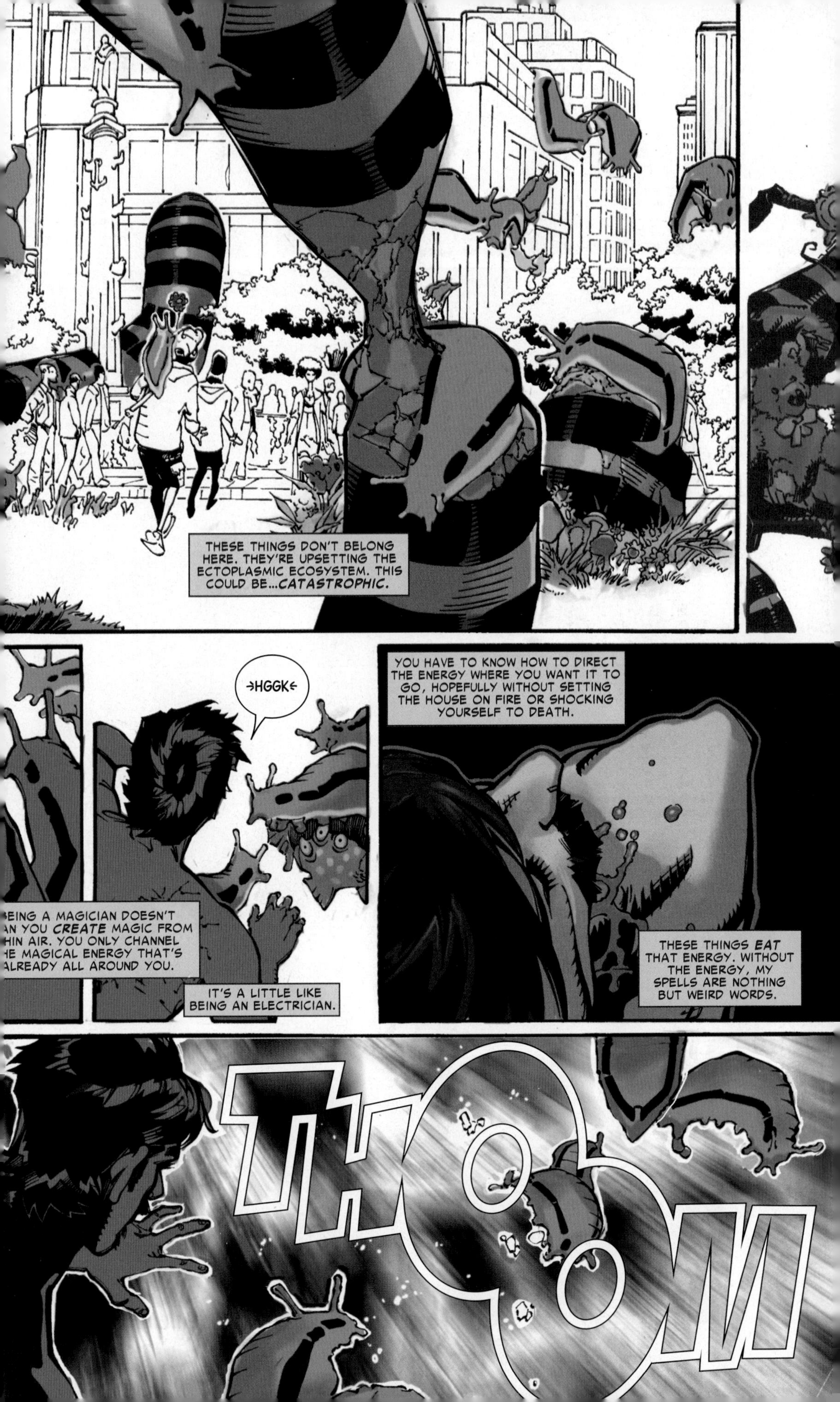

THESE THINGS DON'T BELONG HERE. THEY'RE UPSETTING THE ECTOPLASMIC ECOSYSTEM. THIS COULD BE...*CATASTROPHIC*.
HGGK
BEING A MAGICIAN DOESN'T MEAN YOU *CREATE* MAGIC FROM THIN AIR. YOU ONLY CHANNEL THE MAGICAL ENERGY THAT'S ALREADY ALL AROUND YOU.
IT'S A LITTLE LIKE BEING AN ELECTRICIAN.
YOU HAVE TO KNOW HOW TO DIRECT THE ENERGY WHERE YOU WANT IT TO GO, HOPEFULLY WITHOUT SETTING THE HOUSE ON FIRE OR SHOCKING YOURSELF TO DEATH.
THESE THINGS *EAT* THAT ENERGY. WITHOUT THE ENERGY, MY SPELLS ARE NOTHING BUT WEIRD WORDS.
THOOM

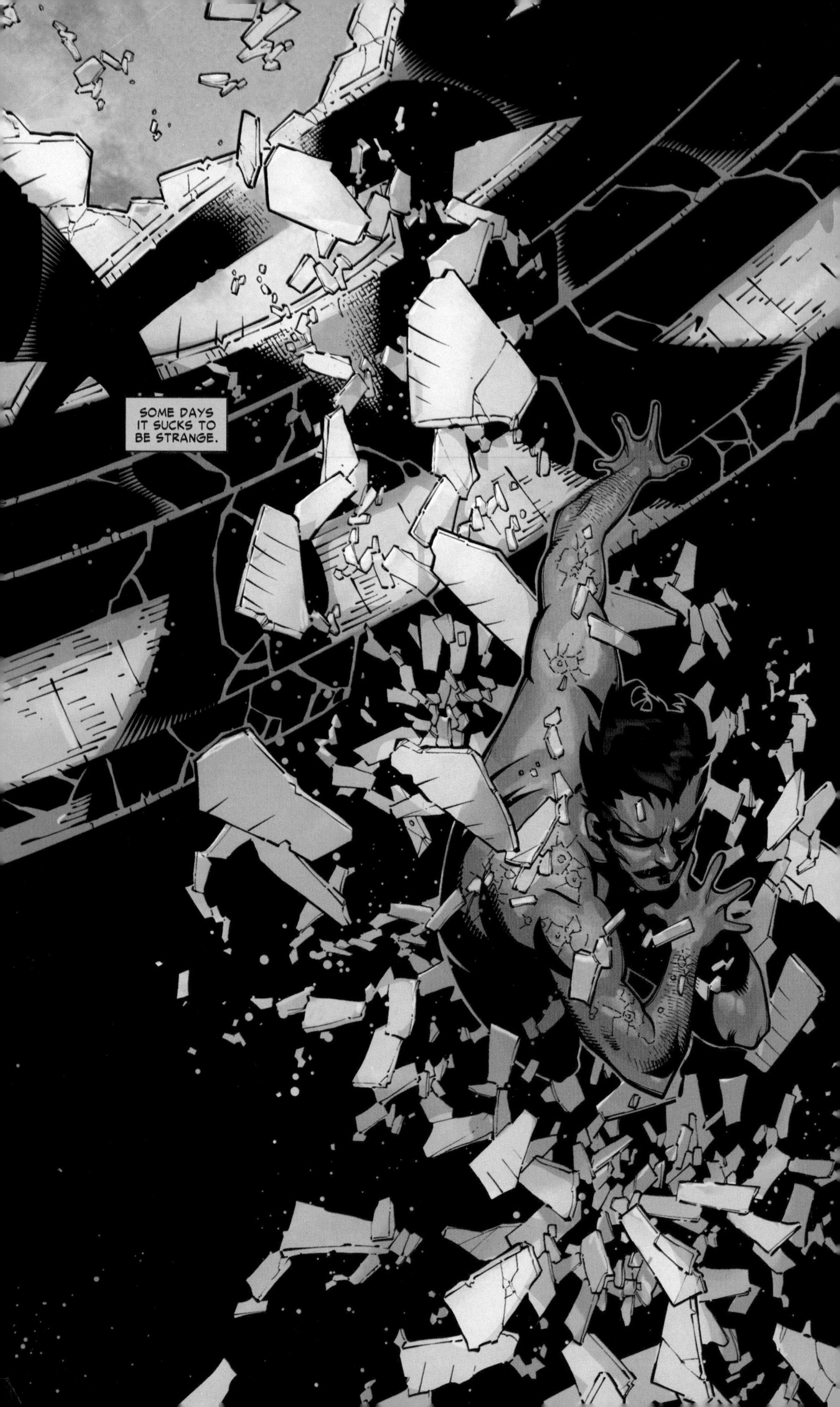
SOME DAYS
IT SUCKS TO
BE STRANGE.

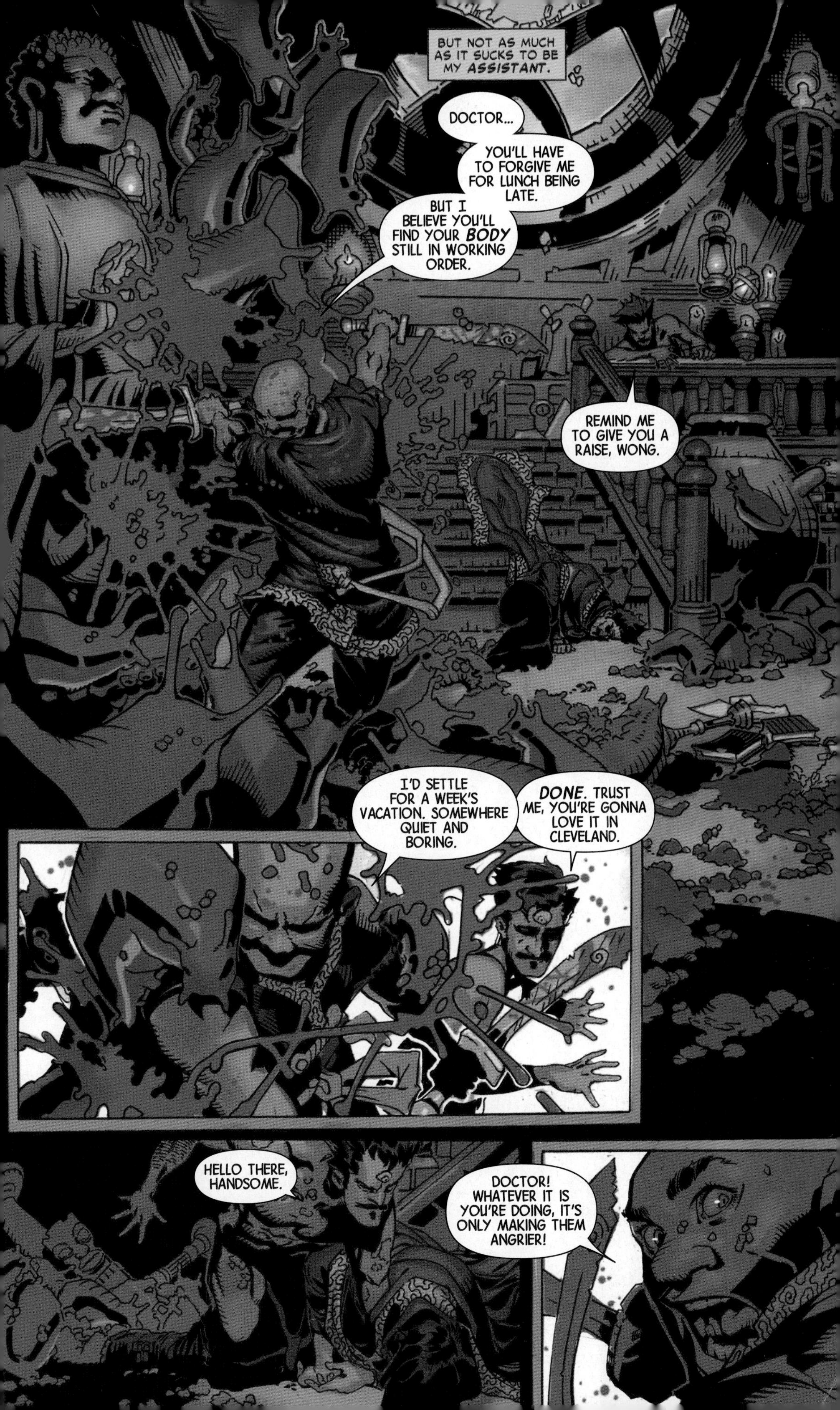

BUT NOT AS MUCH AS IT SUCKS TO BE MY ASSISTANT.
DOCTOR...
YOU'LL HAVE TO FORGIVE ME FOR LUNCH BEING LATE.
BUT I BELIEVE YOU'LL FIND YOUR BODY STILL IN WORKING ORDER.
REMIND ME TO GIVE YOU A RAISE, WONG.
I'D SETTLE FOR A WEEK'S VACATION. SOMEWHERE QUIET AND BORING.
DONE. TRUST ME, YOU'RE GONNA LOVE IT IN CLEVELAND.
HELLO THERE, HANDSOME.
DOCTOR! WHATEVER IT IS YOU'RE DOING, IT'S ONLY MAKING THEM ANGRIER!

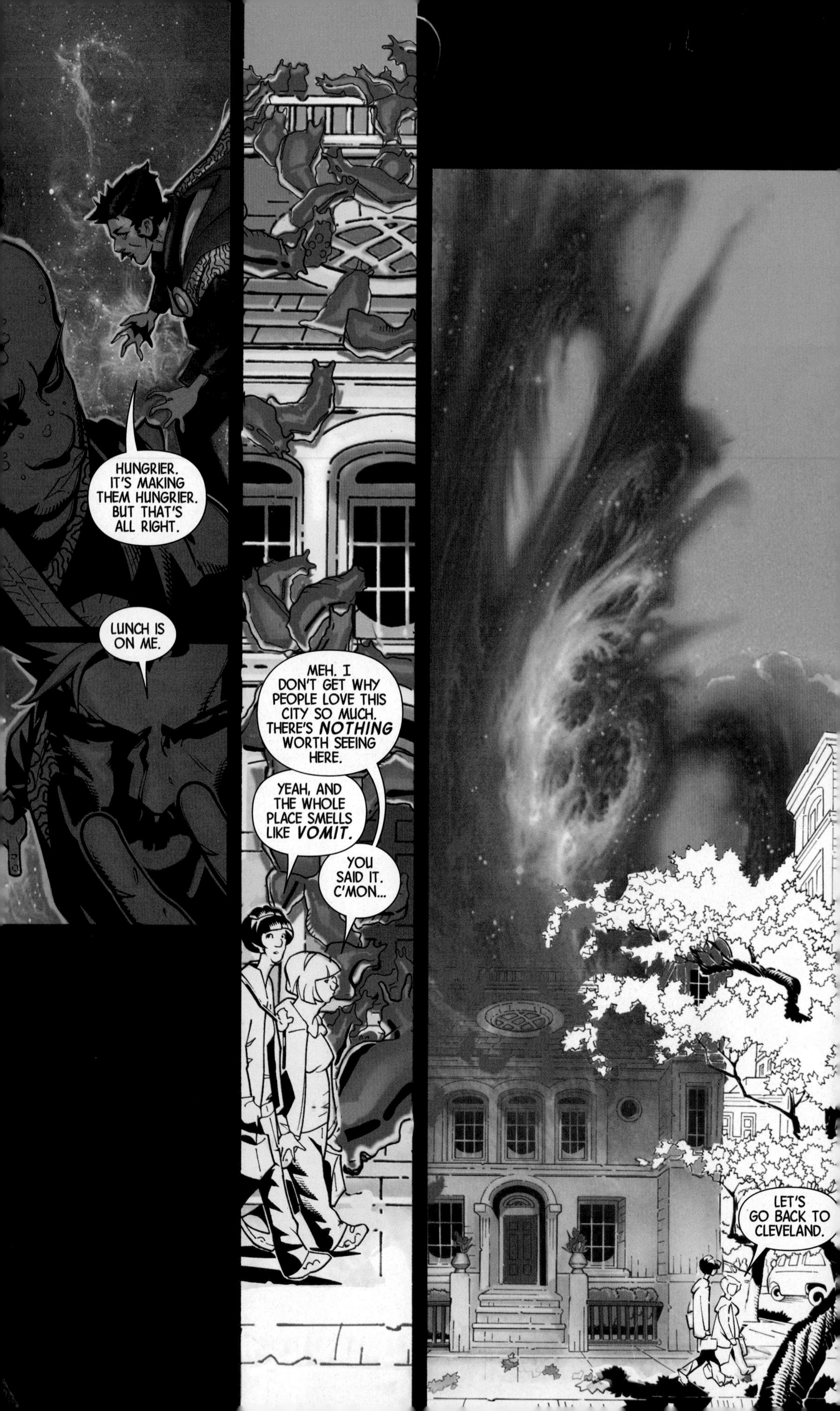
HUNGRIER. IT'S MAKING THEM HUNGRIER. BUT THAT'S ALL RIGHT.
LUNCH IS ON ME.
MEH. I DON'T GET WHY PEOPLE LOVE THIS CITY SO MUCH. THERE'S NOTHING WORTH SEEING HERE.
YEAH, AND THE WHOLE PLACE SMELLS LIKE VOMIT.
YOU SAID IT. C'MON...
LET'S GO BACK TO CLEVELAND.

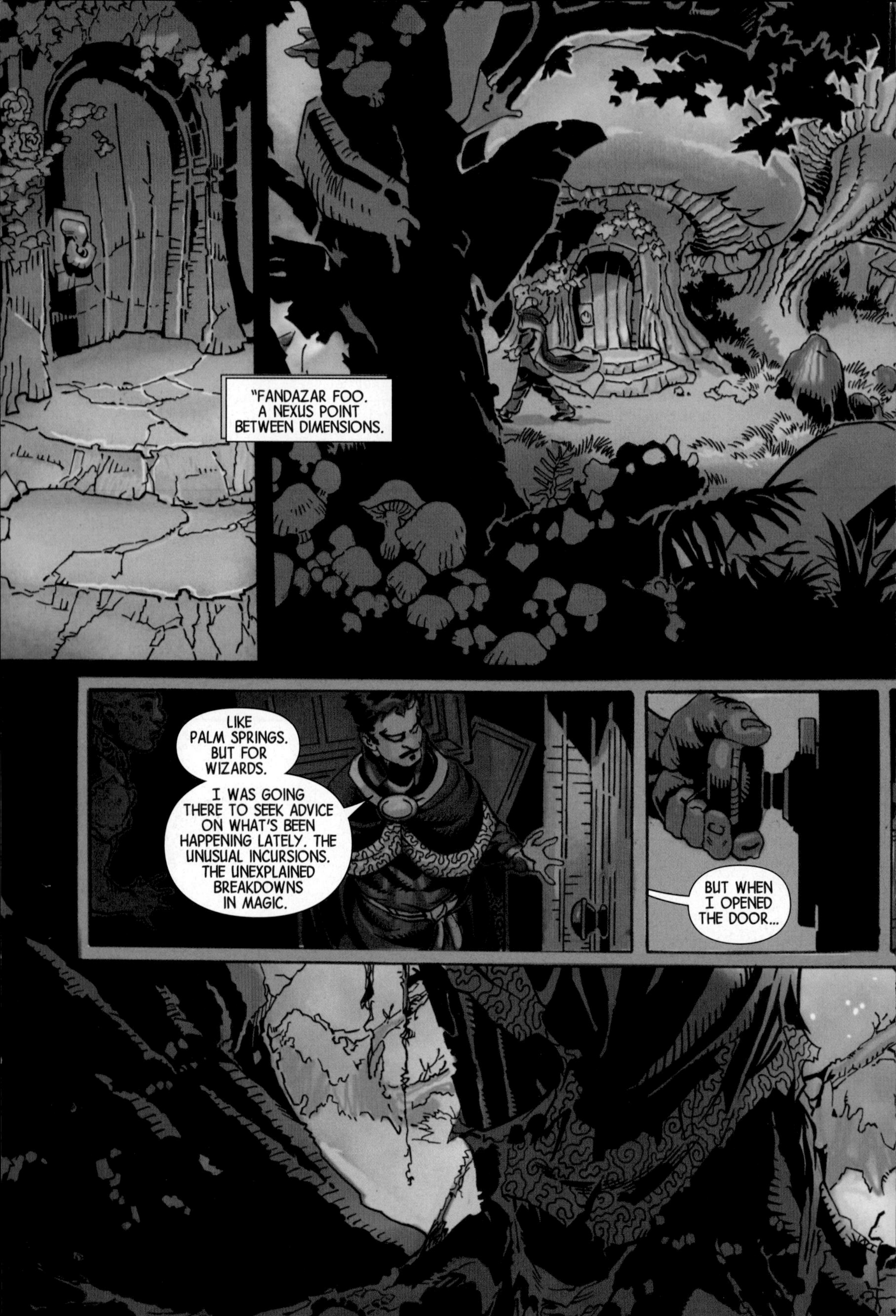
"FANDAZAR FOO. A NEXUS POINT BETWEEN DIMENSIONS.
LIKE PALM SPRINGS. BUT FOR WIZARDS.
I WAS GOING THERE TO SEEK ADVICE ON WHAT'S BEEN HAPPENING LATELY. THE UNUSUAL INCURSIONS. THE UNEXPLAINED BREAKDOWNS IN MAGIC.
BUT WHEN I OPENED THE DOOR...

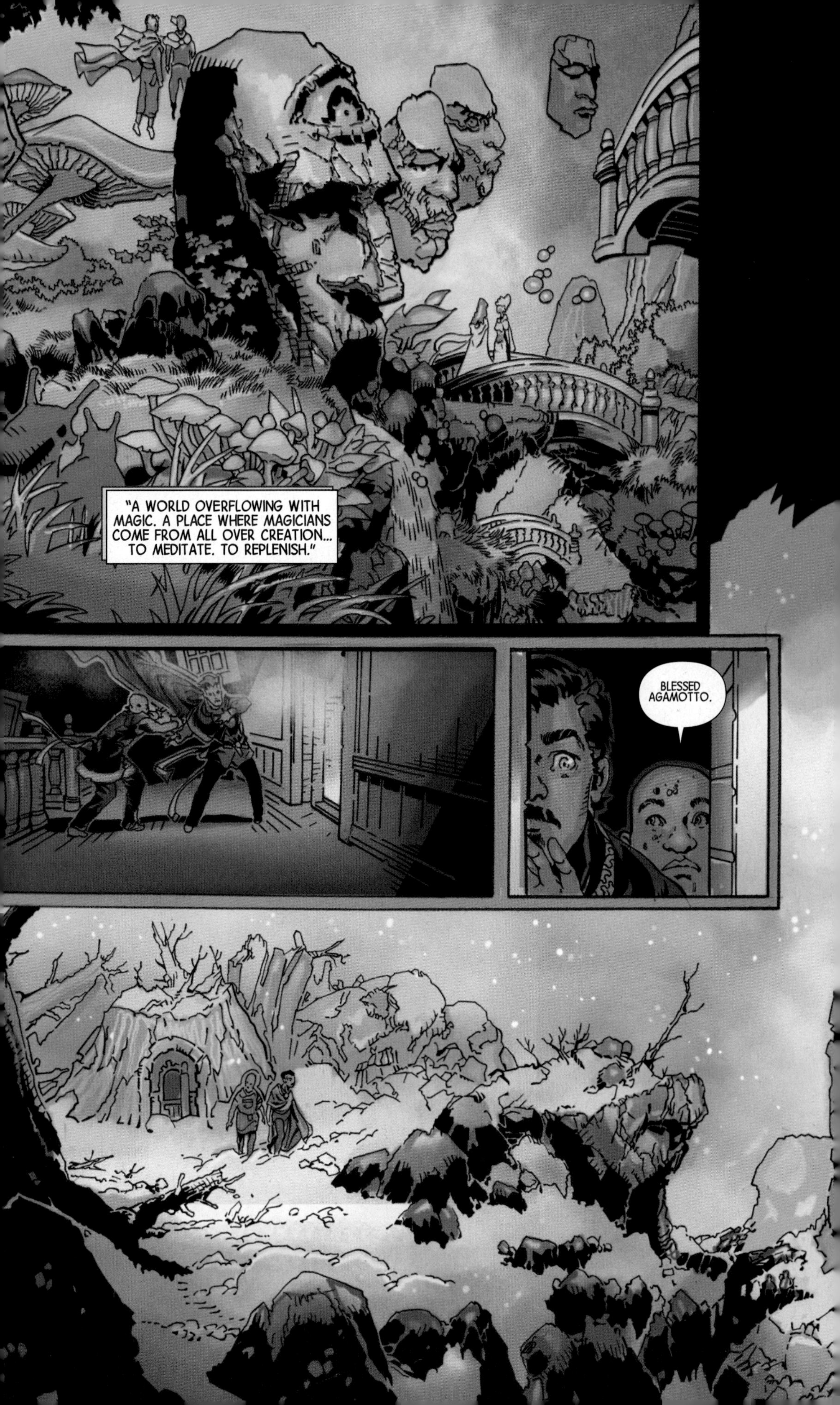
"A WORLD OVERFLOWING WITH MAGIC. A PLACE WHERE MAGICIANS COME FROM ALL OVER CREATION... TO MEDITATE. TO REPLENISH."
BLESSED AGAMOTTO.

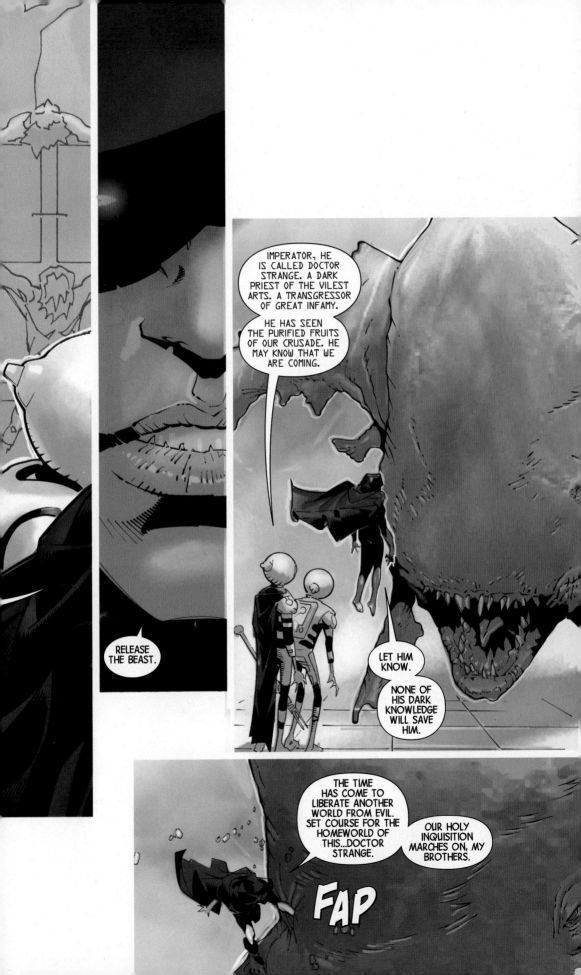

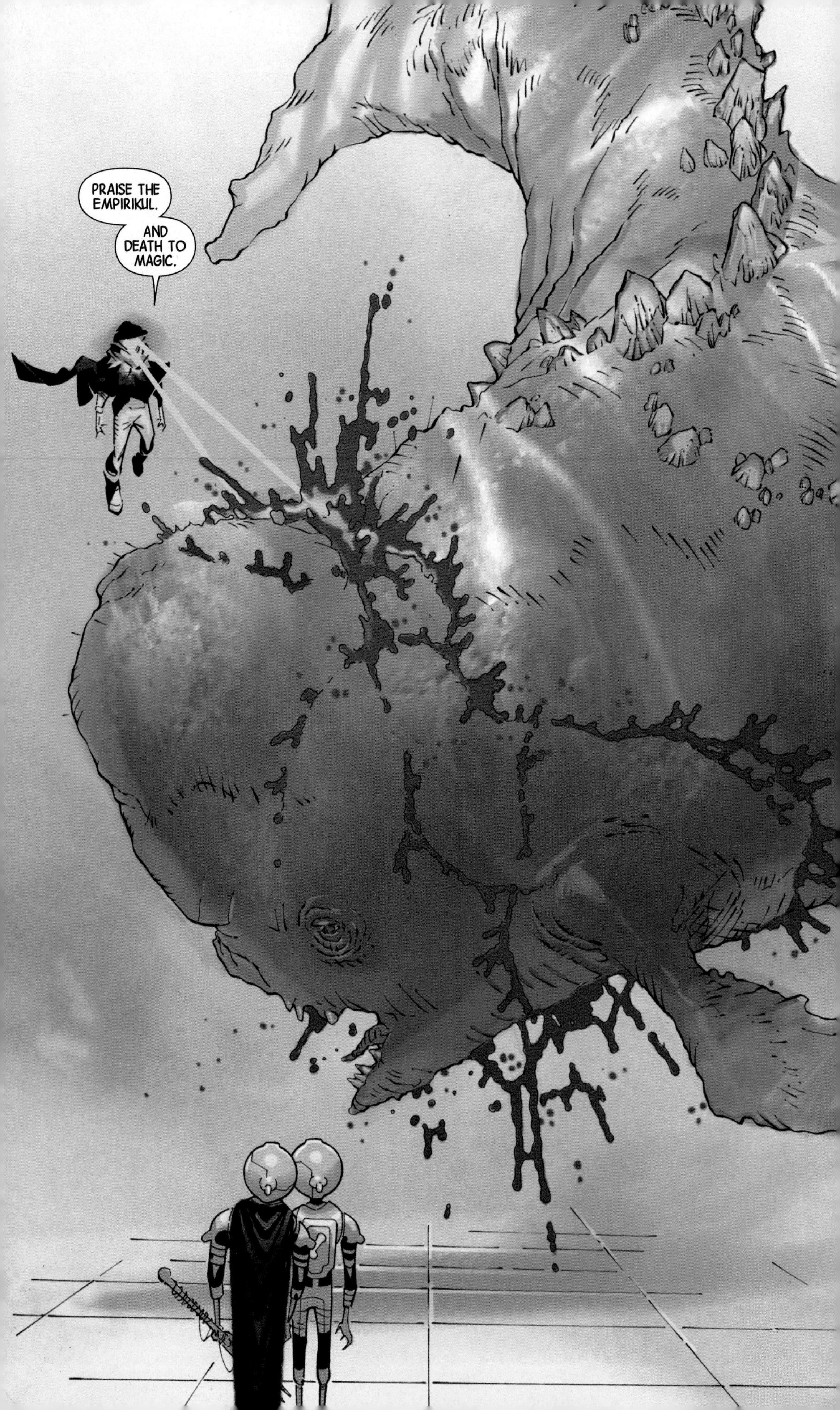
PRAISE THE EMPIRIKUL.
AND DEATH TO MAGIC.

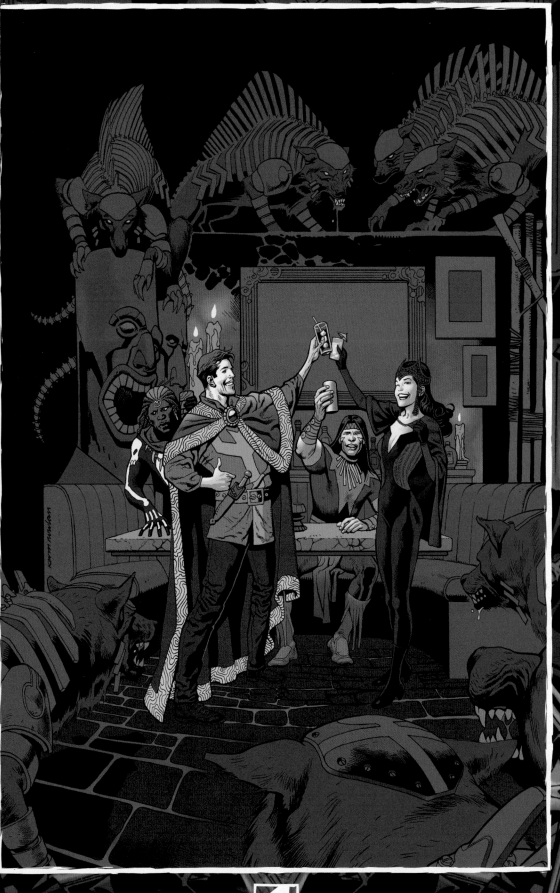

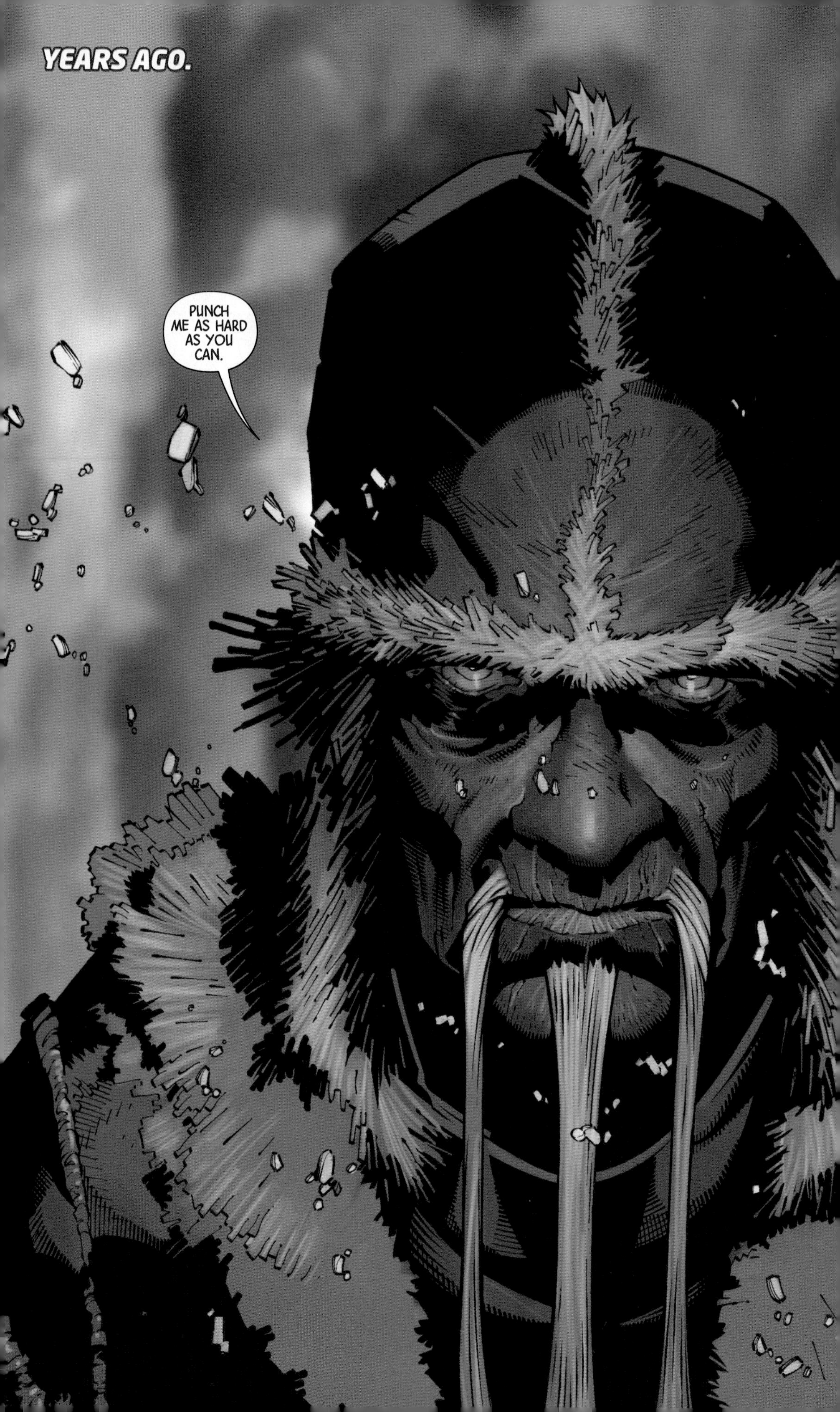
YEARS AGO.
PUNCH ME AS HARD AS YOU CAN.

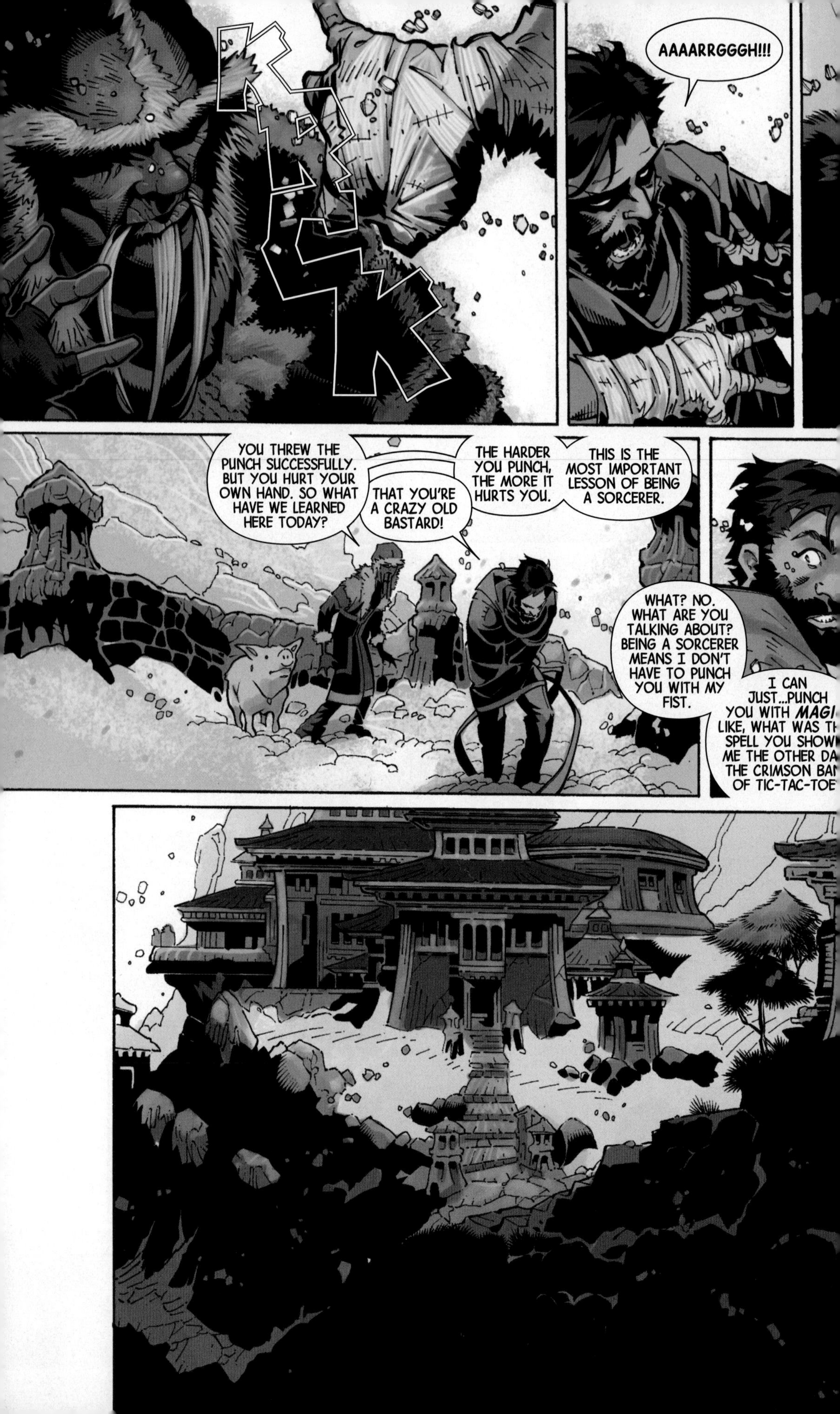
KRAK
AAAARRGGGH!!!
YOU THREW THE PUNCH SUCCESSFULLY. BUT YOU HURT YOUR OWN HAND. SO WHAT HAVE WE LEARNED HERE TODAY?
THAT YOU'RE A CRAZY OLD BASTARD!
THE HARDER YOU PUNCH, THE MORE IT HURTS YOU.
THIS IS THE MOST IMPORTANT LESSON OF BEING A SORCERER.
WHAT? NO. WHAT ARE YOU TALKING ABOUT? BEING A SORCERER MEANS I DON'T HAVE TO PUNCH YOU WITH MY FIST.
I CAN JUST...PUNCH YOU WITH MAGI LIKE, WHAT WAS T SPELL YOU SHOW ME THE OTHER DA THE CRIMSON BA OF TIC-TAC-TOE

WELL DONE. NOW TELL ME... HOW DID THAT *FEEL?*

HOW DO YOU *THINK* IT FELT?!

YOU SAID MY HAND WOULD BE FINE!

IS IT NOT?

NO! IT HURTS LIKE HELL!

THIS IS THE WHOLE REASON I'M HERE, TO FIX THESE STUPID *BROKEN* THINGS AND YOU JUST...!

IF A NORMAL PUNCH TAKES A PHYSICAL TOLL ON THE ONE WHO THROWS IT, WHAT DO YOU IMAGINE THE PRICE OF CASTING A *SPELL* TO BE?

NOTHING. AS FAR AS I CAN TELL. I MEAN, I'VE BEEN CASTING SPELLS ALL WEEK AND I FEEL *PERFECTLY...*

URK!

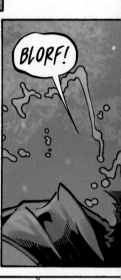

BLORF!

OH GOD. WHY AM I SUDDENLY--

BLARRRGGGH!

CAN'T STOP--

BLHRRRGGGH!

I DON'T REMEMBER EATING--

BLGRRRGGGH!

WHY IS IT GLOWING?!

EVERY PUNCH COMES AT A COST.

NOW YOU KNOW HOW IT FEELS TO BE A MAGICIAN.

BLRRRRGGGH!

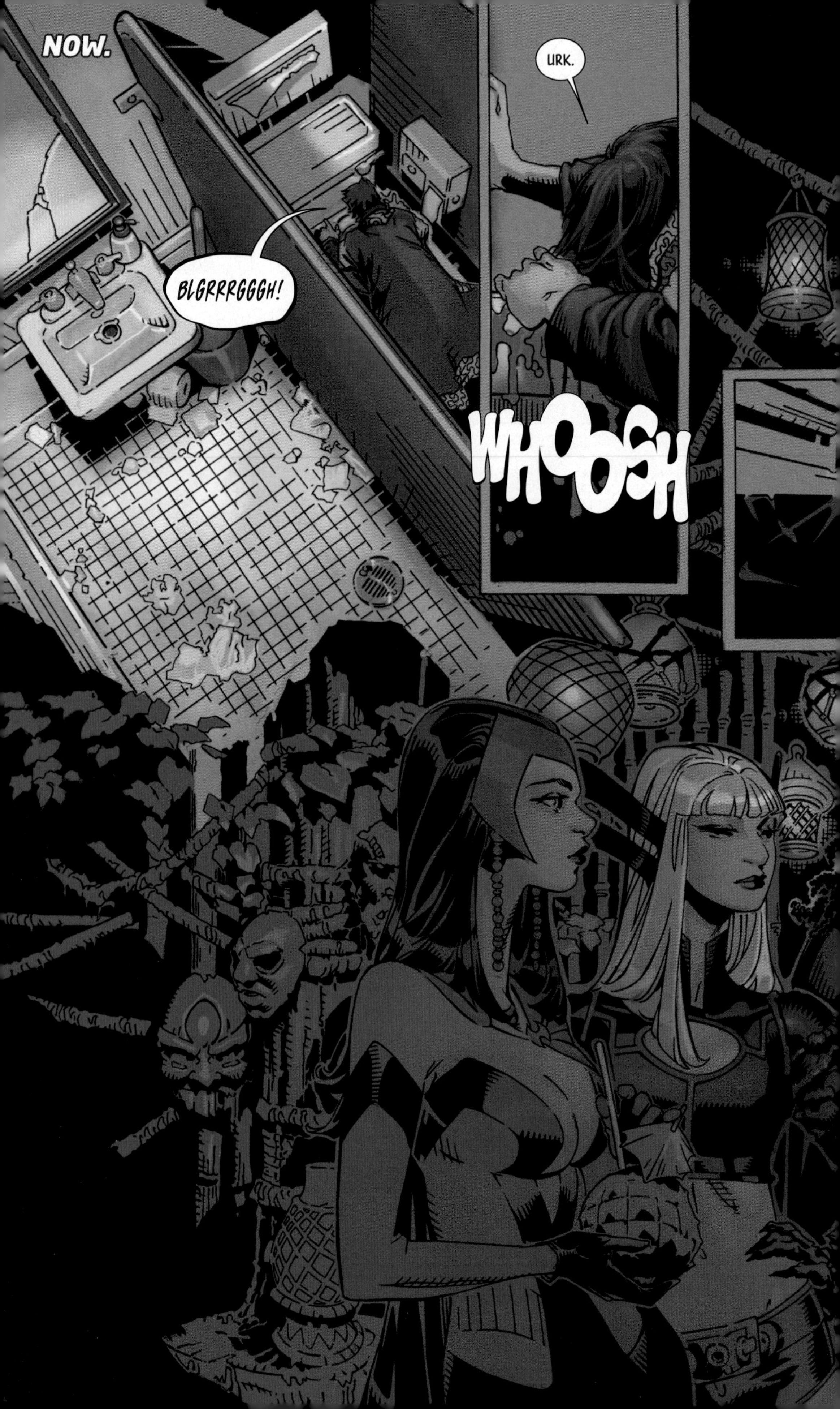
NOW.
BLGRRRGGGH!
URK.
WHOOSH

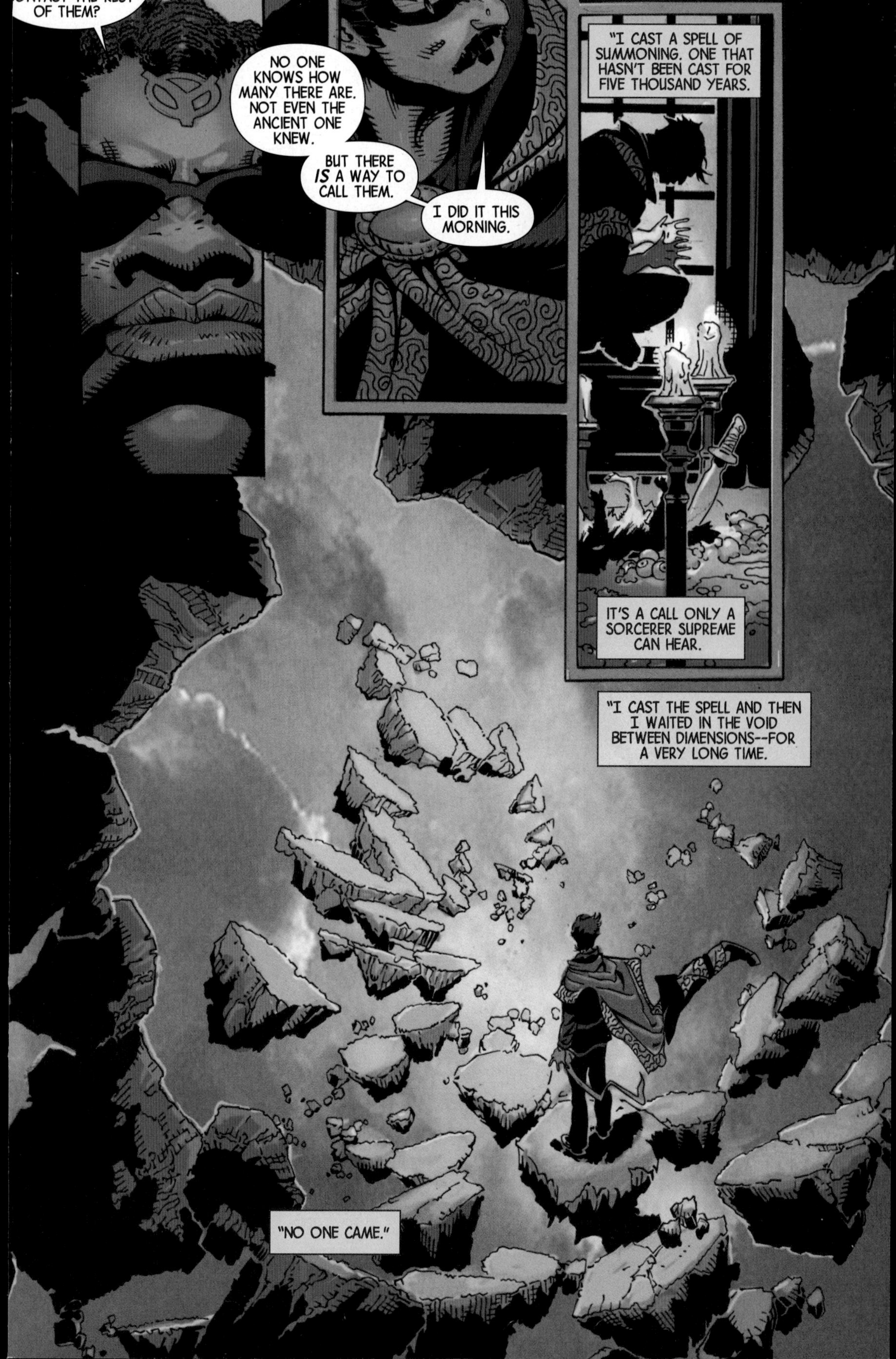
OF THEM?
NO ONE KNOWS HOW MANY THERE ARE. NOT EVEN THE ANCIENT ONE KNEW.
BUT THERE *IS* A WAY TO CALL THEM.
I DID IT THIS MORNING.
"I CAST A SPELL OF SUMMONING. ONE THAT HASN'T BEEN CAST FOR FIVE THOUSAND YEARS.
IT'S A CALL ONLY A SORCERER SUPREME CAN HEAR.
"I CAST THE SPELL AND THEN I WAITED IN THE VOID BETWEEN DIMENSIONS--FOR A VERY LONG TIME.
"NO ONE CAME."

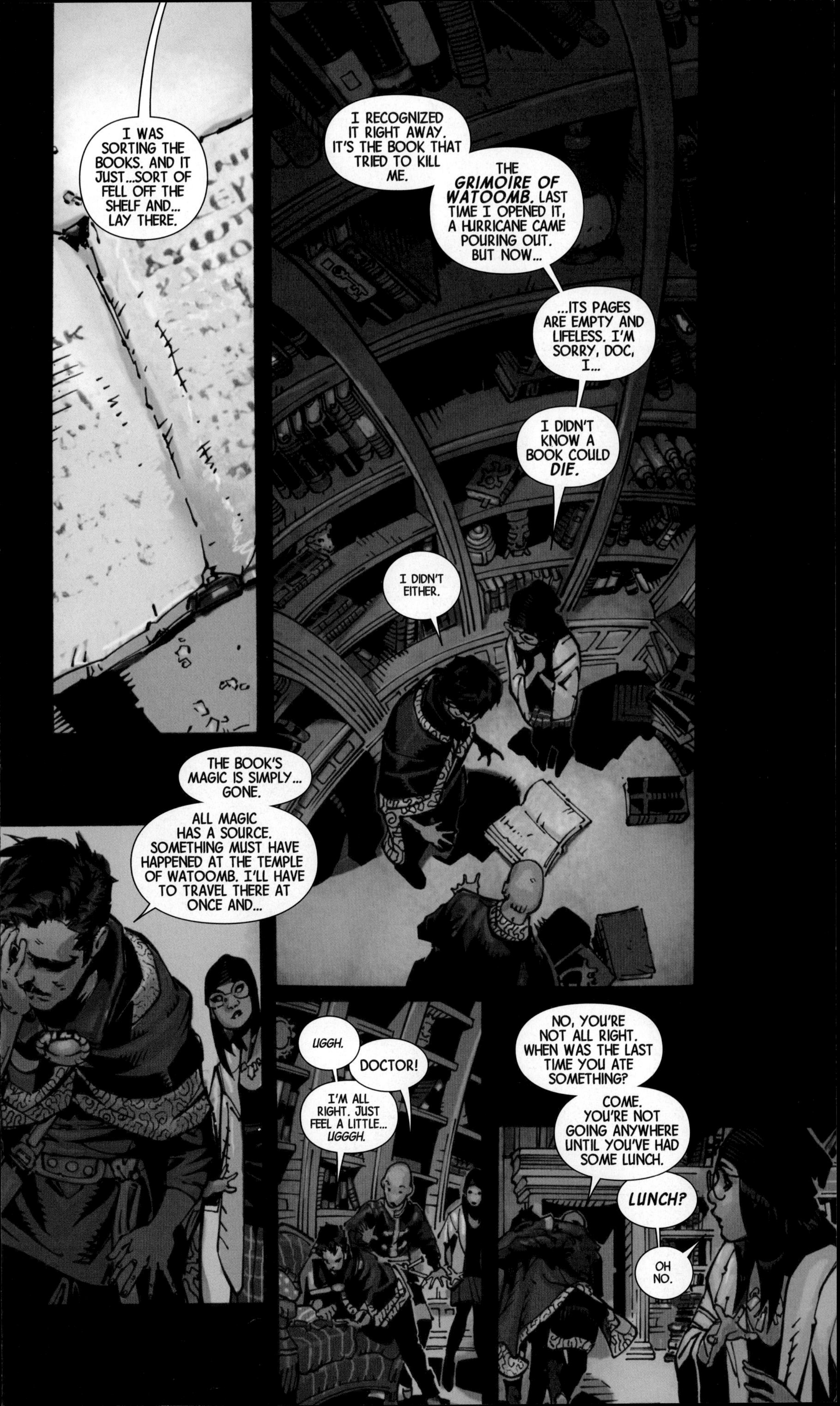
I WAS SORTING THE BOOKS. AND IT JUST...SORT OF FELL OFF THE SHELF AND... LAY THERE.
I RECOGNIZED IT RIGHT AWAY. IT'S THE BOOK THAT TRIED TO KILL ME.
THE GRIMOIRE OF WATOOMB. LAST TIME I OPENED IT, A HURRICANE CAME POURING OUT. BUT NOW...
...ITS PAGES ARE EMPTY AND LIFELESS. I'M SORRY, DOC, I...
I DIDN'T KNOW A BOOK COULD DIE.
I DIDN'T EITHER.
THE BOOK'S MAGIC IS SIMPLY... GONE.
ALL MAGIC HAS A SOURCE. SOMETHING MUST HAVE HAPPENED AT THE TEMPLE OF WATOOMB. I'LL HAVE TO TRAVEL THERE AT ONCE AND...
UGGH.
DOCTOR!
I'M ALL RIGHT. JUST FEEL A LITTLE... UGGGH.
NO, YOU'RE NOT ALL RIGHT. WHEN WAS THE LAST TIME YOU ATE SOMETHING?
COME. YOU'RE NOT GOING ANYWHERE UNTIL YOU'VE HAD SOME LUNCH.
LUNCH?
OH NO.

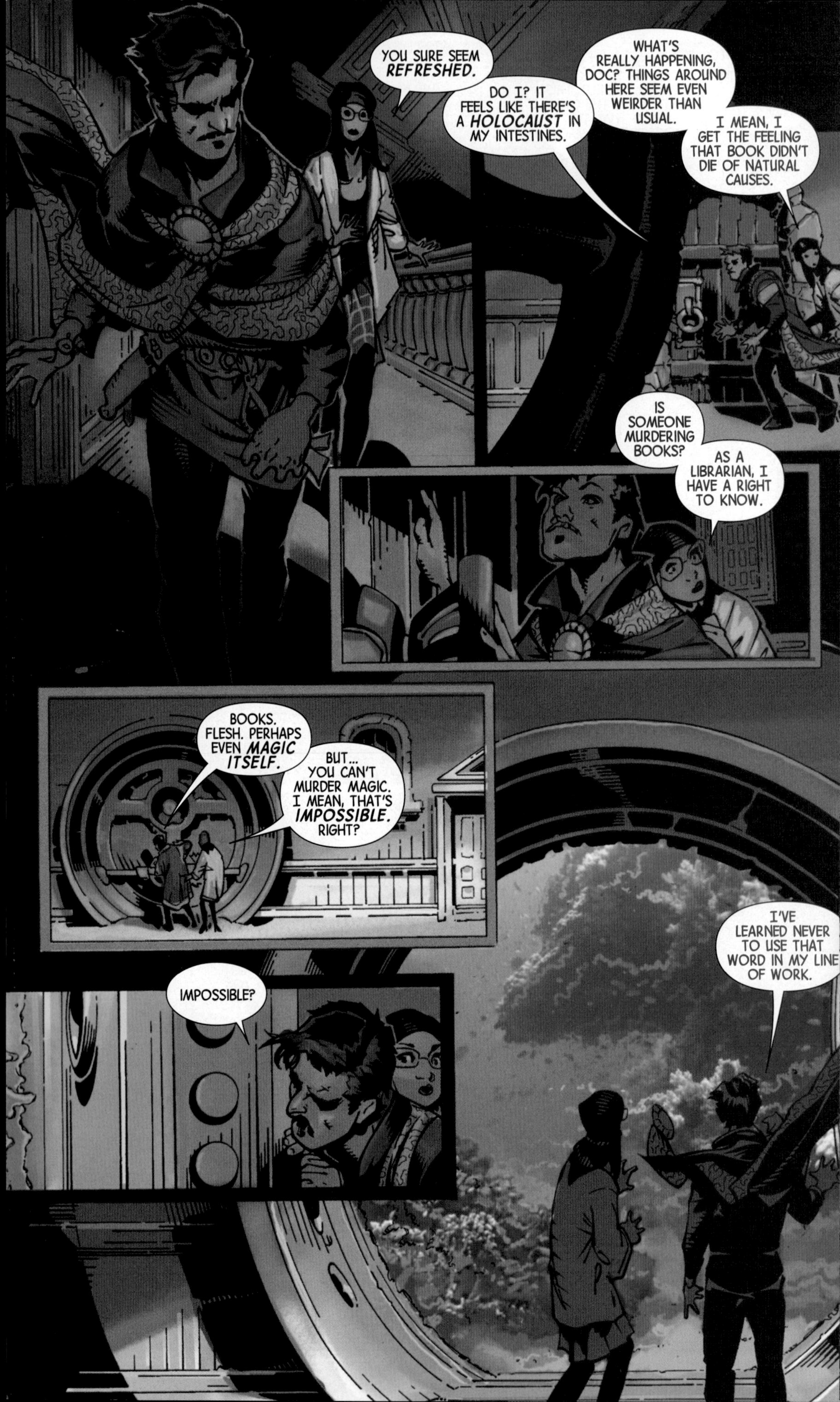
YOU SURE SEEM REFRESHED.
DO I? IT FEELS LIKE THERE'S A HOLOCAUST IN MY INTESTINES.
WHAT'S REALLY HAPPENING, DOC? THINGS AROUND HERE SEEM EVEN WEIRDER THAN USUAL.
I MEAN, I GET THE FEELING THAT BOOK DIDN'T DIE OF NATURAL CAUSES.
IS SOMEONE MURDERING BOOKS?
AS A LIBRARIAN, I HAVE A RIGHT TO KNOW.
BOOKS. FLESH. PERHAPS EVEN MAGIC ITSELF.
BUT... YOU CAN'T MURDER MAGIC. I MEAN, THAT'S IMPOSSIBLE. RIGHT?
IMPOSSIBLE?
I'VE LEARNED NEVER TO USE THAT WORD IN MY LINE OF WORK.

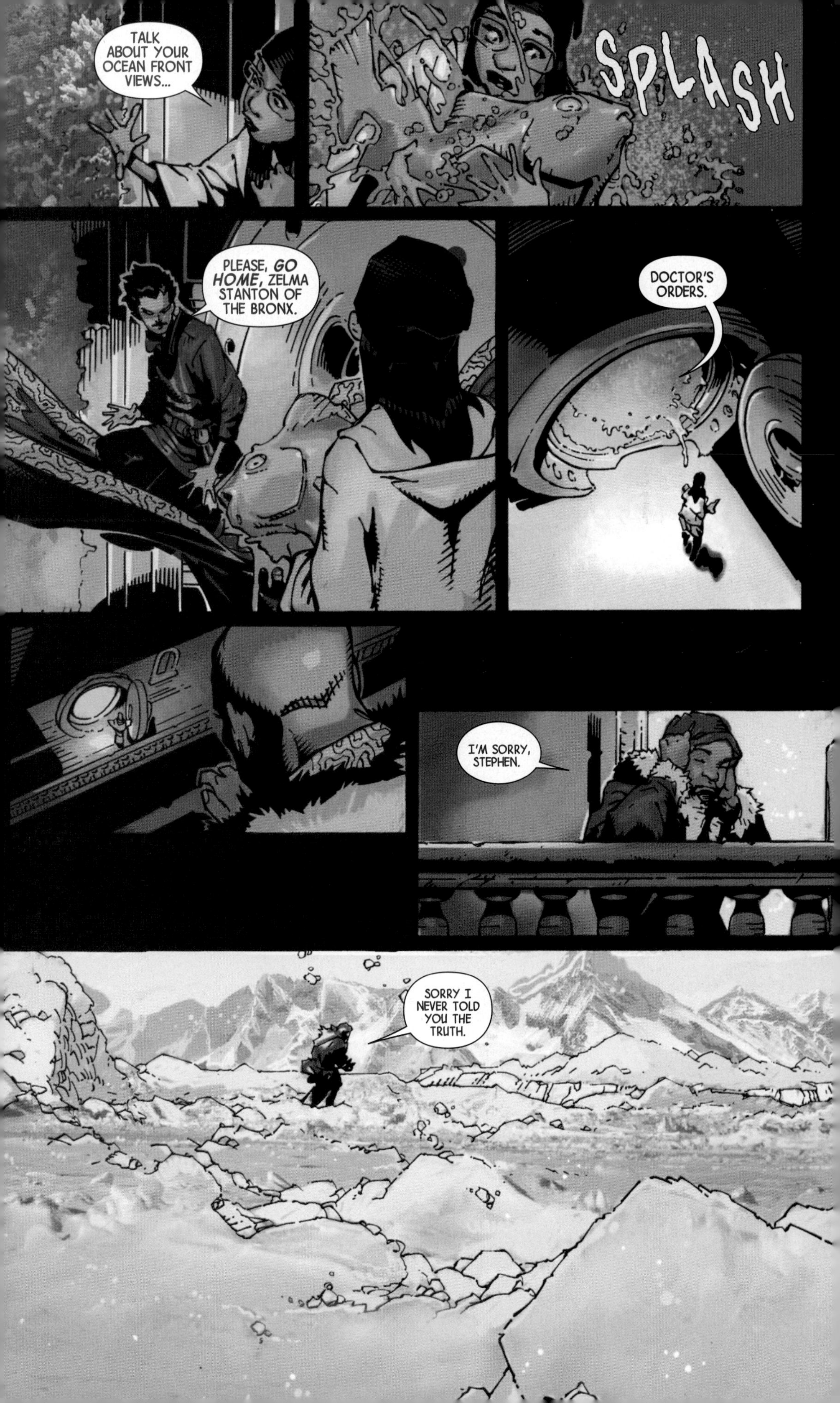
TALK ABOUT YOUR OCEAN FRONT VIEWS...
SPLASH
PLEASE, GO HOME, ZELMA STANTON OF THE BRONX.
DOCTOR'S ORDERS.
I'M SORRY, STEPHEN.
SORRY I NEVER TOLD YOU THE TRUTH.

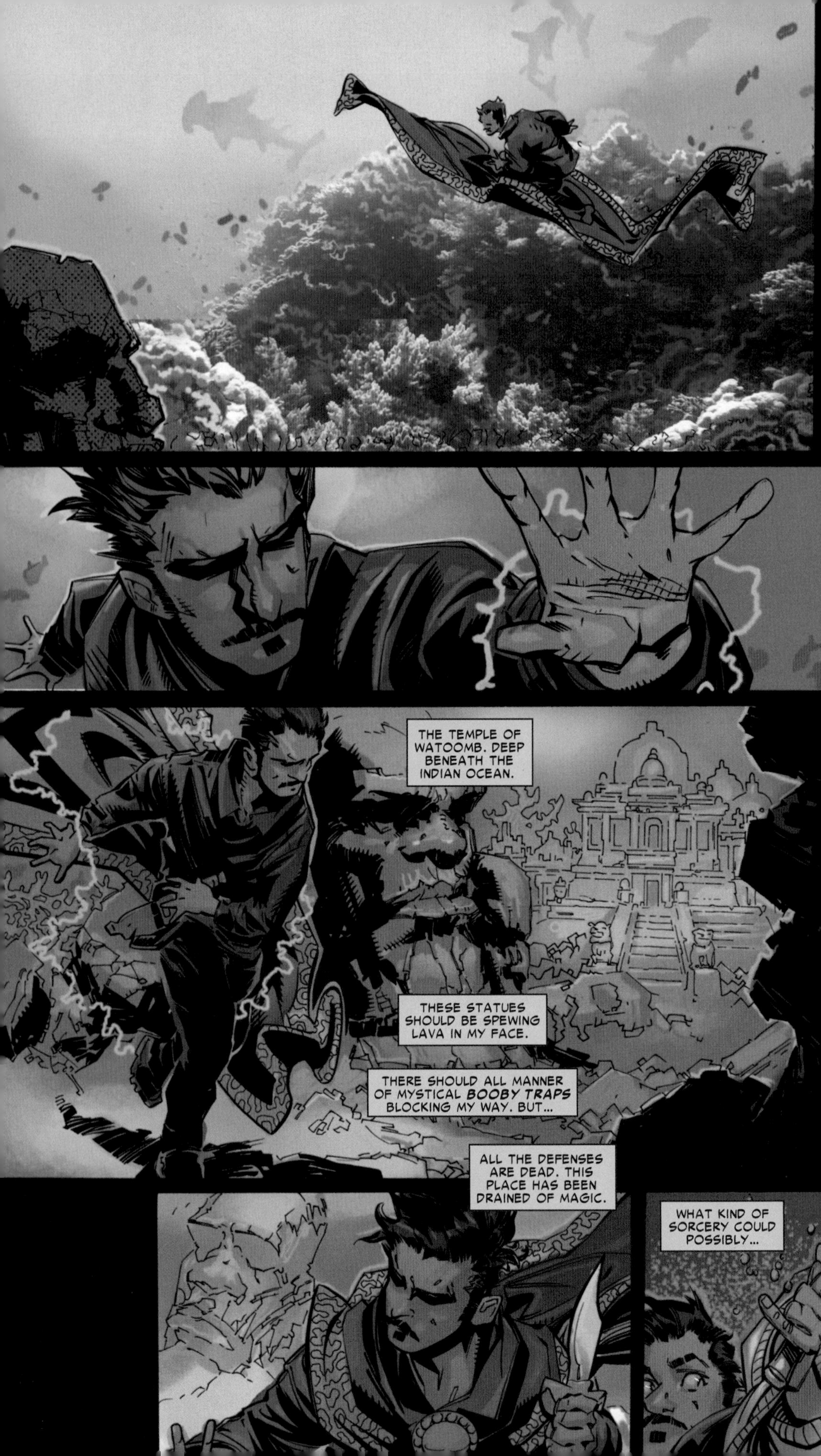

THE TEMPLE OF WATOOMB. DEEP BENEATH THE INDIAN OCEAN.
THESE STATUES SHOULD BE SPEWING LAVA IN MY FACE.
THERE SHOULD ALL MANNER OF MYSTICAL *BOOBY TRAPS* BLOCKING MY WAY. BUT...
ALL THE DEFENSES ARE DEAD. THIS PLACE HAS BEEN DRAINED OF MAGIC.
WHAT KIND OF SORCERY COULD POSSIBLY...

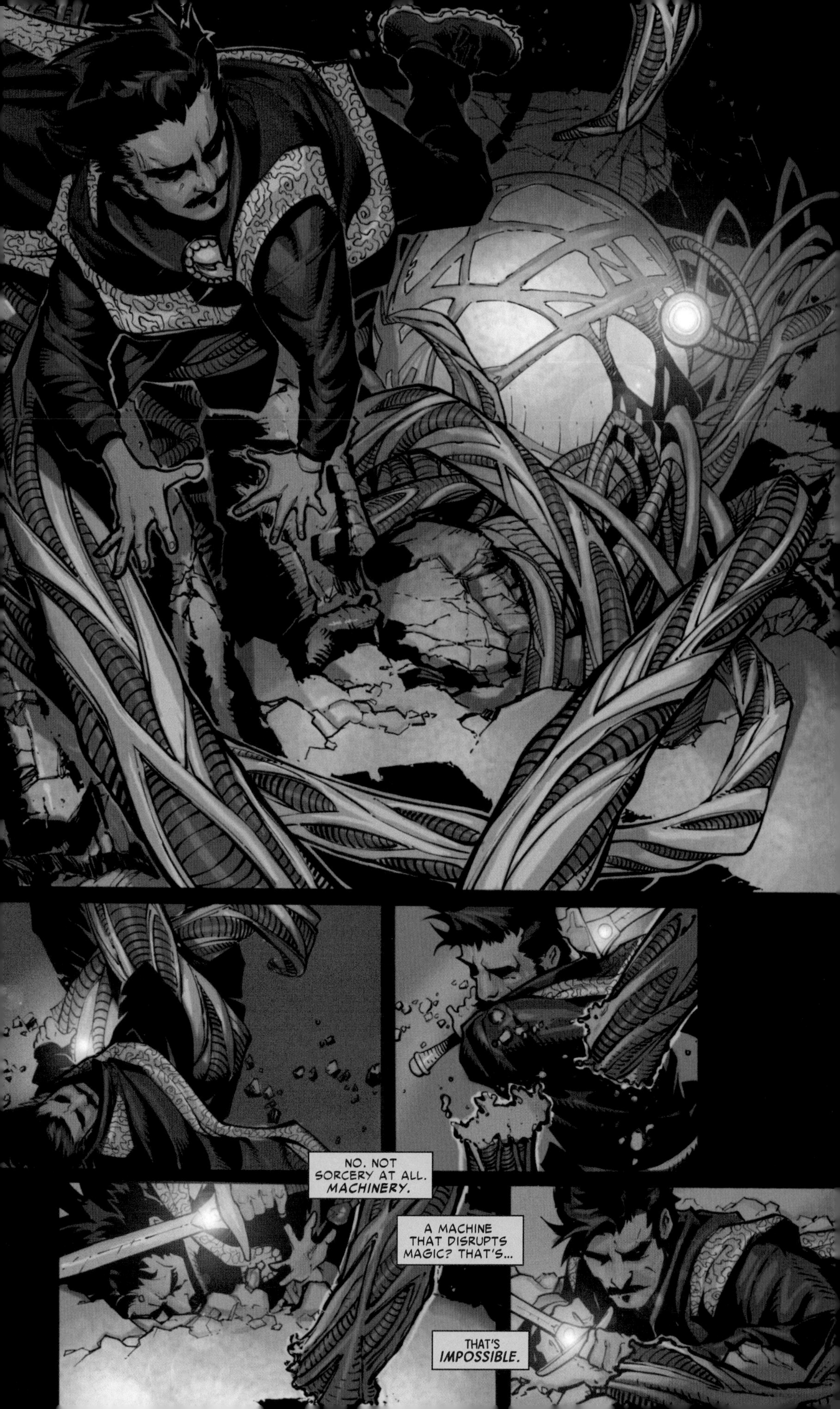
NO. NOT SORCERY AT ALL. MACHINERY.
A MACHINE THAT DISRUPTS MAGIC? THAT'S...
THAT'S IMPOSSIBLE.

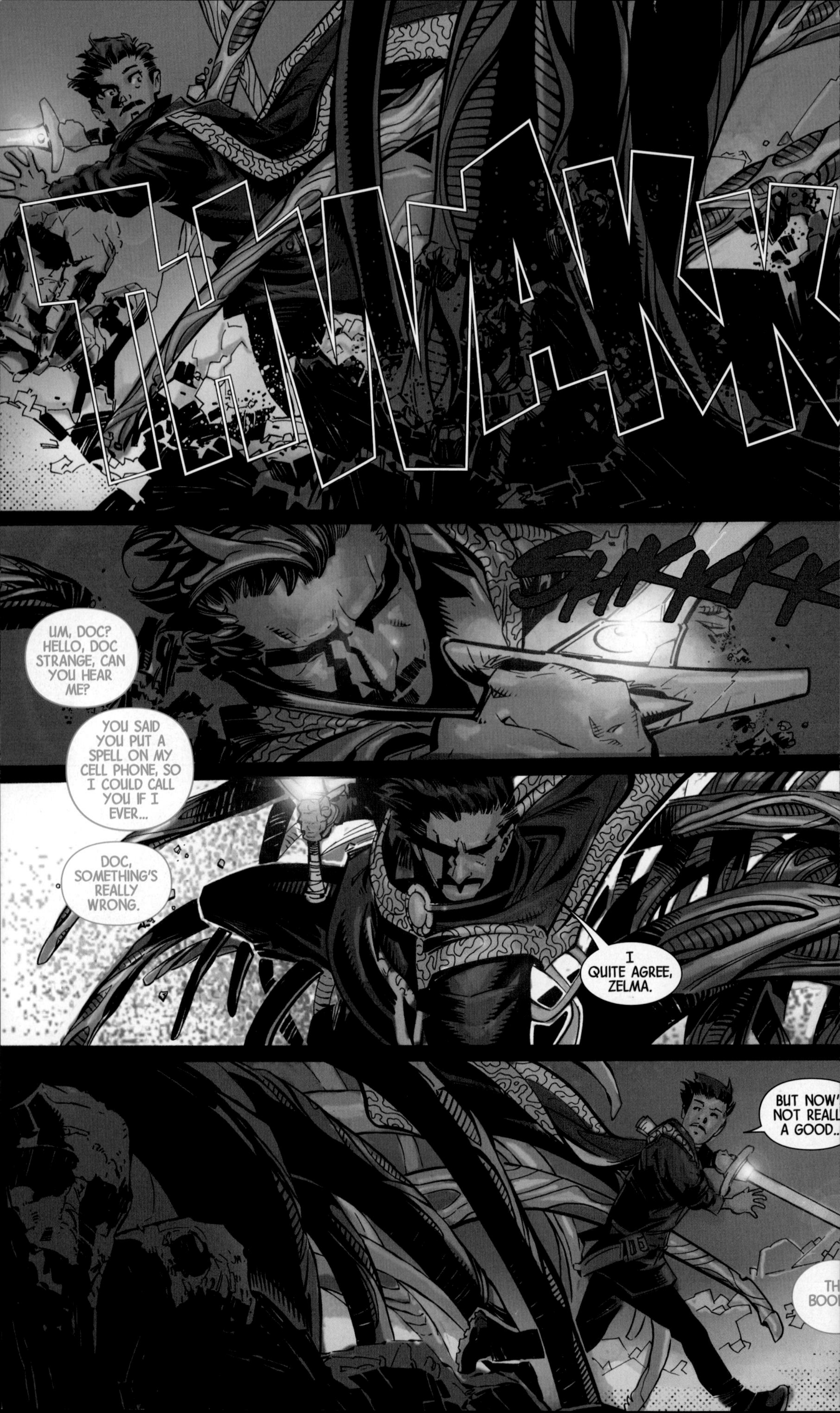
THWAKK
SHKKK
UM, DOC? HELLO, DOC STRANGE, CAN YOU HEAR ME?
YOU SAID YOU PUT A SPELL ON MY CELL PHONE, SO I COULD CALL YOU IF I EVER...
DOC, SOMETHING'S REALLY WRONG.
I QUITE AGREE, ZELMA.
BUT NOW' NOT REALL A GOOD...

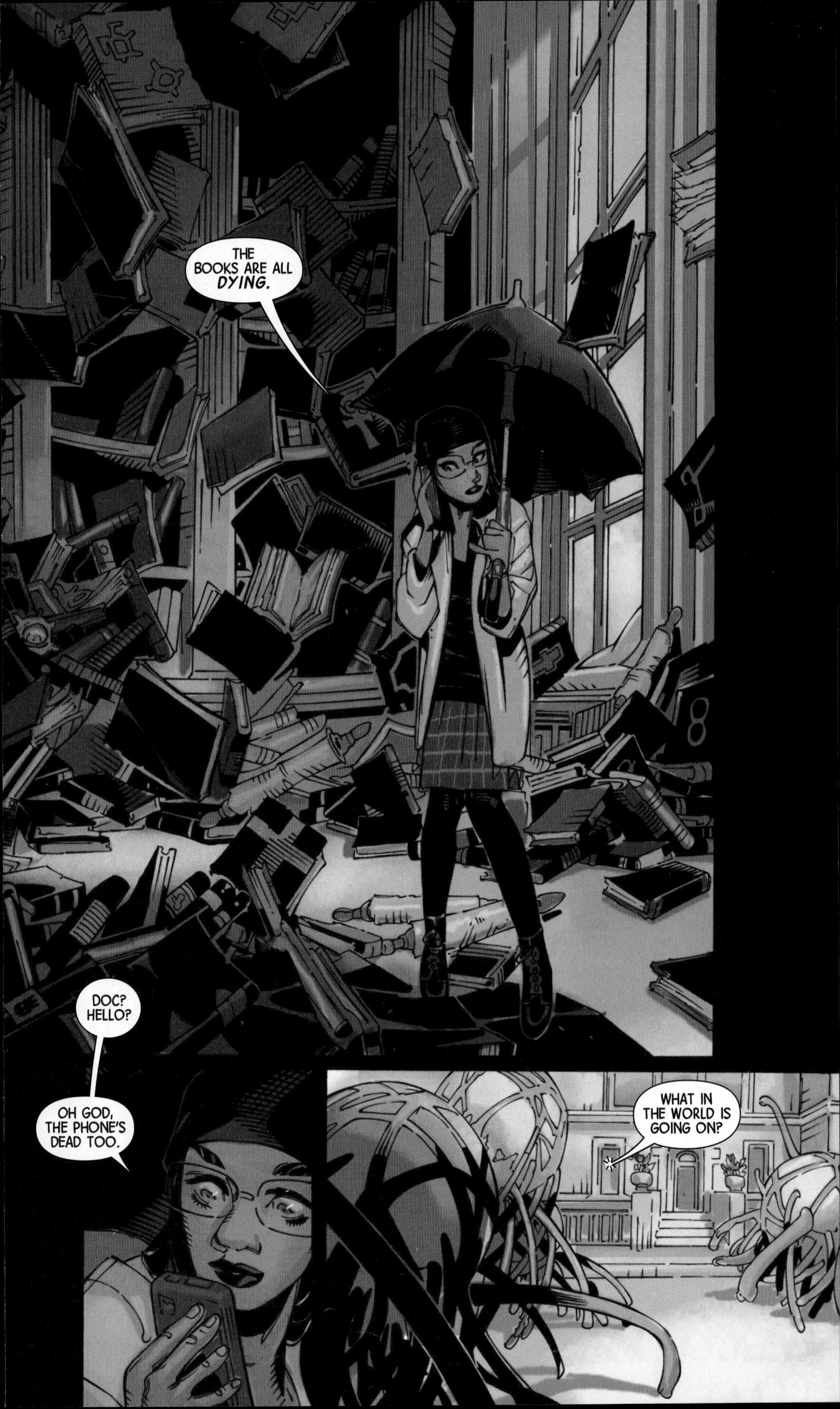
THE BOOKS ARE ALL DYING.
DOC? HELLO?
OH GOD, THE PHONE'S DEAD TOO.
WHAT IN THE WORLD IS GOING ON?

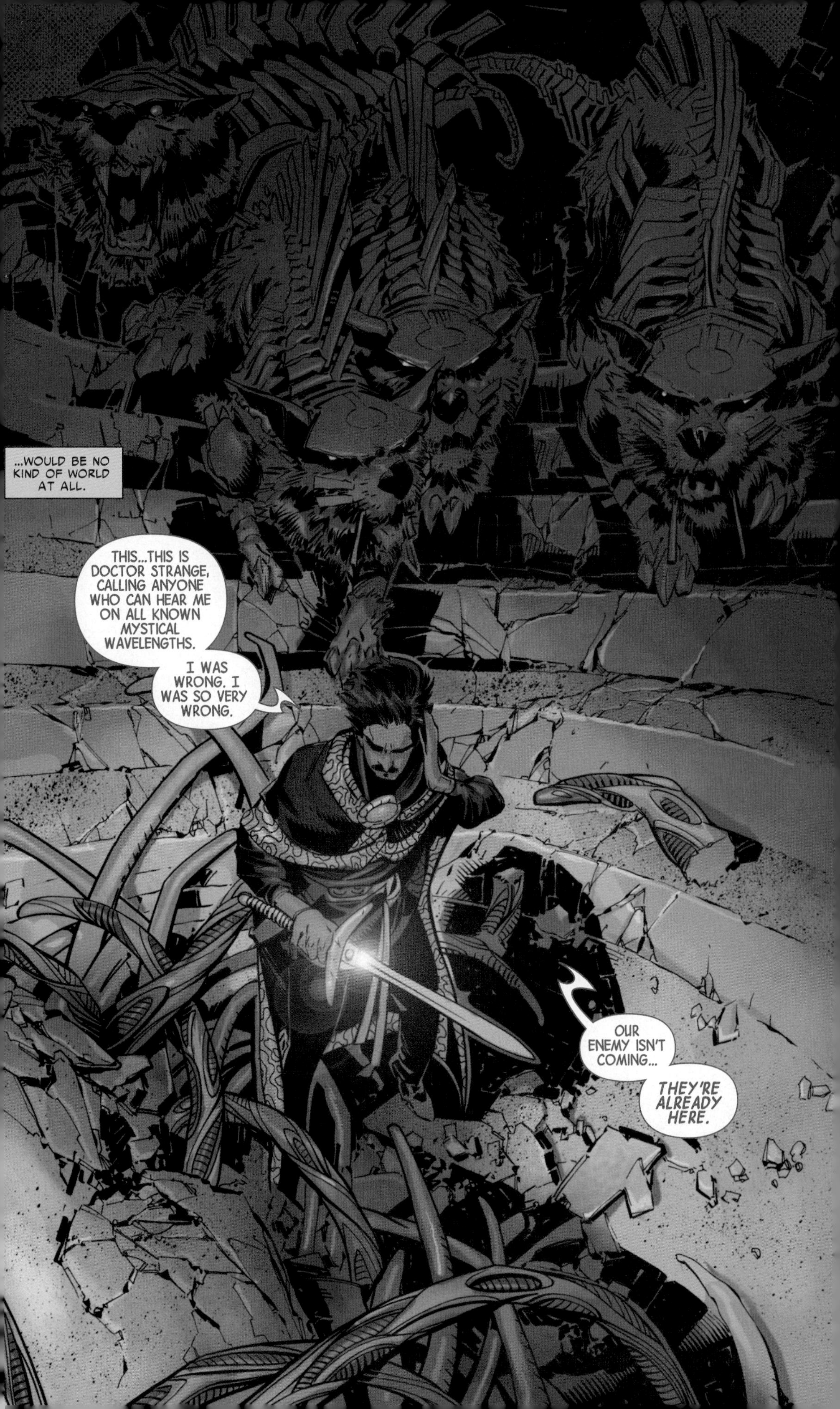
...WOULD BE NO KIND OF WORLD AT ALL.
THIS...THIS IS DOCTOR STRANGE, CALLING ANYONE WHO CAN HEAR ME ON ALL KNOWN MYSTICAL WAVELENGTHS.
I WAS WRONG. I WAS SO VERY WRONG.
OUR ENEMY ISN'T COMING...
THEY'RE ALREADY HERE.

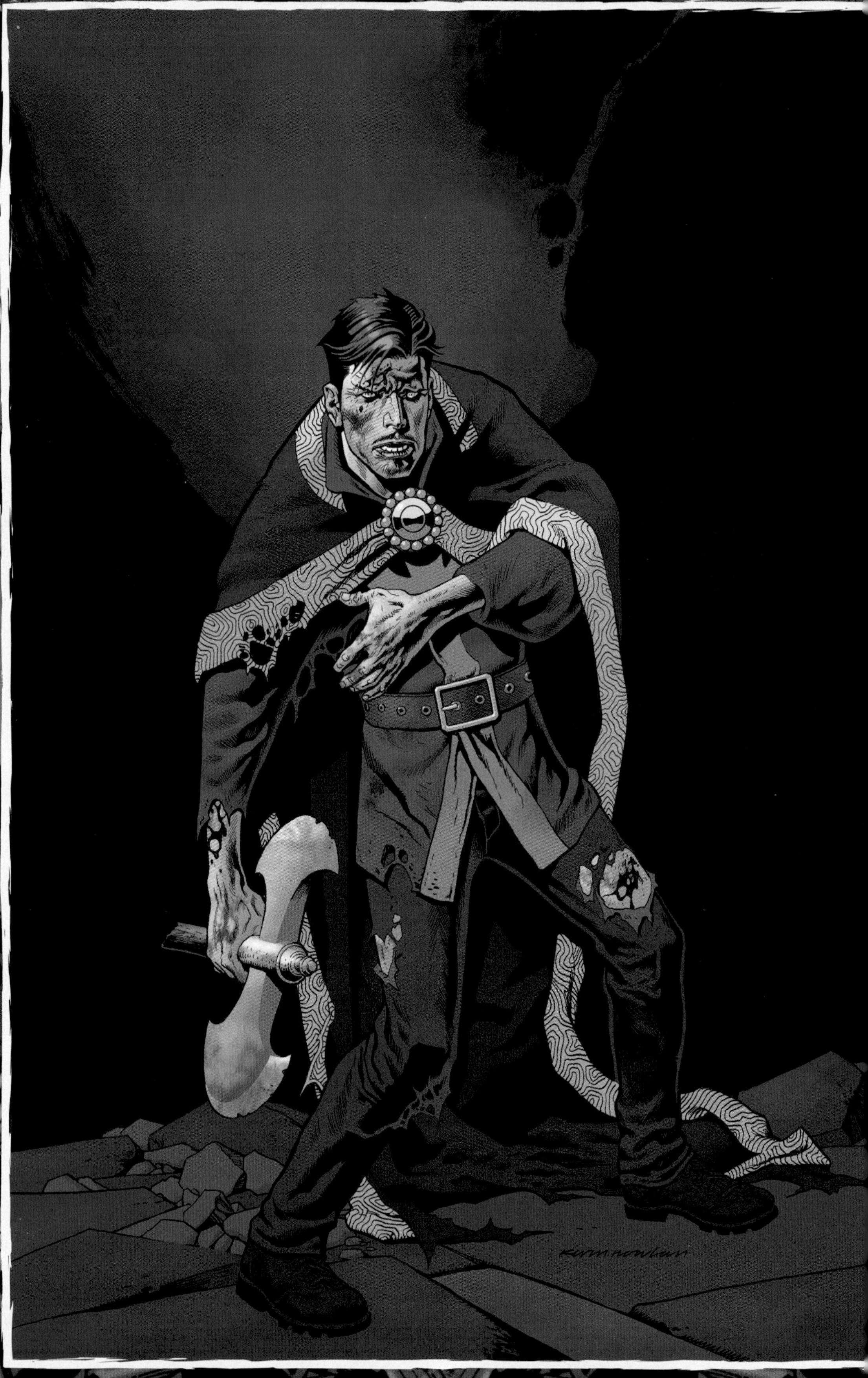

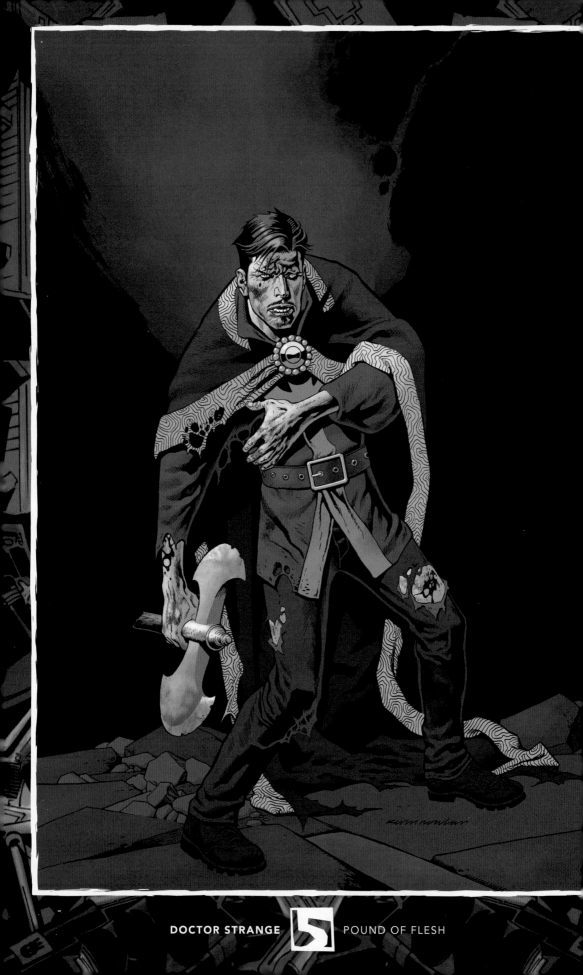

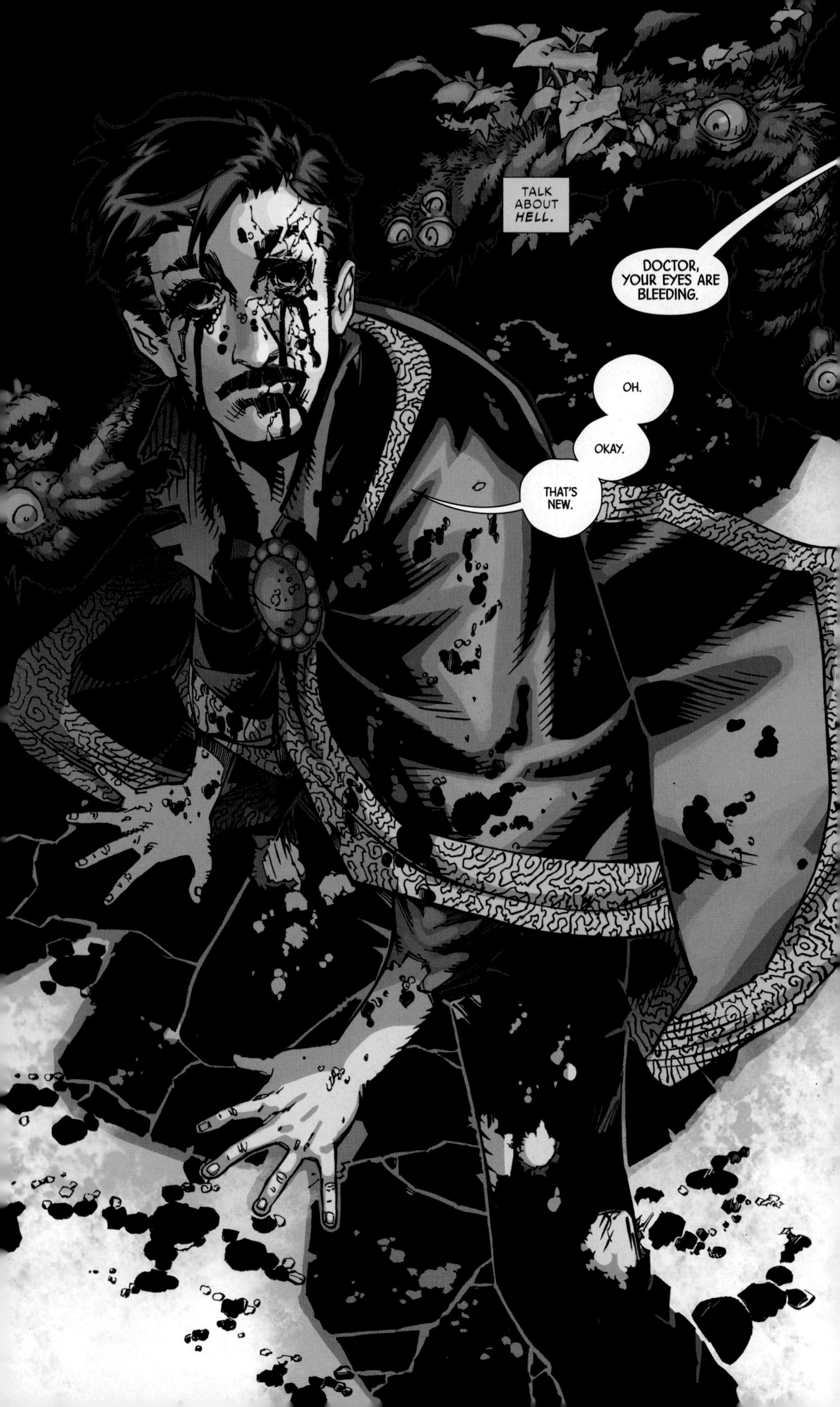
TALK ABOUT *HELL.*
DOCTOR, YOUR EYES ARE BLEEDING.
OH.
OKAY.
THAT'S NEW.

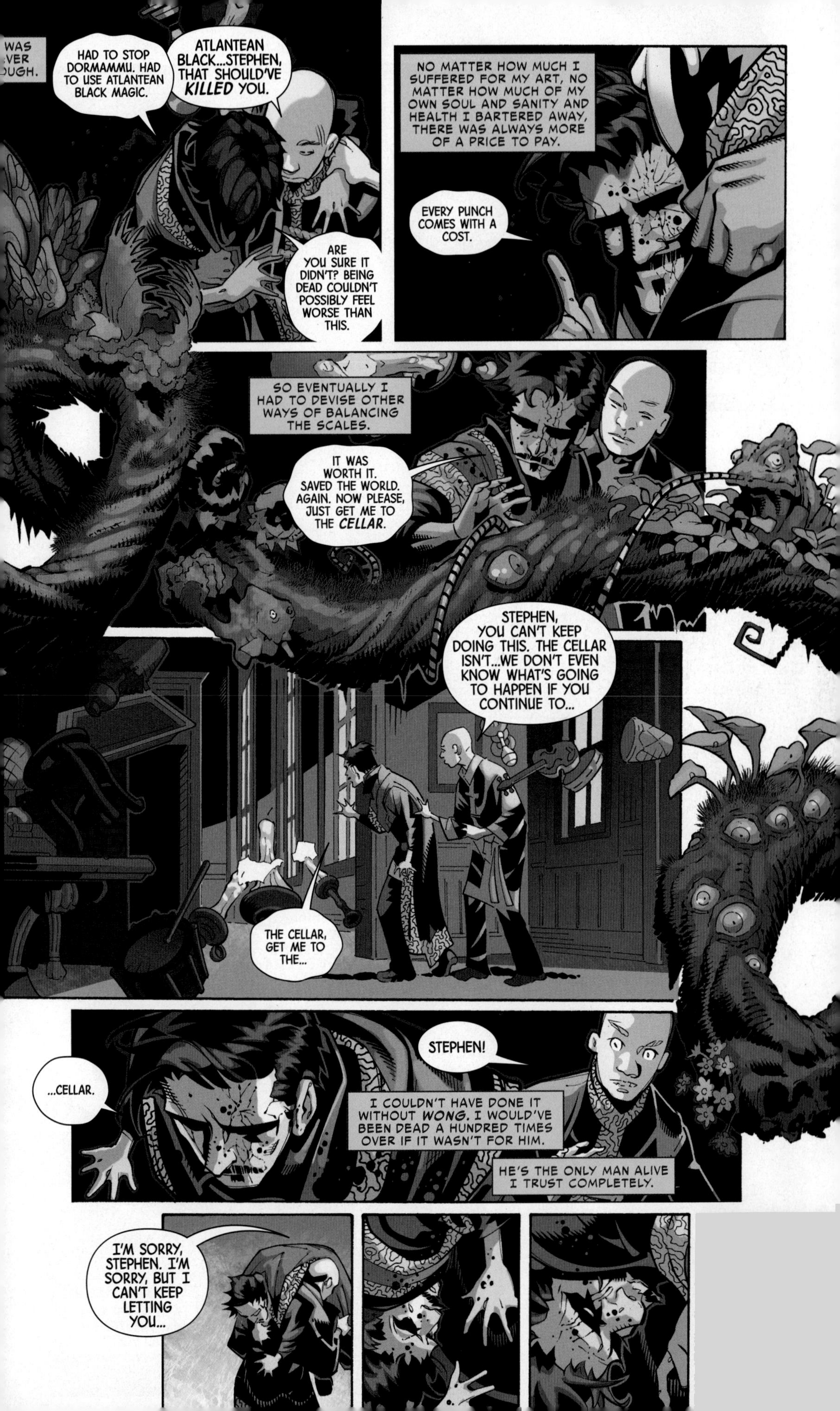

WAS
VER
UGH.
HAD TO STOP DORMAMMU. HAD TO USE ATLANTEAN BLACK MAGIC.
ATLANTEAN BLACK...STEPHEN, THAT SHOULD'VE *KILLED* YOU.
ARE YOU SURE IT DIDN'T? BEING DEAD COULDN'T POSSIBLY FEEL WORSE THAN THIS.
NO MATTER HOW MUCH I SUFFERED FOR MY ART, NO MATTER HOW MUCH OF MY OWN SOUL AND SANITY AND HEALTH I BARTERED AWAY, THERE WAS ALWAYS MORE OF A PRICE TO PAY.
EVERY PUNCH COMES WITH A COST.
SO EVENTUALLY I HAD TO DEVISE OTHER WAYS OF BALANCING THE SCALES.
IT WAS WORTH IT. SAVED THE WORLD. AGAIN. NOW PLEASE, JUST GET ME TO THE *CELLAR*.
STEPHEN, YOU CAN'T KEEP DOING THIS. THE CELLAR ISN'T...WE DON'T EVEN KNOW WHAT'S GOING TO HAPPEN IF YOU CONTINUE TO...
THE CELLAR, GET ME TO THE...
...CELLAR.
STEPHEN!
I COULDN'T HAVE DONE IT WITHOUT *WONG*. I WOULD'VE BEEN DEAD A HUNDRED TIMES OVER IF IT WASN'T FOR HIM.
HE'S THE ONLY MAN ALIVE I TRUST COMPLETELY.
I'M SORRY, STEPHEN. I'M SORRY, BUT I CAN'T KEEP LETTING YOU...

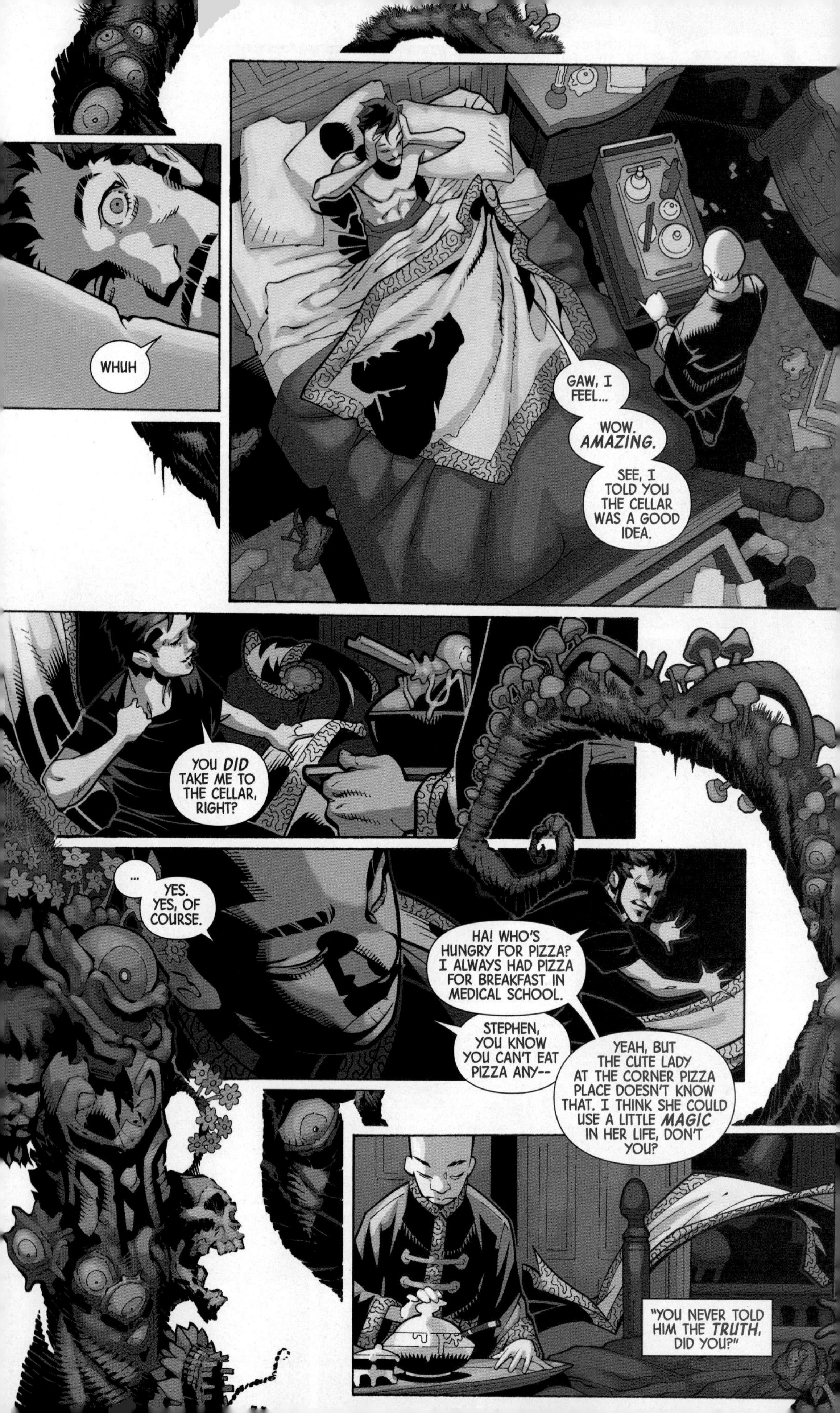
WHUH
GAW, I FEEL...
WOW. AMAZING.
SEE, I TOLD YOU THE CELLAR WAS A GOOD IDEA.
YOU DID TAKE ME TO THE CELLAR, RIGHT?
... YES. YES, OF COURSE.
HA! WHO'S HUNGRY FOR PIZZA? I ALWAYS HAD PIZZA FOR BREAKFAST IN MEDICAL SCHOOL.
STEPHEN, YOU KNOW YOU CAN'T EAT PIZZA ANY--
YEAH, BUT THE CUTE LADY AT THE CORNER PIZZA PLACE DOESN'T KNOW THAT. I THINK SHE COULD USE A LITTLE MAGIC IN HER LIFE, DON'T YOU?
"YOU NEVER TOLD HIM THE TRUTH, DID YOU?"

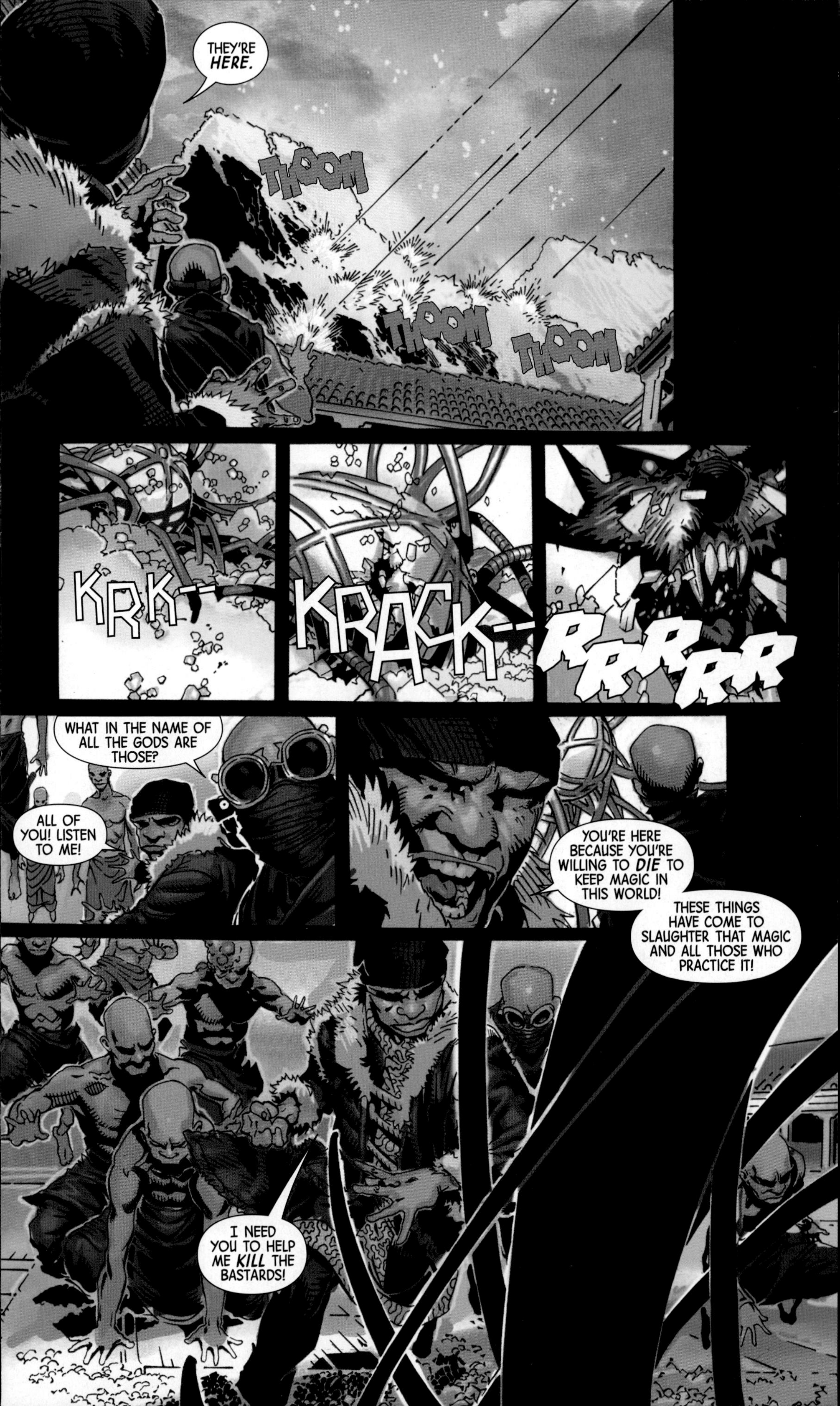
THEY'RE *HERE.*
THOOM
THOOM
THOOM
KRK--
KRACK--
RRRRR
WHAT IN THE NAME OF ALL THE GODS ARE THOSE?
ALL OF YOU! LISTEN TO ME!
YOU'RE HERE BECAUSE YOU'RE WILLING TO *DIE* TO KEEP MAGIC IN THIS WORLD!
THESE THINGS HAVE COME TO SLAUGHTER THAT MAGIC AND ALL THOSE WHO PRACTICE IT!
I NEED YOU TO HELP ME *KILL* THE BASTARDS!

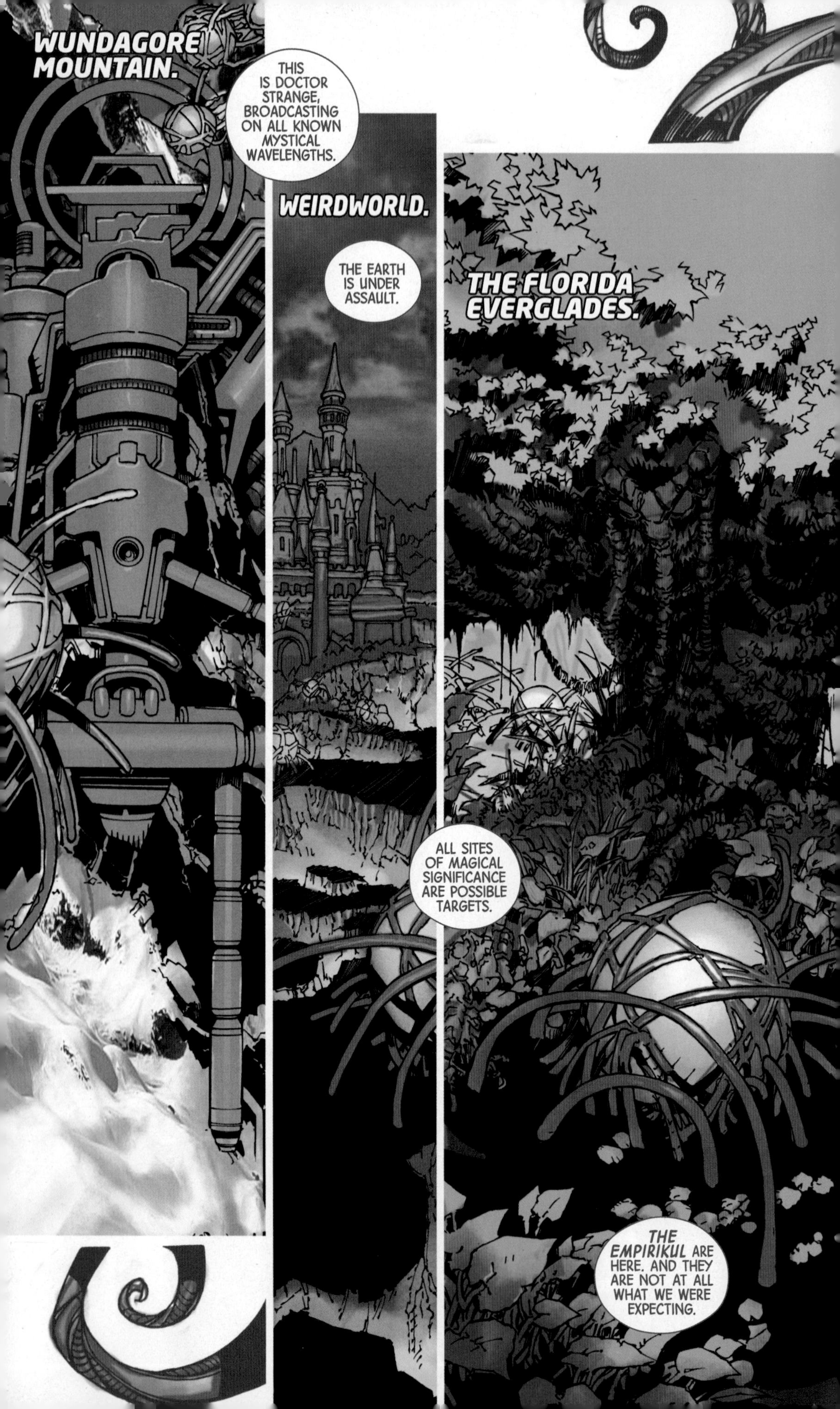
WUNDAGORE MOUNTAIN.
THIS IS DOCTOR STRANGE, BROADCASTING ON ALL KNOWN MYSTICAL WAVELENGTHS.
WEIRDWORLD.
THE EARTH IS UNDER ASSAULT.
THE FLORIDA EVERGLADES.
ALL SITES OF MAGICAL SIGNIFICANCE ARE POSSIBLE TARGETS.
THE EMPIRIKUL ARE HERE. AND THEY ARE NOT AT ALL WHAT WE WERE EXPECTING.

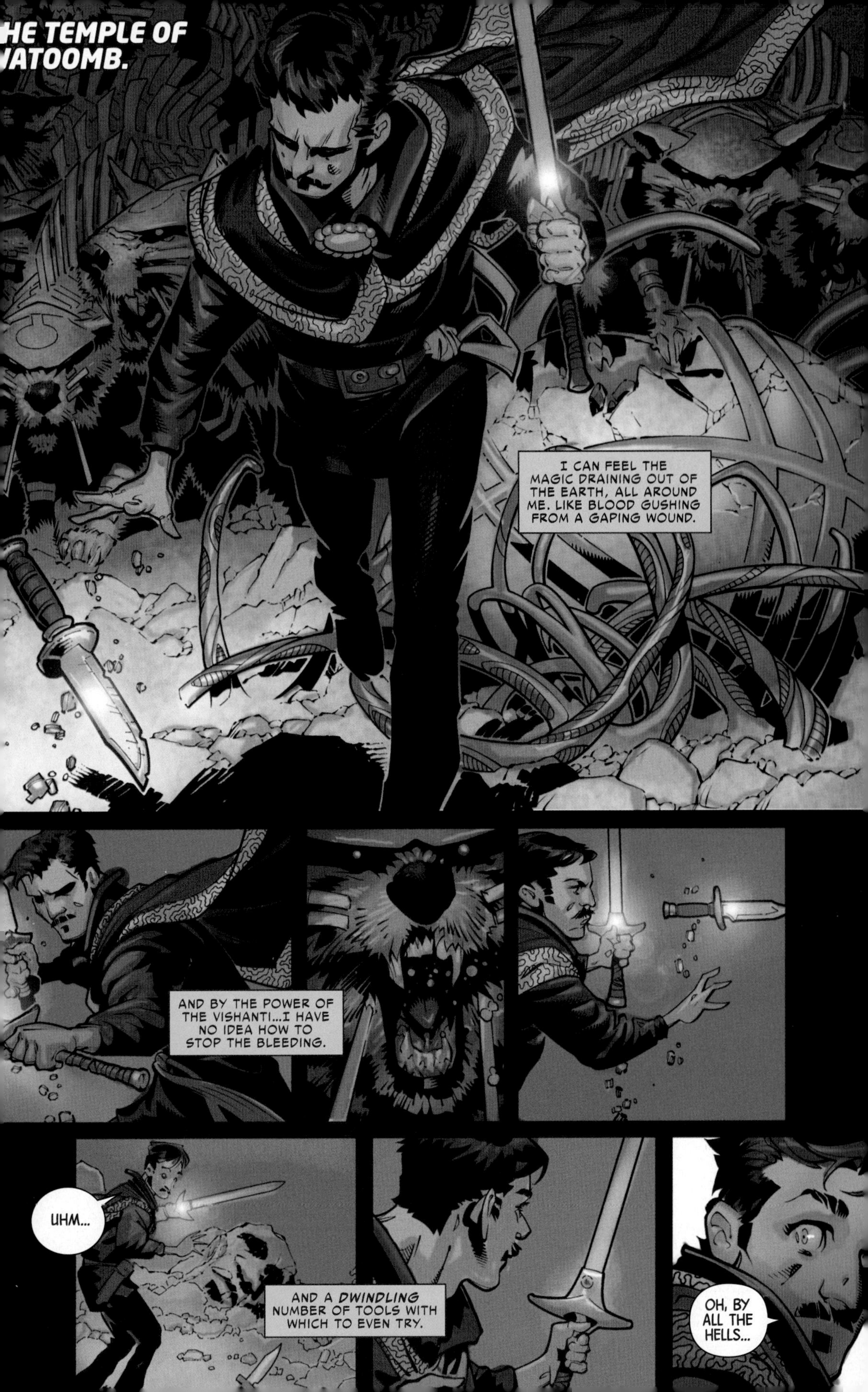

HE TEMPLE OF
/ATOOMB.
I CAN FEEL THE MAGIC DRAINING OUT OF THE EARTH, ALL AROUND ME. LIKE BLOOD GUSHING FROM A GAPING WOUND.
AND BY THE POWER OF THE VISHANTI...I HAVE NO IDEA HOW TO STOP THE BLEEDING.
UHM...
AND A *DWINDLING* NUMBER OF TOOLS WITH WHICH TO EVEN TRY.
OH, BY ALL THE HELLS...

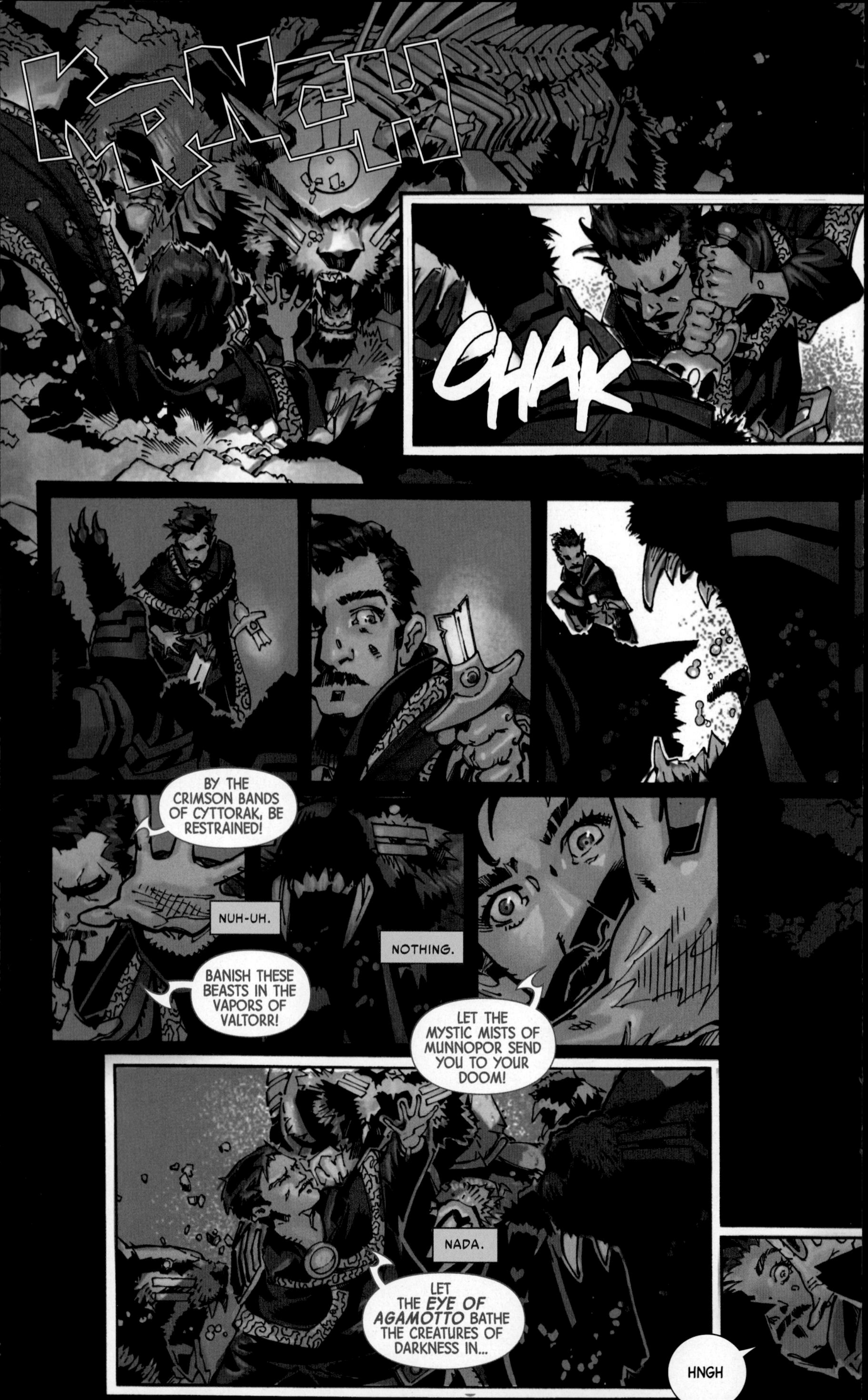
KRANCH
CHAK
BY THE CRIMSON BANDS OF CYTTORAK, BE RESTRAINED!
NUH-UH.
NOTHING.
BANISH THESE BEASTS IN THE VAPORS OF VALTORR!
LET THE MYSTIC MISTS OF MUNNOPOR SEND YOU TO YOUR DOOM!
NADA.
LET THE *EYE OF AGAMOTTO* BATHE THE CREATURES OF DARKNESS IN...
HNGH

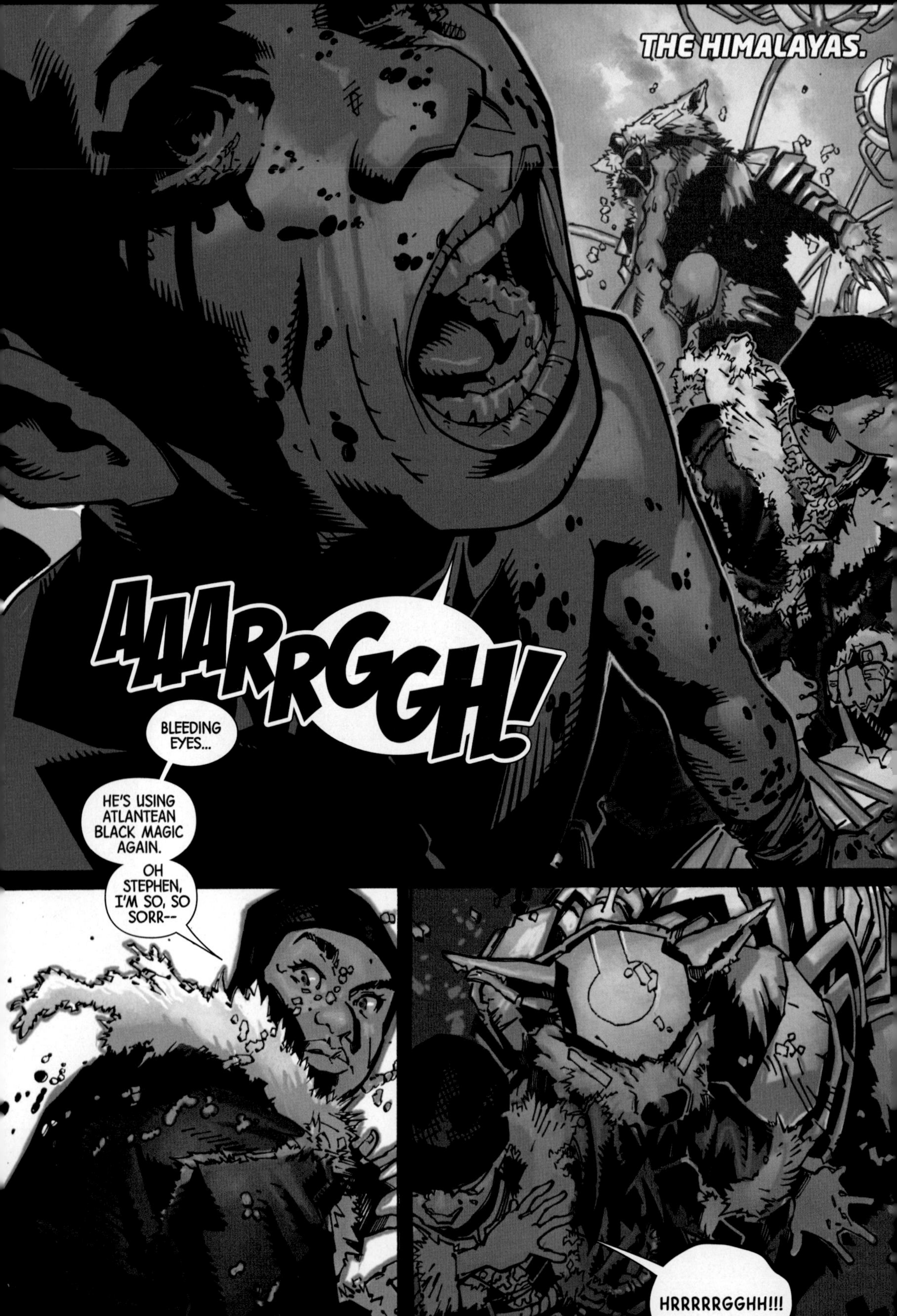
THE HIMALAYAS.
AAARRGGH!
BLEEDING EYES...
HE'S USING ATLANTEAN BLACK MAGIC AGAIN.
OH STEPHEN, I'M SO, SO SORR--
HRRRRRGGHH!!!

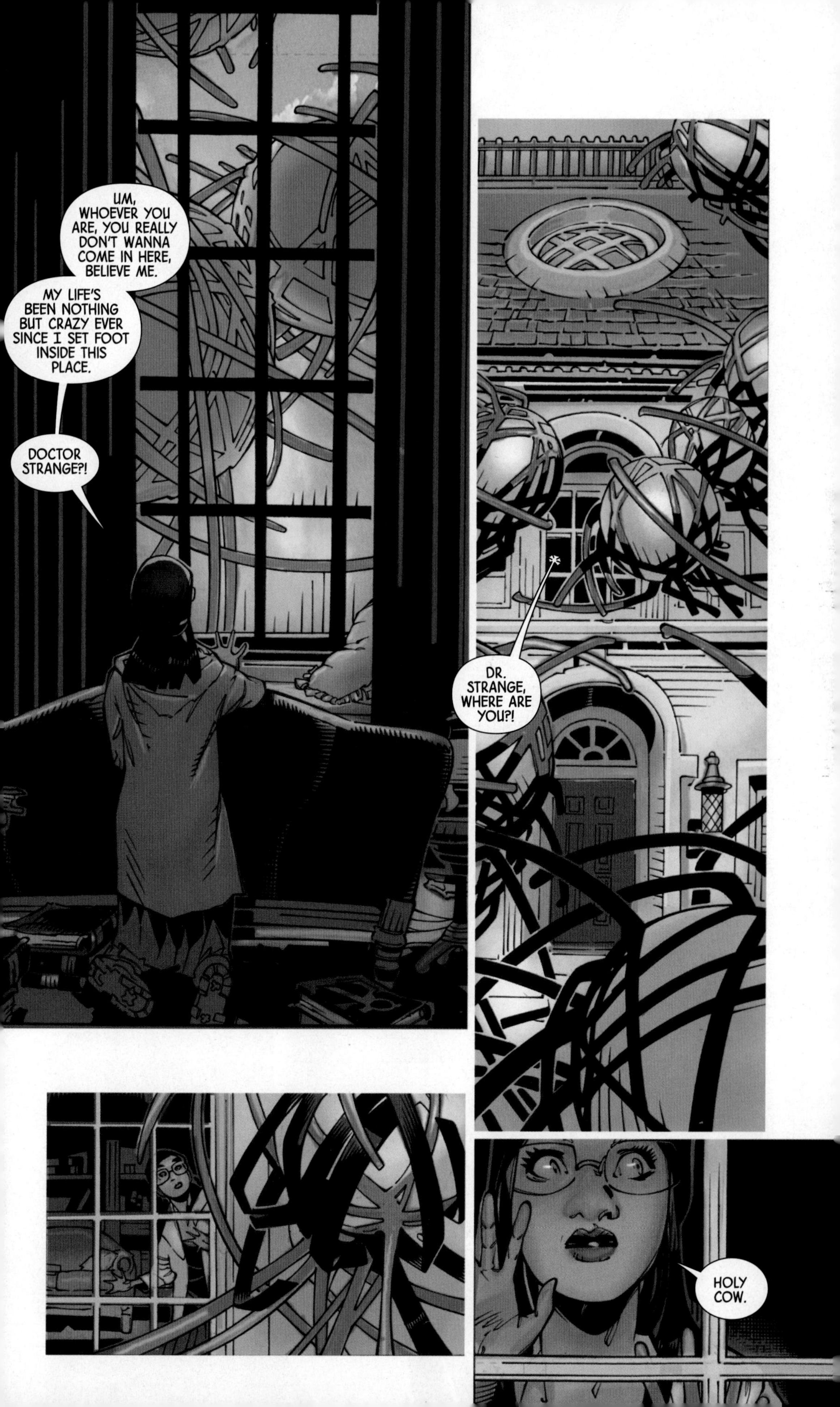
UM, WHOEVER YOU ARE, YOU REALLY DON'T WANNA COME IN HERE, BELIEVE ME.
MY LIFE'S BEEN NOTHING BUT CRAZY EVER SINCE I SET FOOT INSIDE THIS PLACE.
DOCTOR STRANGE?!
DR. STRANGE, WHERE ARE YOU?!
HOLY COW.

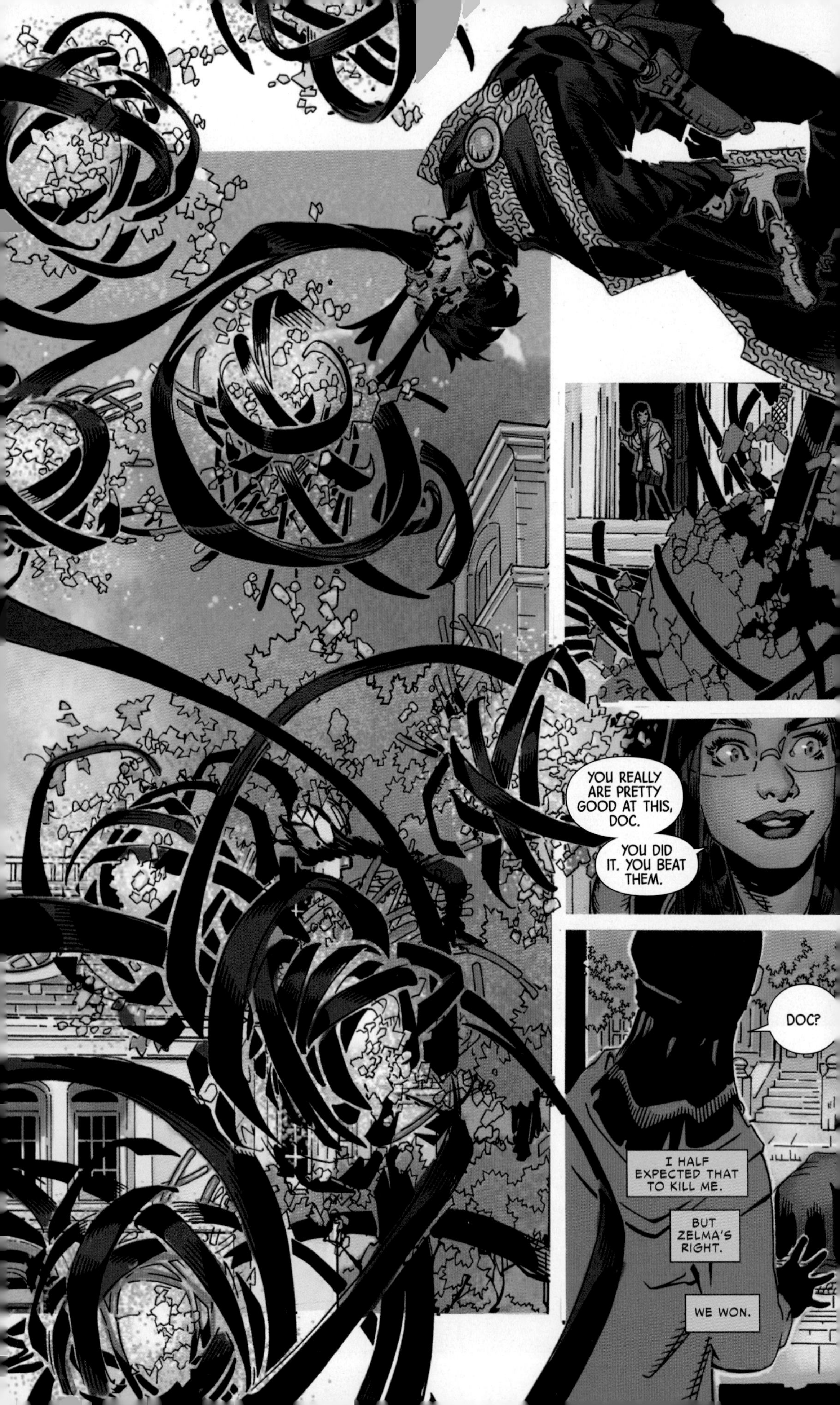

YOU REALLY ARE PRETTY GOOD AT THIS, DOC.
YOU DID IT. YOU BEAT THEM.
DOC?
I HALF EXPECTED THAT TO KILL ME.
BUT ZELMA'S RIGHT.
WE WON.

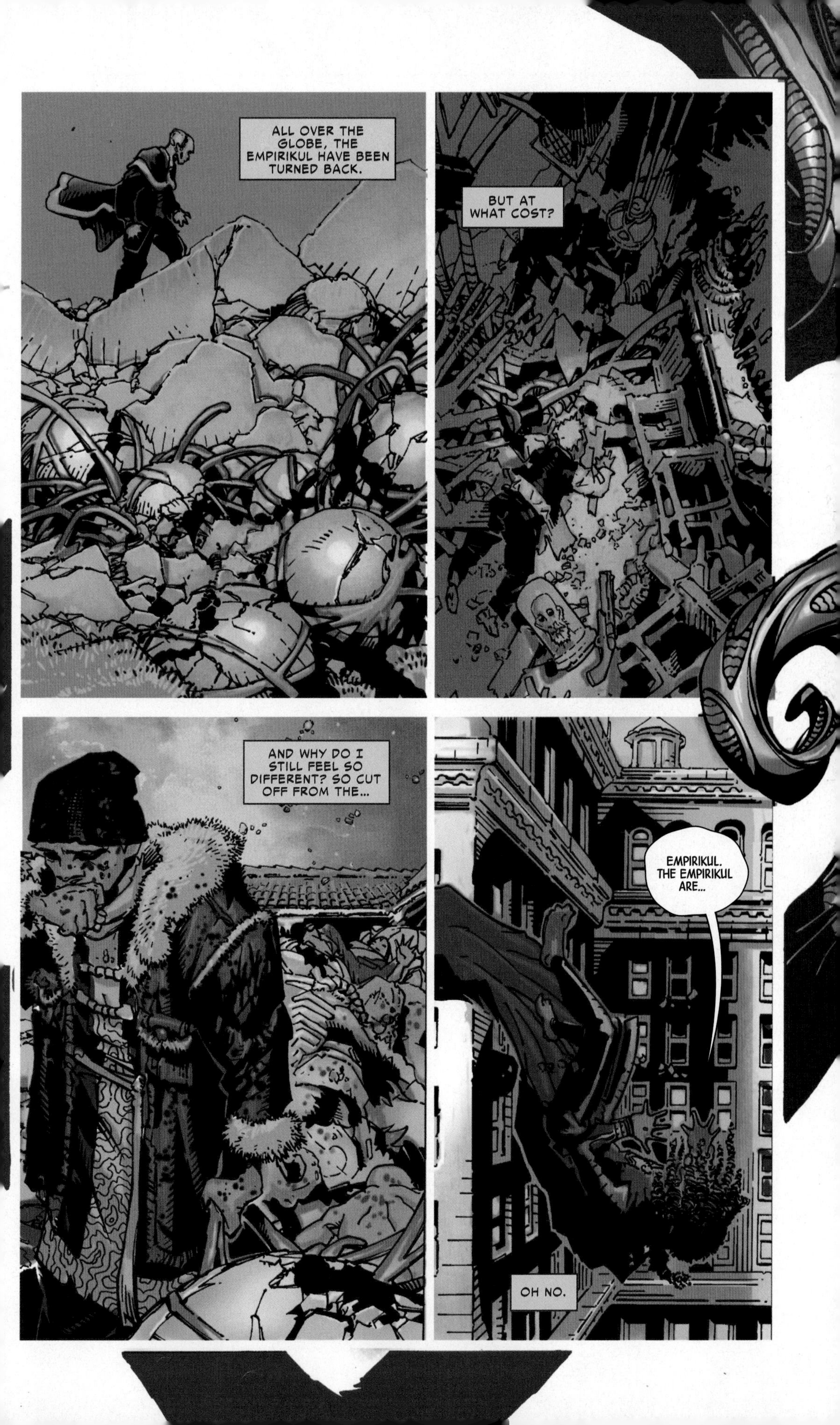
ALL OVER THE GLOBE, THE EMPIRIKUL HAVE BEEN TURNED BACK.
BUT AT WHAT COST?
AND WHY DO I STILL FEEL SO DIFFERENT? SO CUT OFF FROM THE...
EMPIRIKUL. THE EMPIRIKUL ARE...
OH NO.

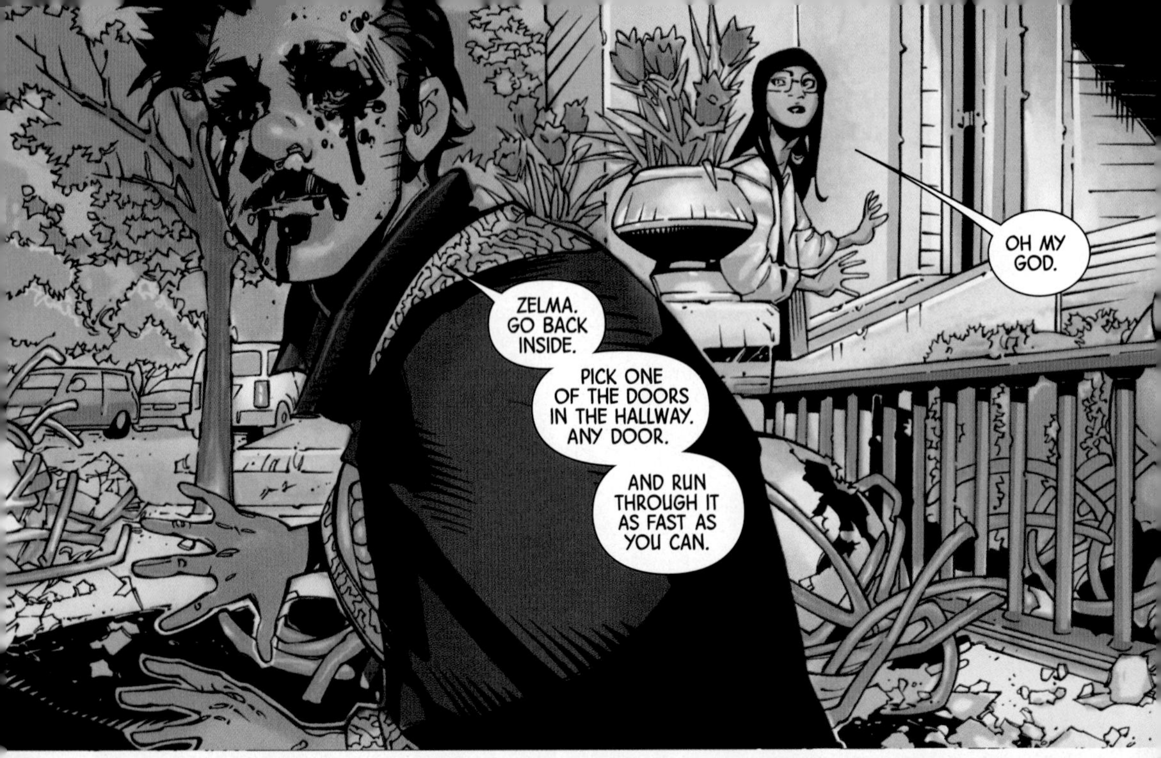
OH MY GOD.
ZELMA. GO BACK INSIDE.
PICK ONE OF THE DOORS IN THE HALLWAY. ANY DOOR.
AND RUN THROUGH IT AS FAST AS YOU CAN.

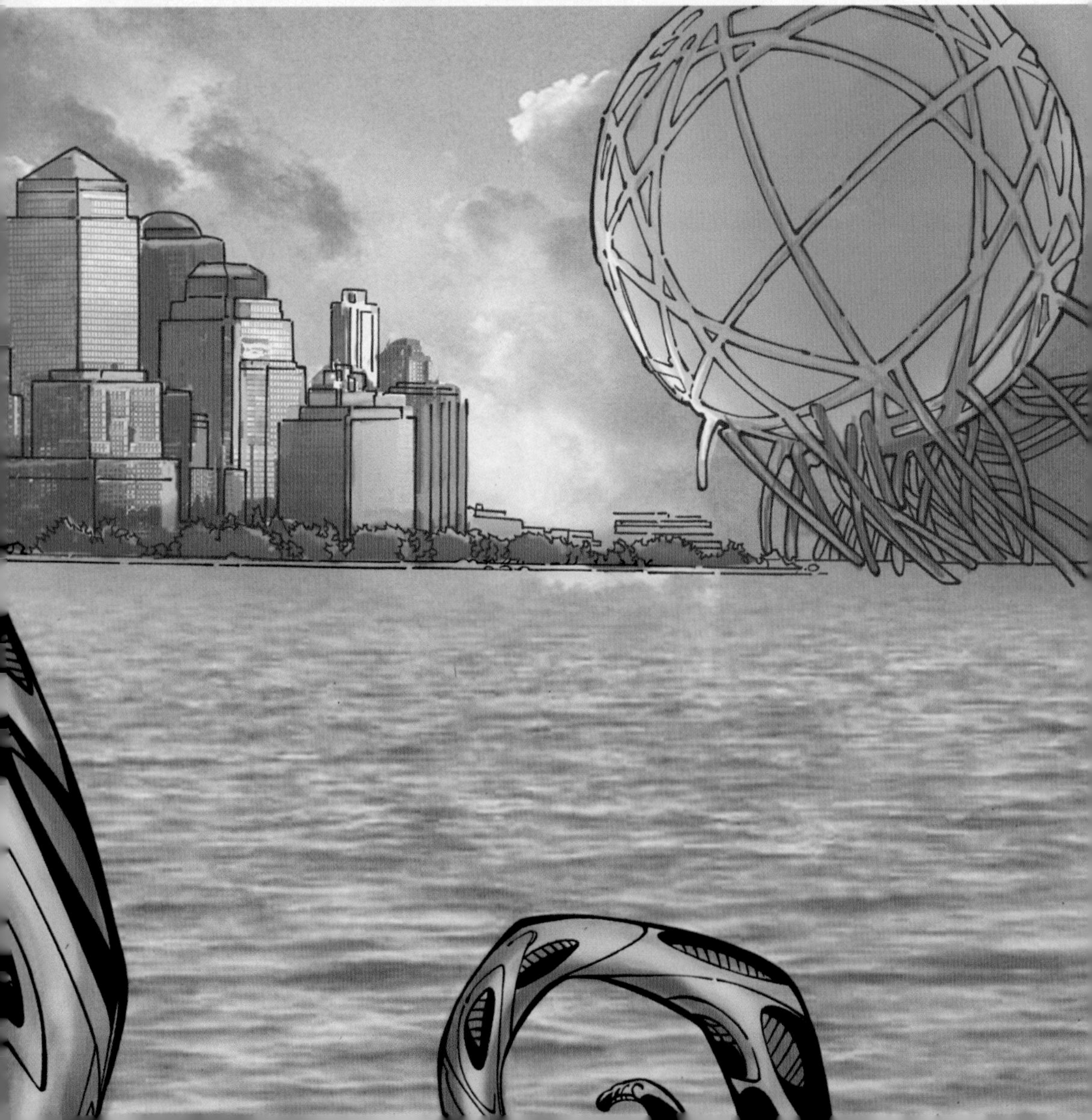

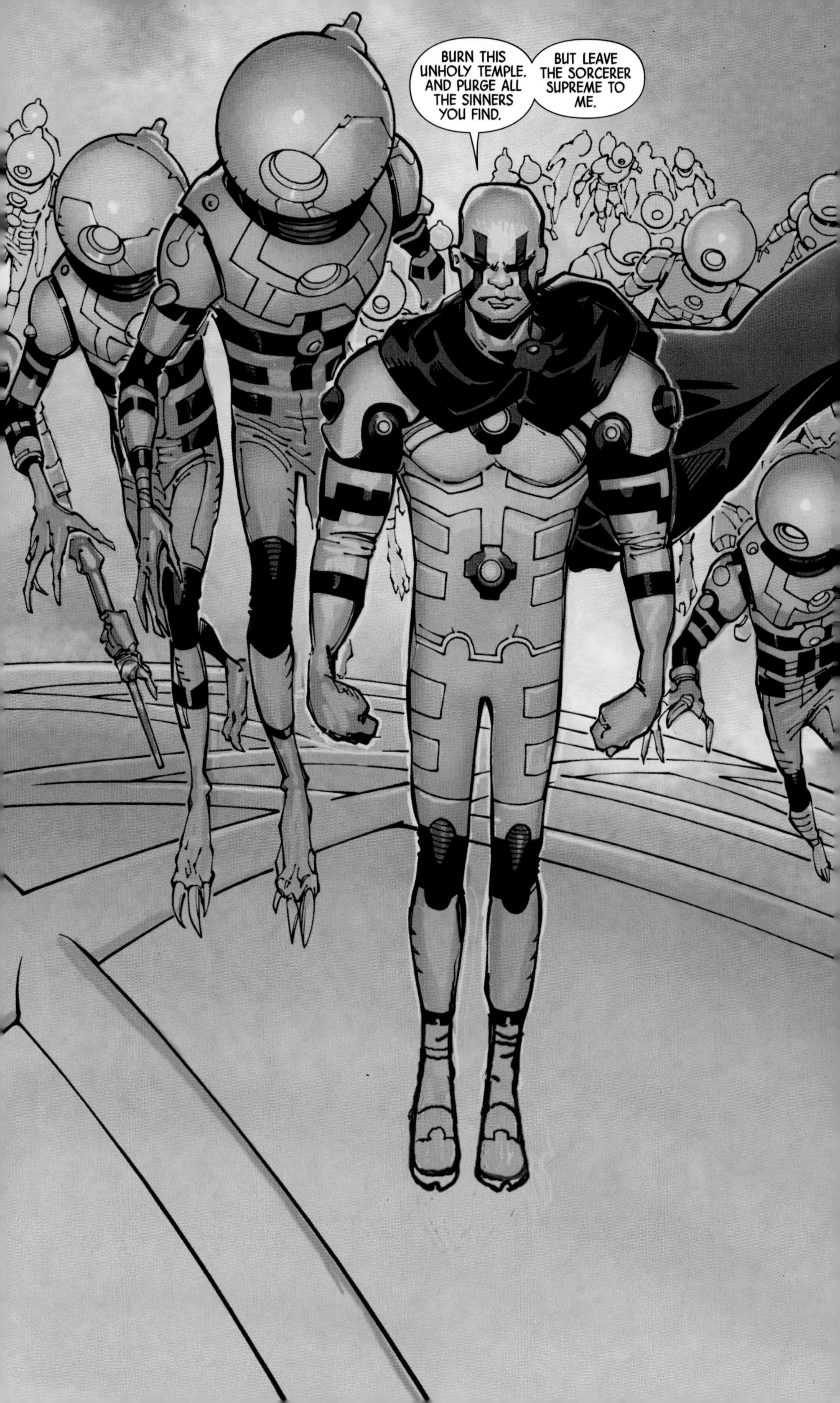

BURN THIS UNHOLY TEMPLE. AND PURGE ALL THE SINNERS YOU FIND.
BUT LEAVE THE SORCERER SUPREME TO ME.

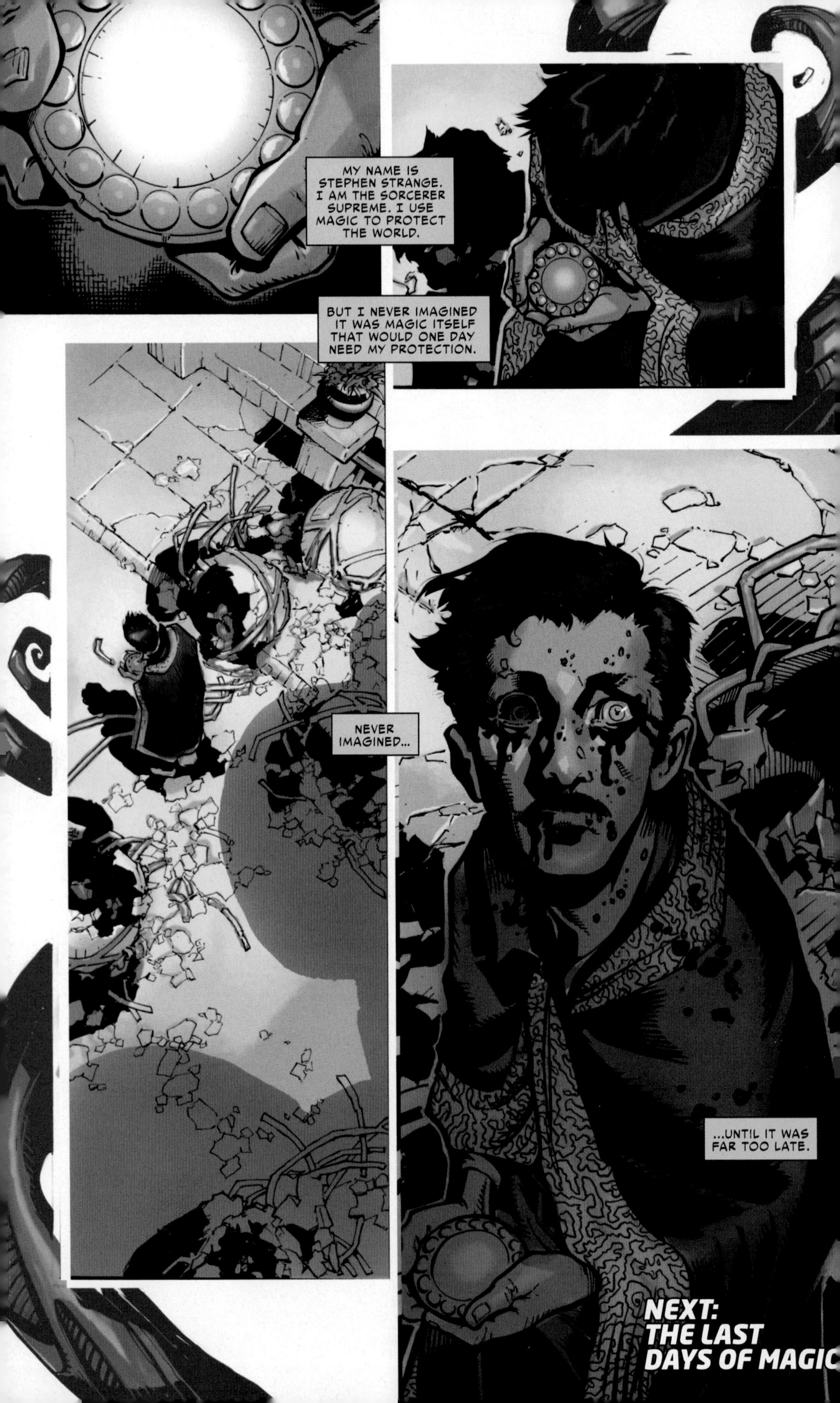
MY NAME IS STEPHEN STRANGE. I AM THE SORCERER SUPREME. I USE MAGIC TO PROTECT THE WORLD.
BUT I NEVER IMAGINED IT WAS MAGIC ITSELF THAT WOULD ONE DAY NEED MY PROTECTION.
NEVER IMAGINED...
...UNTIL IT WAS FAR TOO LATE.
NEXT: THE LAST DAYS OF MAGIC

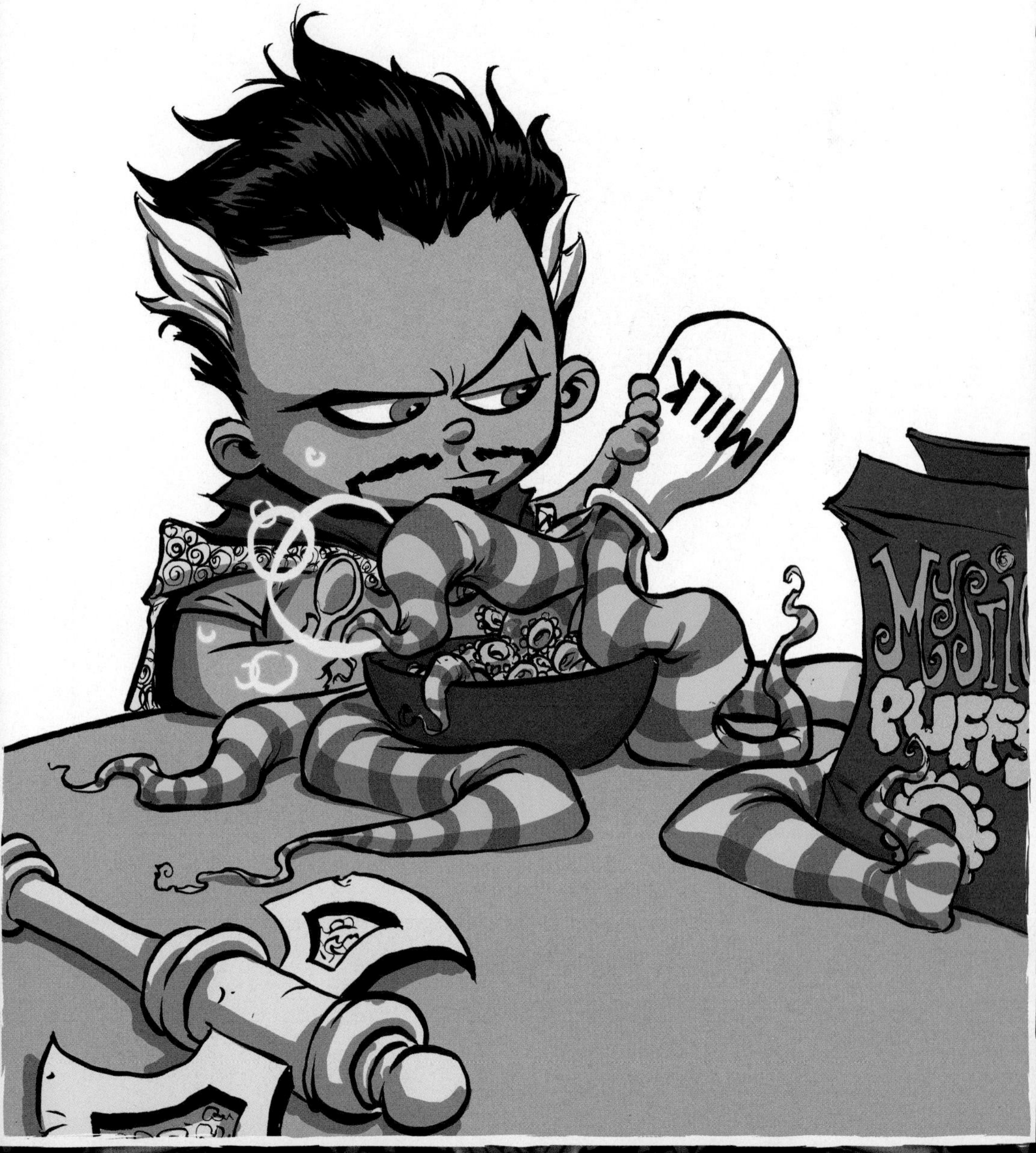
MILK
MYSTIC
PUFFS
#1 VARIANT BY **SKOTTIE YOUNG**

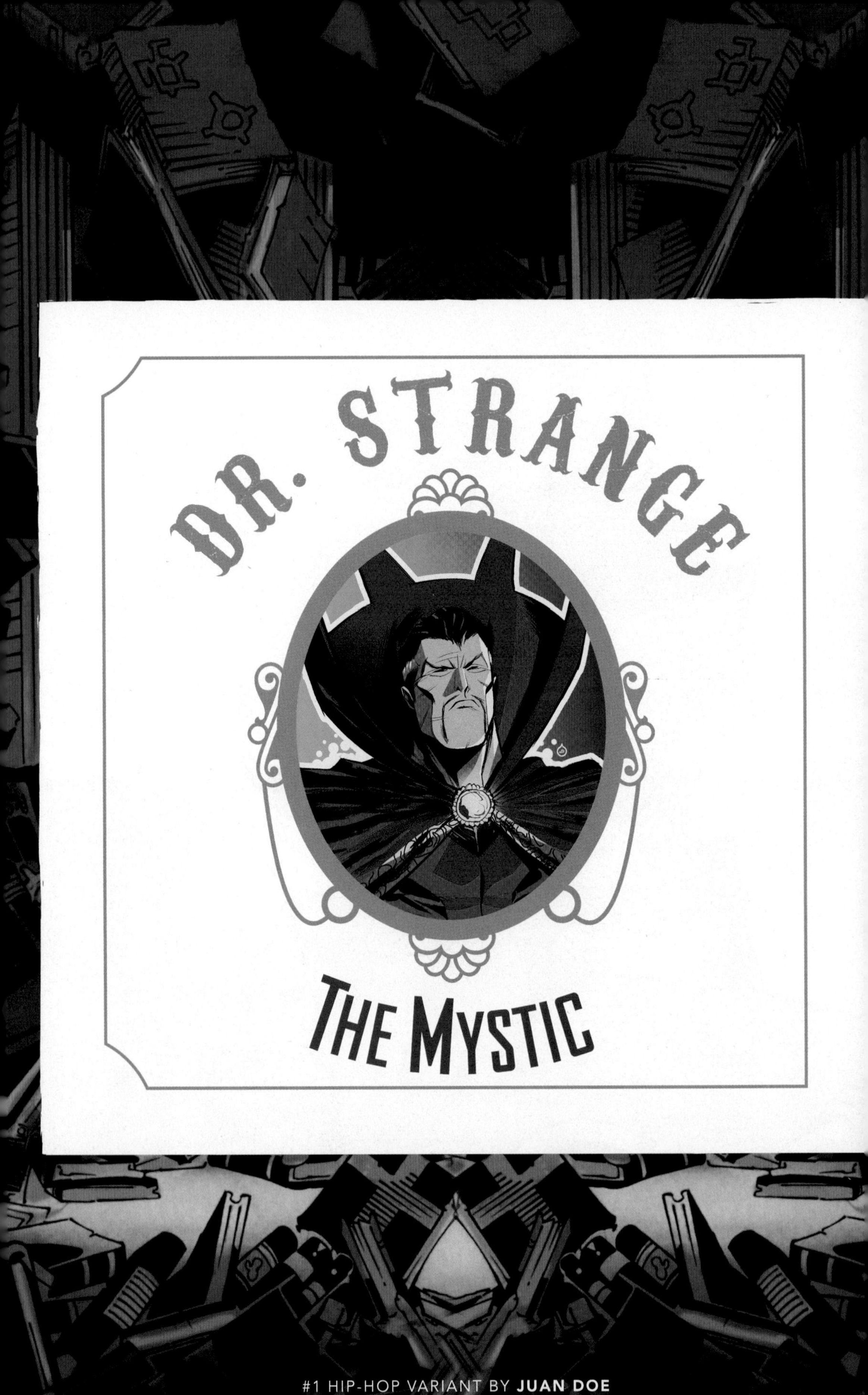
DR. STRANGE
THE MYSTIC

#1 HIP-HOP VARIANT BY **JUAN DOE**

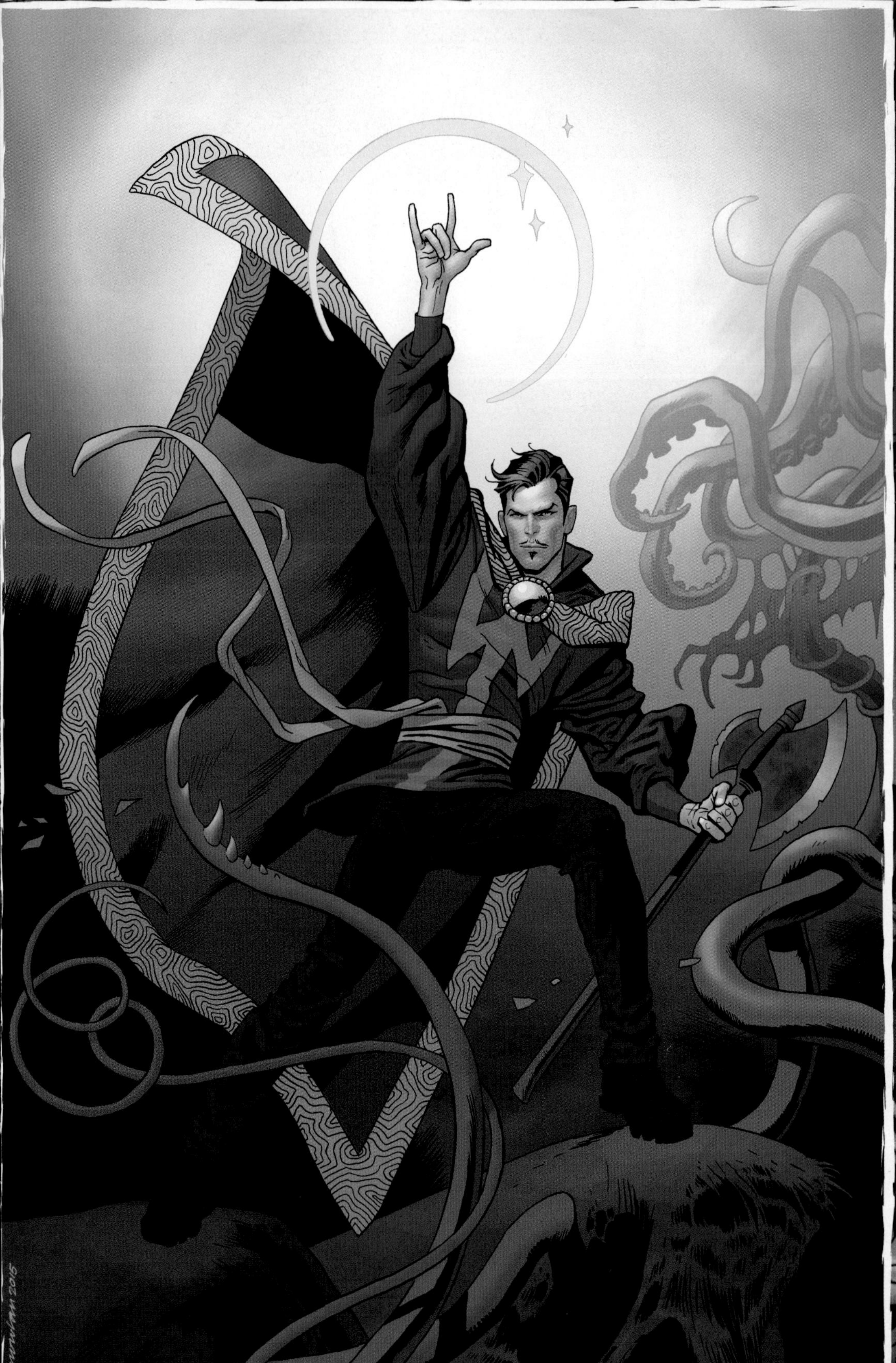

#1 VARIANT BY **KEVIN NOWLAN**

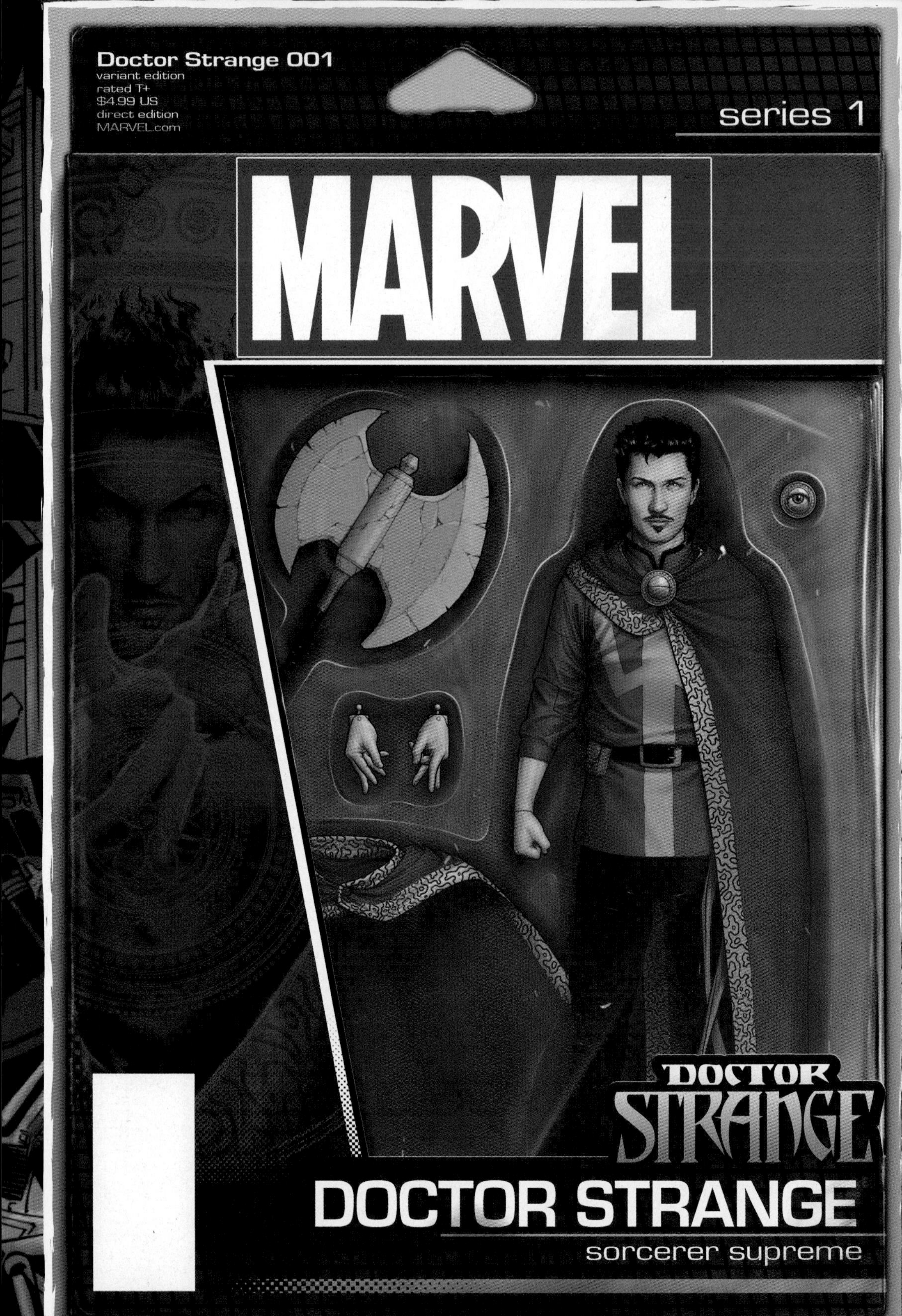
Doctor Strange 001
variant edition
rated T+
$4.99 US
direct edition
MARVEL.com
series 1
MARVEL
DOCTOR STRANGE
DOCTOR STRANGE
sorcerer supreme

#1 ACTION FIGURE VARIANT BY **JOHN TYLER CHRISTOPHER**

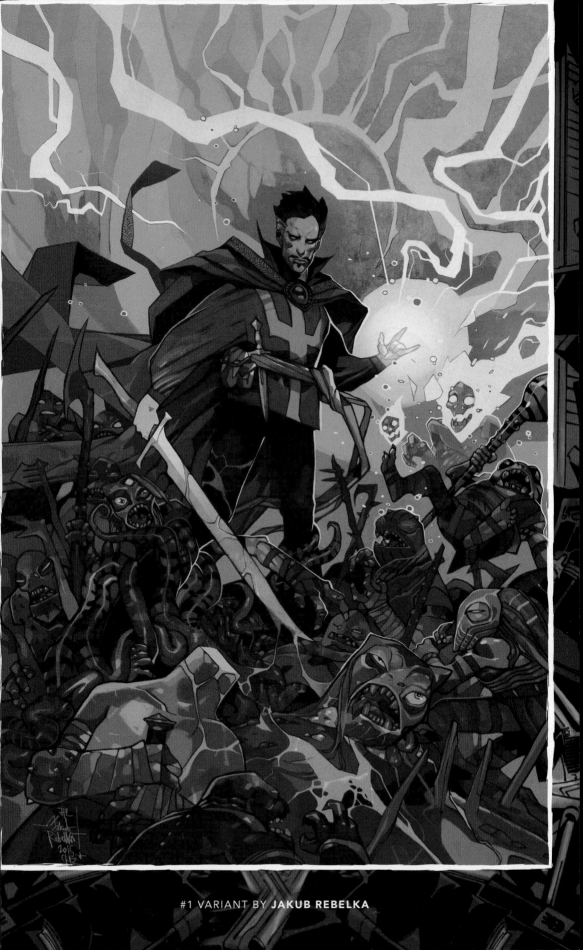

#1 VARIANT BY **JAKUB REBELKA**

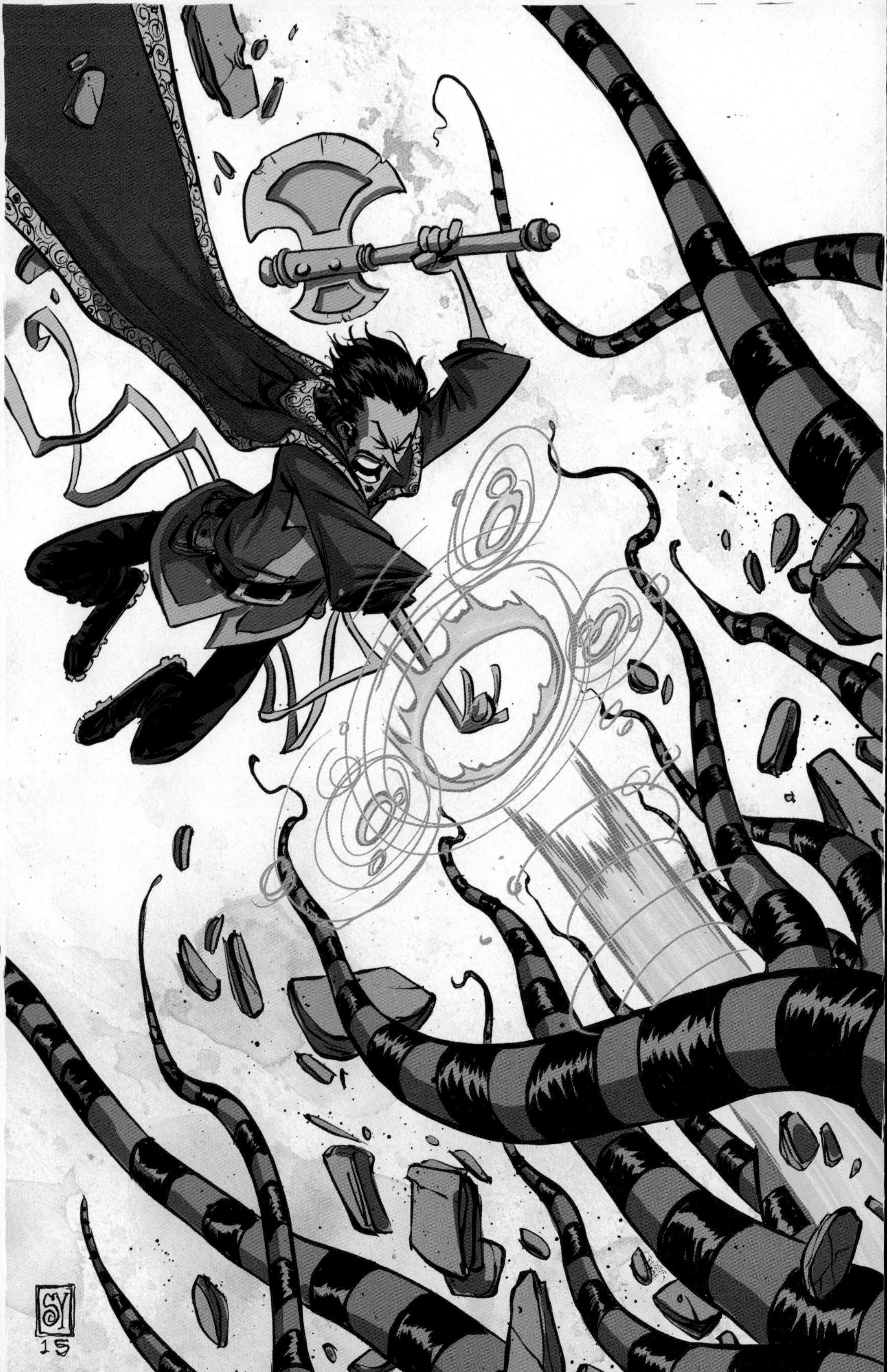
SY
15

#2 VARIANT BY **SKOTTIE YOUNG**

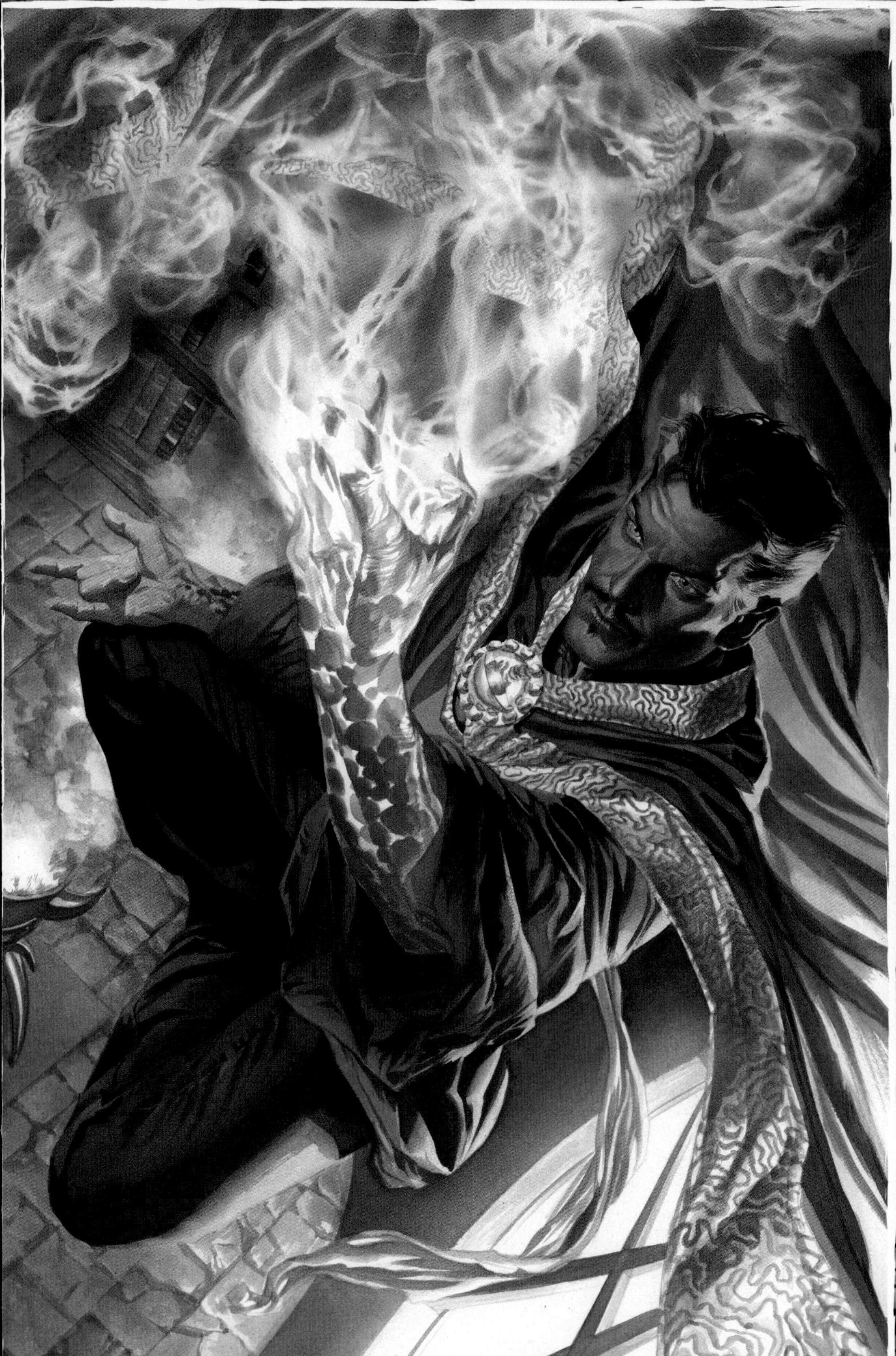

#2 VARIANT BY **ALEX ROSS**

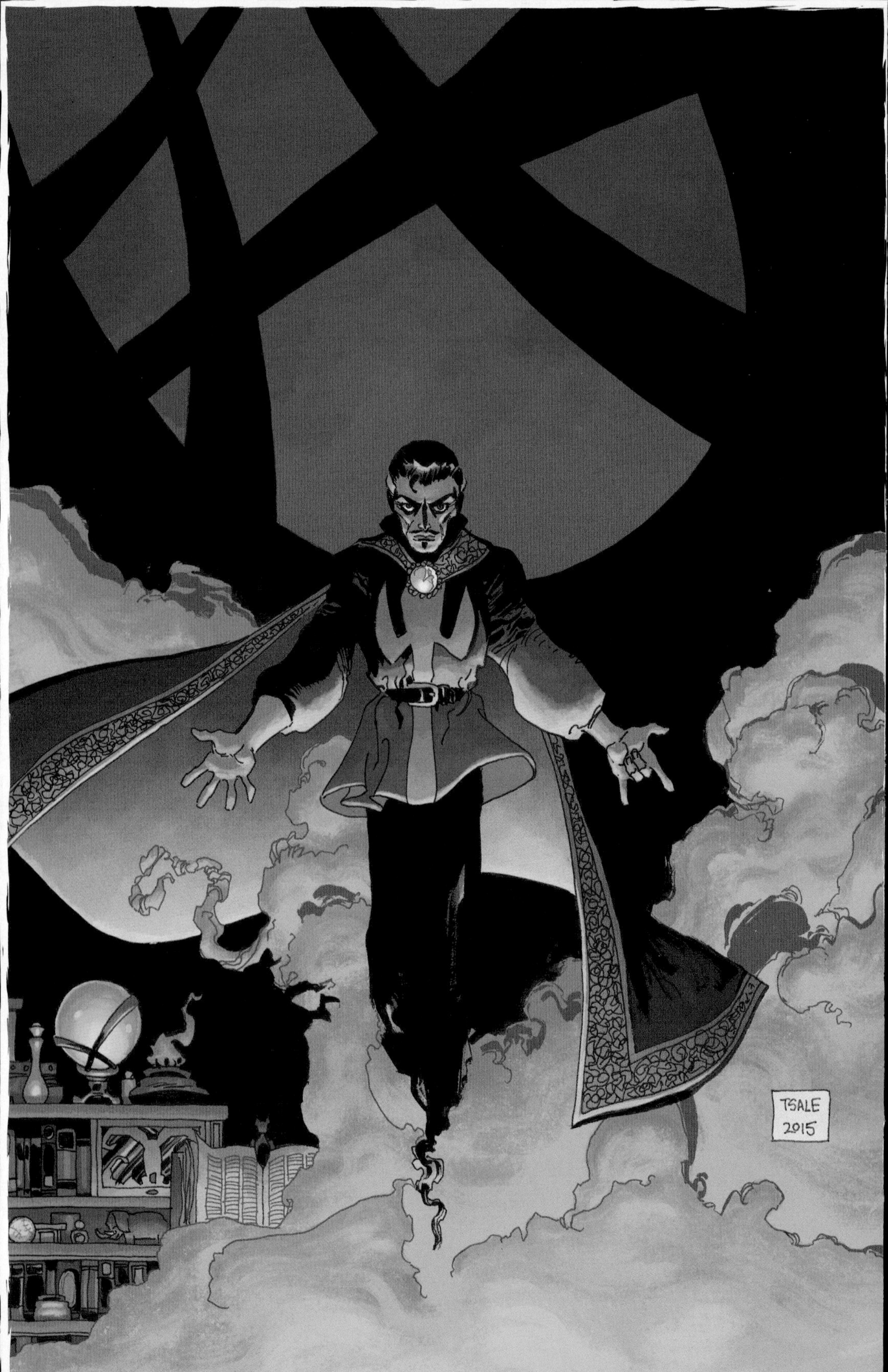
TSALE
2015

#3 VARIANT BY **TIM SALE**

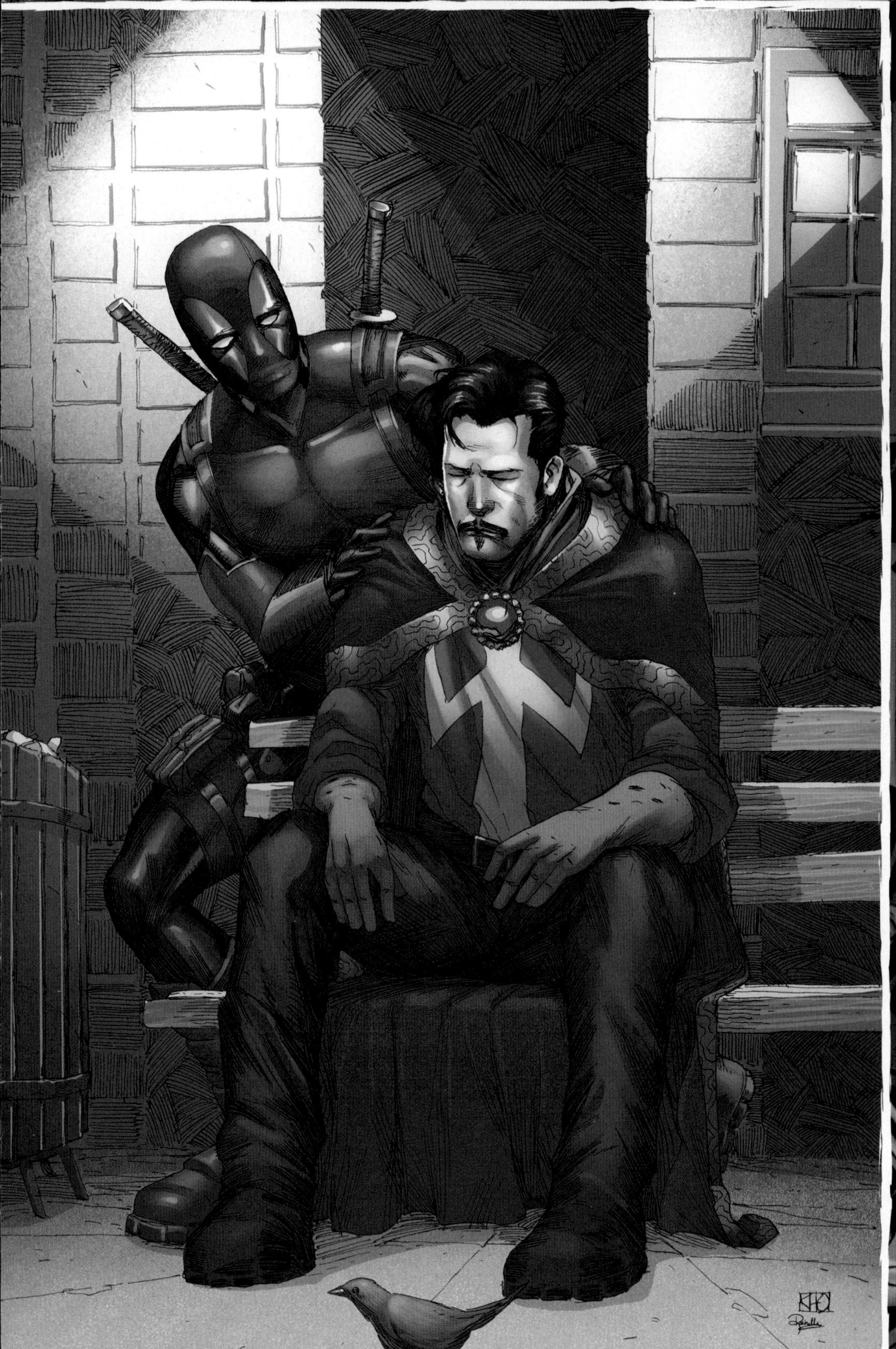

#4 DEADPOOL VARIANT BY **KHOI PHAM** & **RACHELLE ROSENBERG**

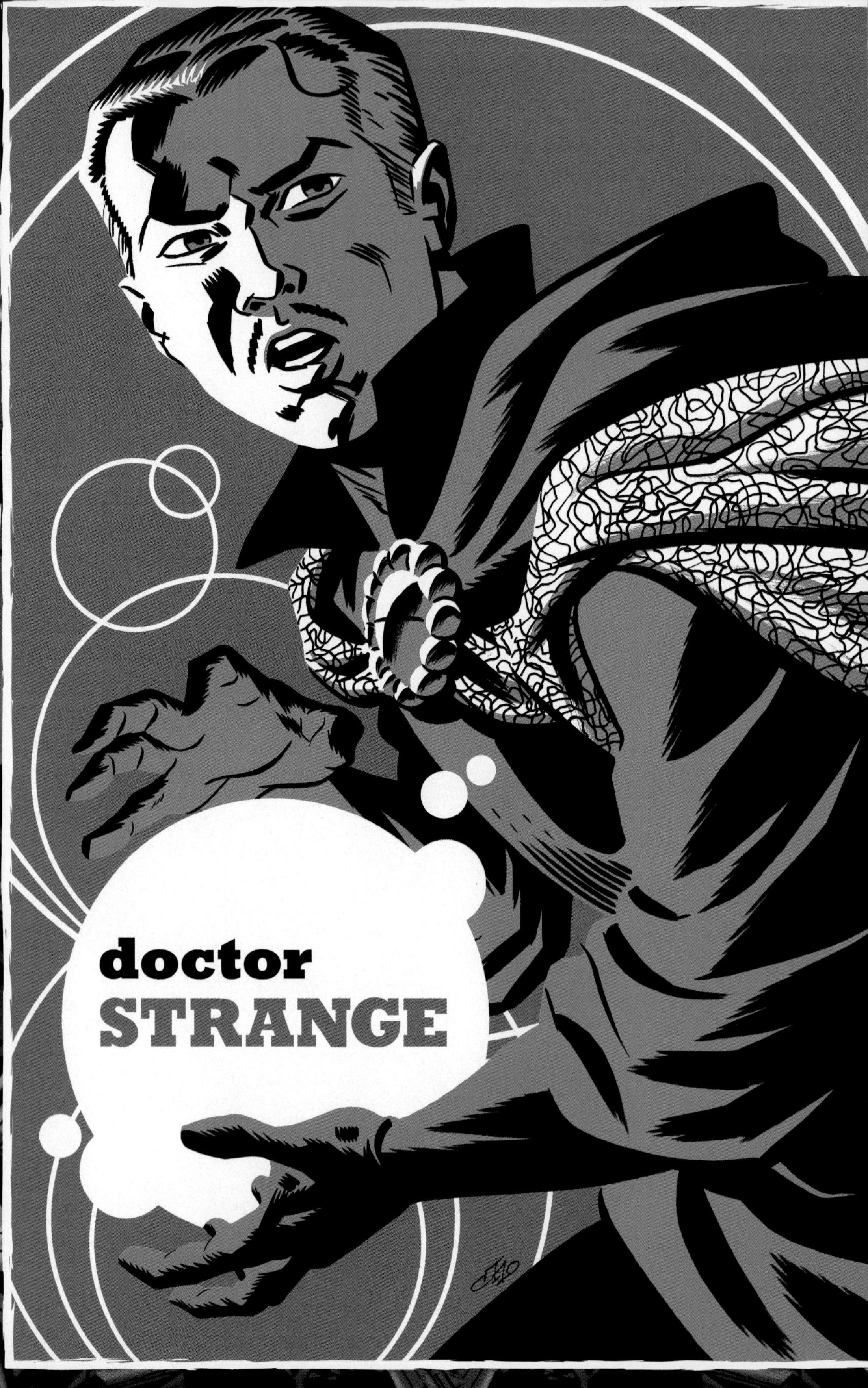
doctor
STRANGE

#5 VARIANT BY **MICHAEL CHO**

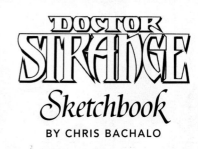

DOCTOR STRANGE
Sketchbook
BY CHRIS BACHALO

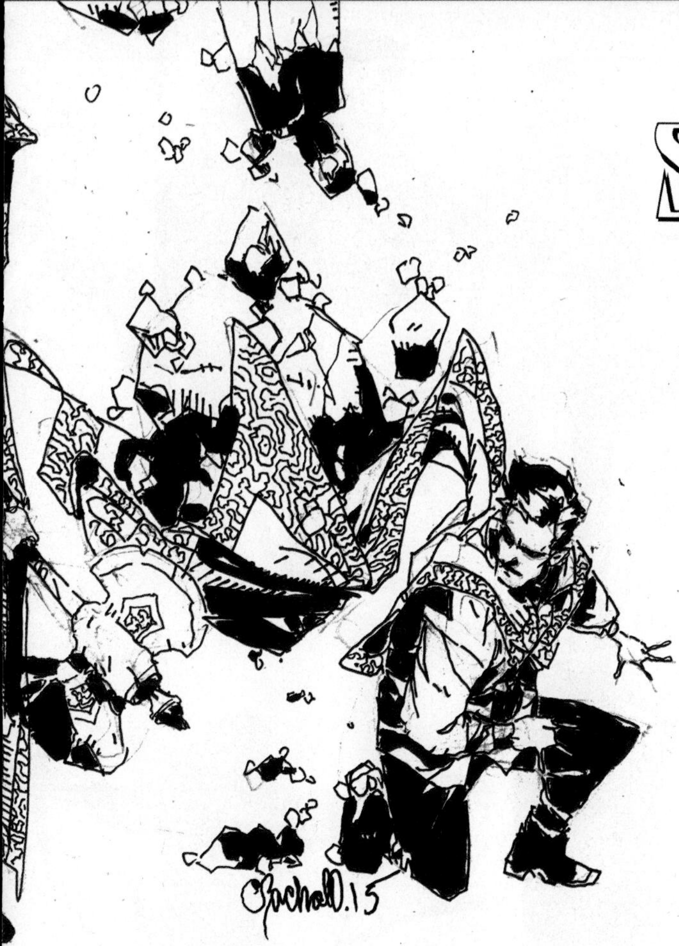

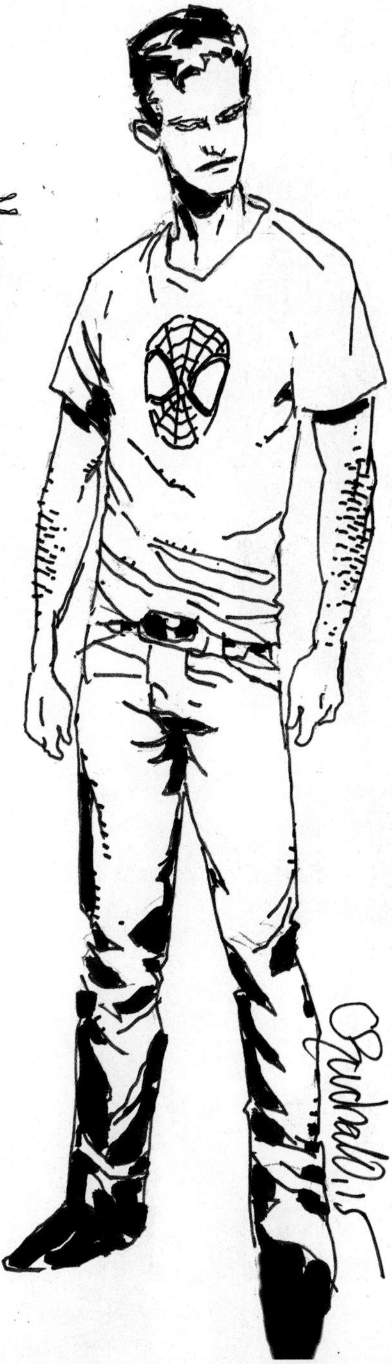

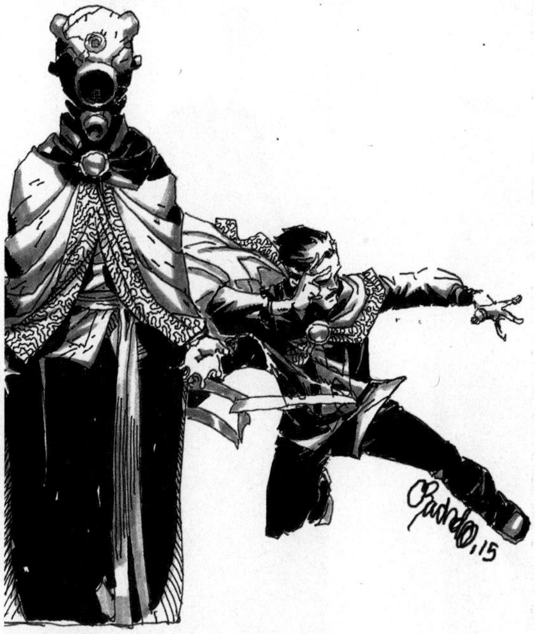

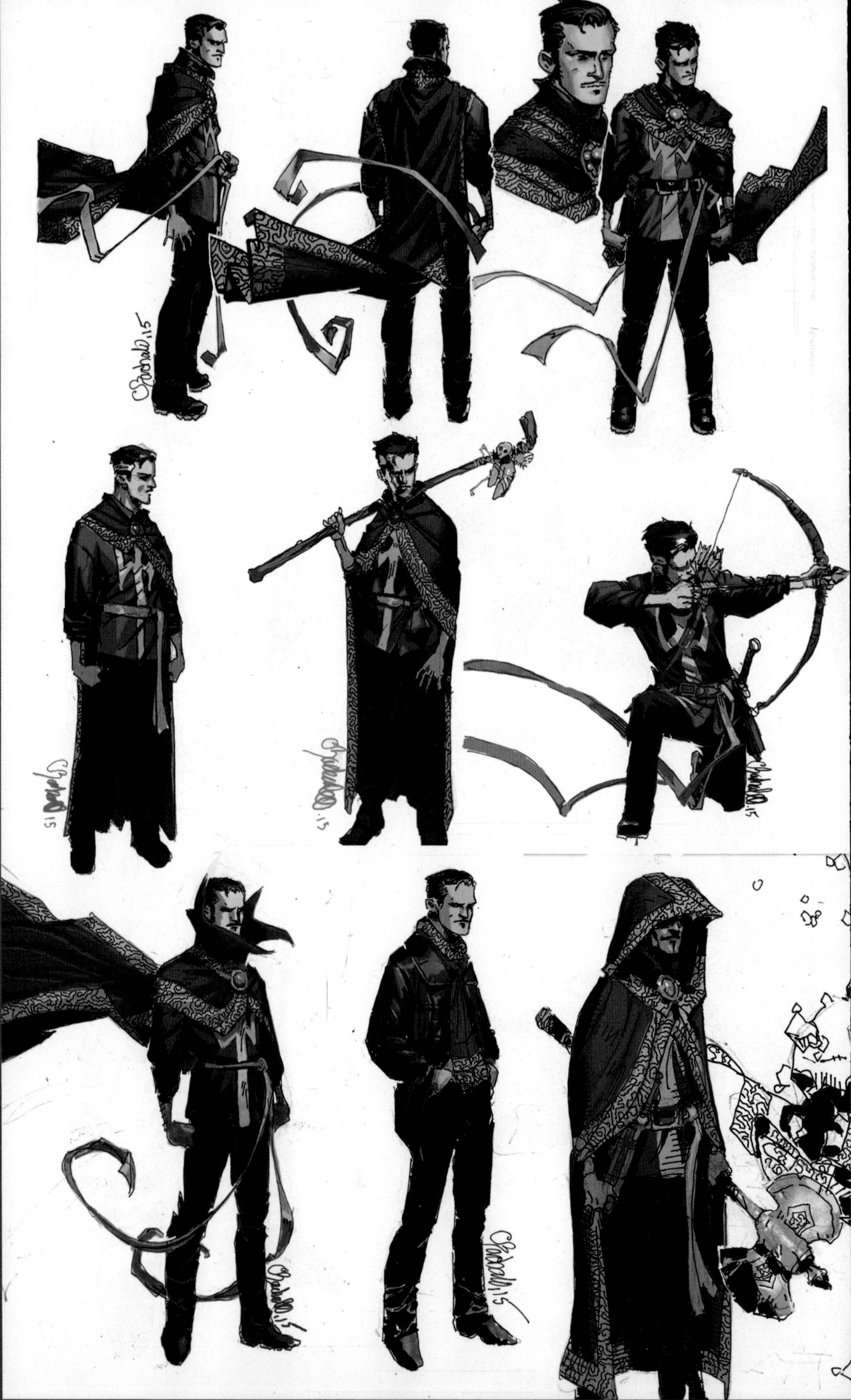

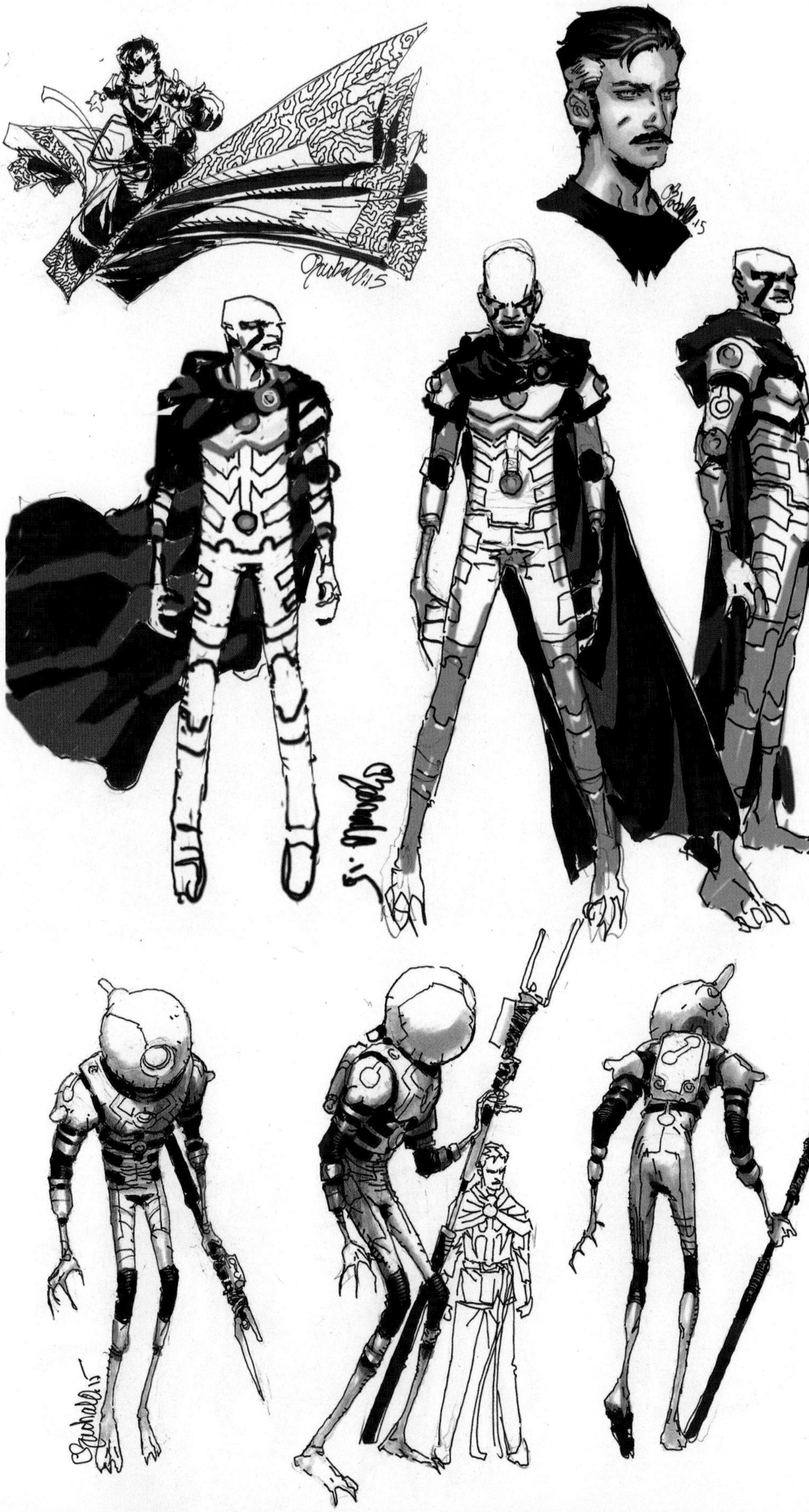

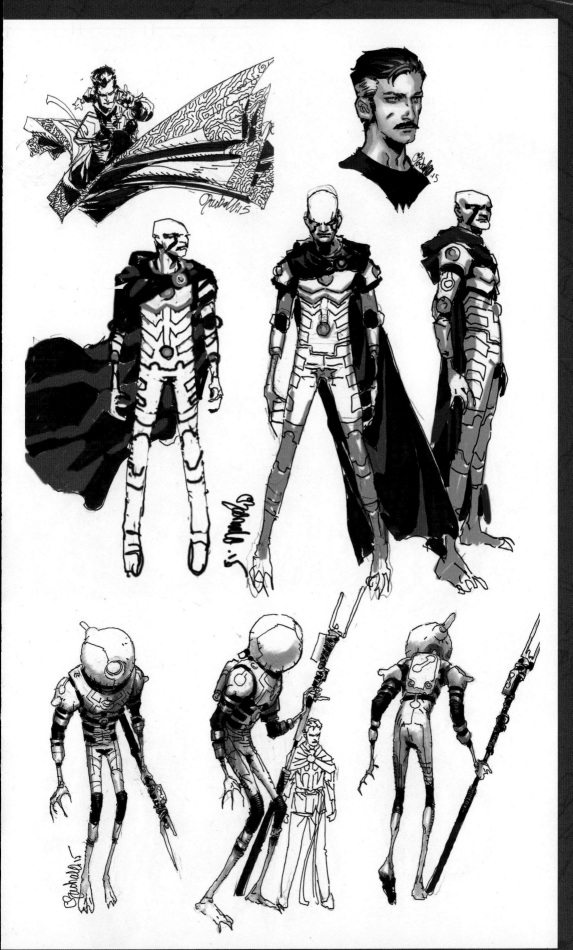

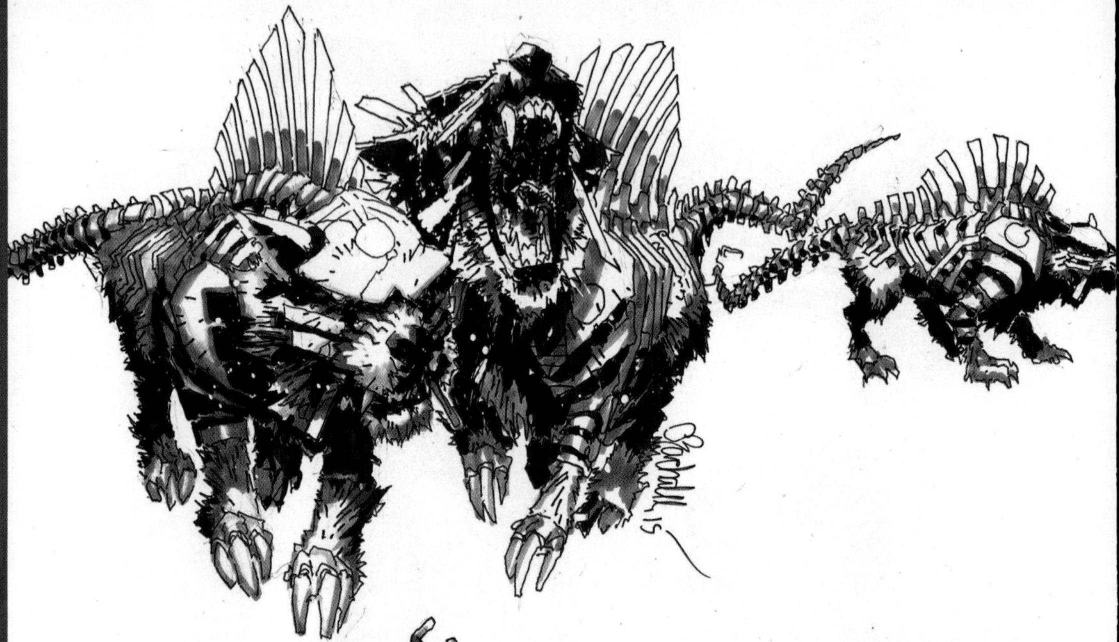

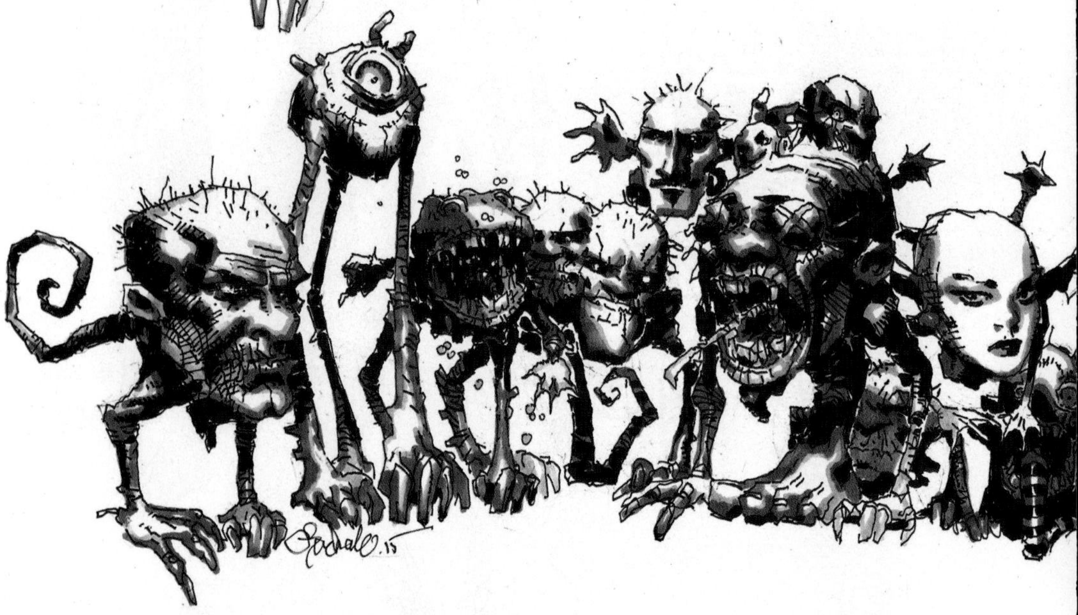

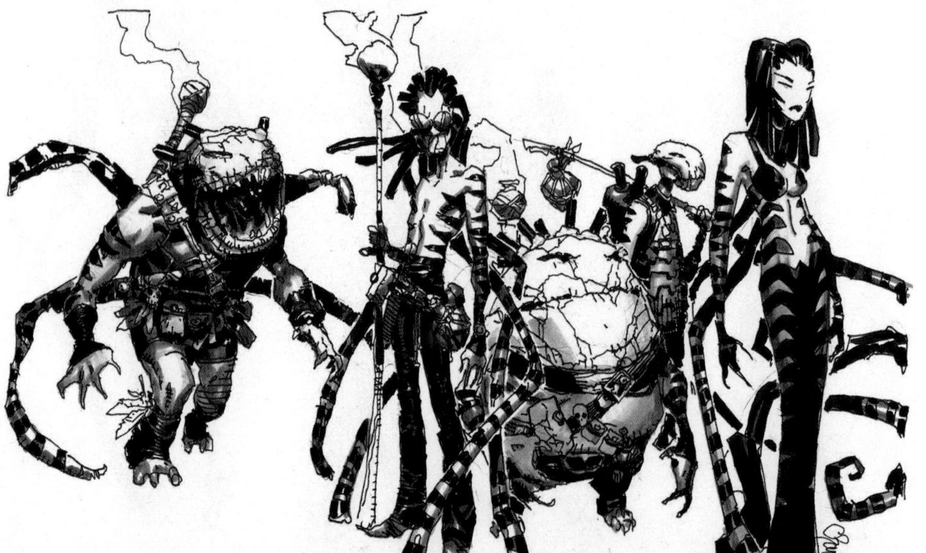

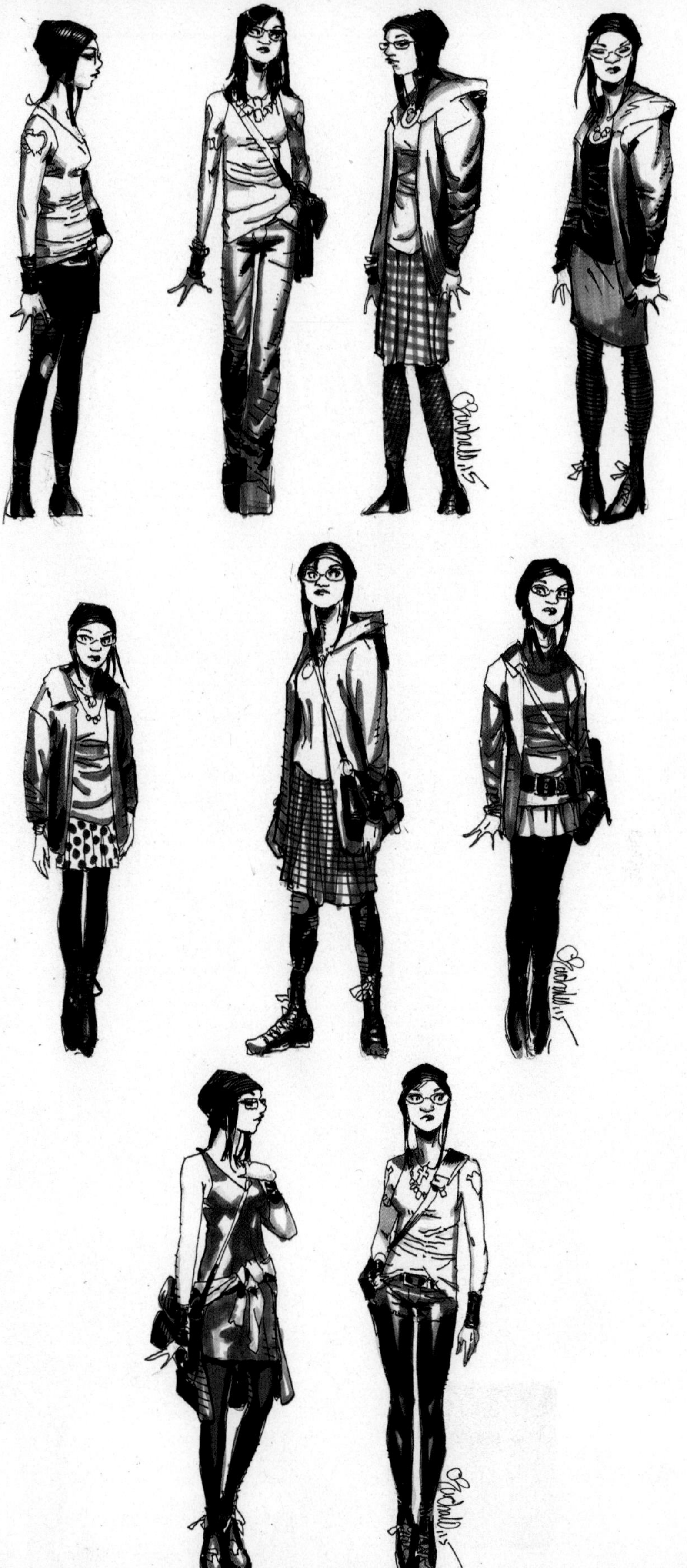

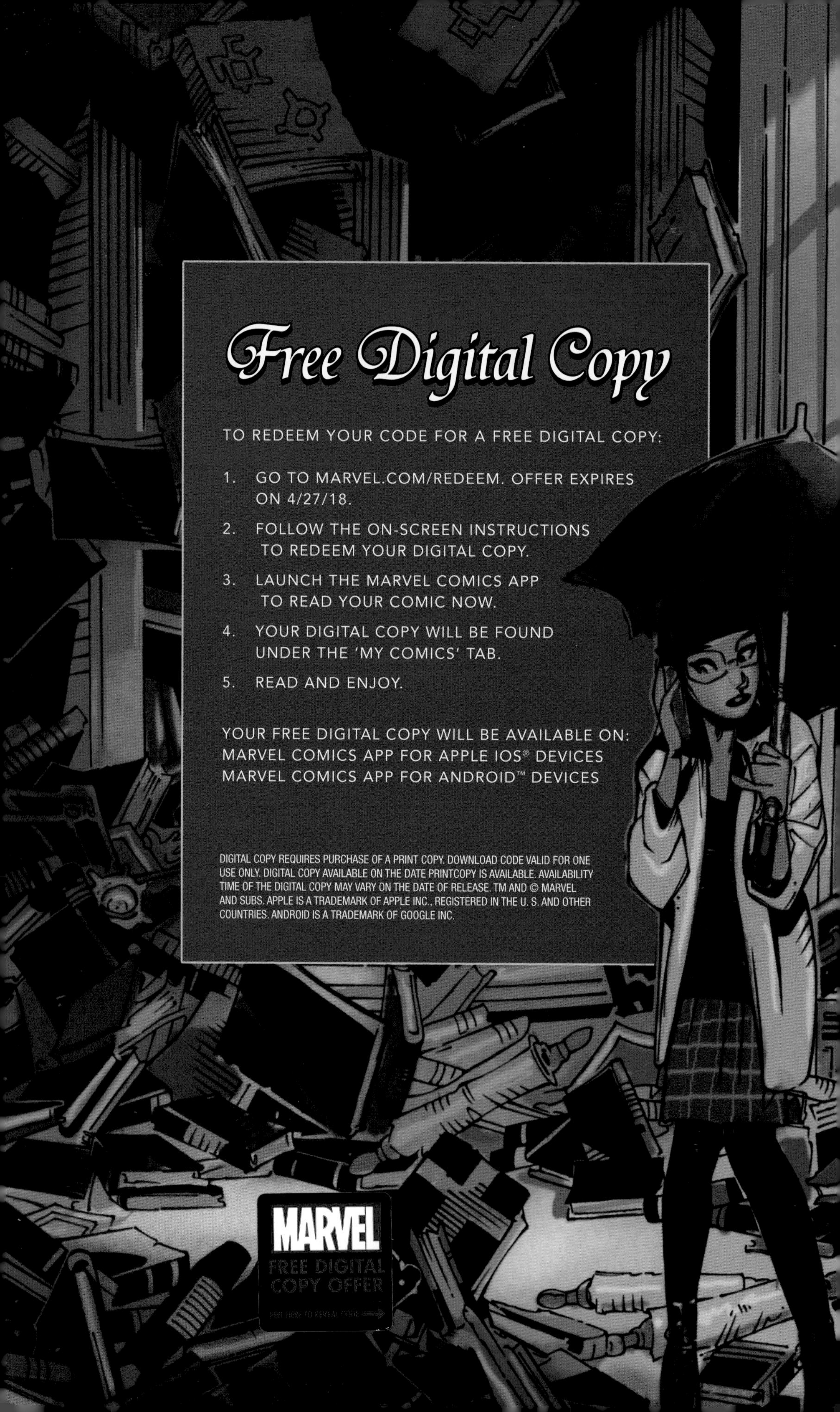
Free Digital Copy
TO REDEEM YOUR CODE FOR A FREE DIGITAL COPY:
1. GO TO MARVEL.COM/REDEEM. OFFER EXPIRES ON 4/27/18.
2. FOLLOW THE ON-SCREEN INSTRUCTIONS TO REDEEM YOUR DIGITAL COPY.
3. LAUNCH THE MARVEL COMICS APP TO READ YOUR COMIC NOW.
4. YOUR DIGITAL COPY WILL BE FOUND UNDER THE 'MY COMICS' TAB.
5. READ AND ENJOY.
YOUR FREE DIGITAL COPY WILL BE AVAILABLE ON:
MARVEL COMICS APP FOR APPLE IOS® DEVICES
MARVEL COMICS APP FOR ANDROID™ DEVICES
DIGITAL COPY REQUIRES PURCHASE OF A PRINT COPY. DOWNLOAD CODE VALID FOR ONE USE ONLY. DIGITAL COPY AVAILABLE ON THE DATE PRINTCOPY IS AVAILABLE. AVAILABILITY TIME OF THE DIGITAL COPY MAY VARY ON THE DATE OF RELEASE. TM AND © MARVEL AND SUBS. APPLE IS A TRADEMARK OF APPLE INC., REGISTERED IN THE U. S. AND OTHER COUNTRIES. ANDROID IS A TRADEMARK OF GOOGLE INC.
MARVEL
FREE DIGITAL COPY OFFER